Raymond Fox, PhD

Elements of the Helping Process
A Guide for Clinicians
Second Edition

D0060776

"In *Elements of the Helping Process*, Dr. Fox communicates the experience of encounter in social work practice with a voice that is humanistic, poetic, and client-centered. Beginning, for example, with the metaphor of a safe house capable of holding, sheltering, and structuring the client and the social worker in their work together, Dr. Fox infuses the 'elements of practice' with clinically informed images and playful acronyms: relationship as 'AGAPE'—Acceptance, Genuineness, Actuality, Positive regard, and Empathy; assessment as a 'jigsaw puzzle' in which one assembles a coherent picture from disparate pieces; or the alliterative 'Spheres of Strength' that direct the worker to explore resources of self, society, and the spiritual. Dr. Fox weaves the analytic and the associative, nimbly connecting the two with emergent heuristics and practice guidelines that are easily absorbed. Each chapter reads like a well-taught class where one is engaged, inspired, transformed, and effortlessly instructed. How wonderful, for example, to include the narratives of four resilient men who overcame trauma as a way to teach the reader about what works in treatment and what does not. This epitomizes client-centered learning, an approach Dr. Fox continuously helps the reader experience through the tenor of his text, full of warmth, respect, care, and personal sharing. Dr. Fox is interested in, and succeeds in, presenting social work practice as craft and art. His groundbreaking chapter on the clinical use of metaphor will encourage students and professionals to use clinical intuition creatively and effectively and his invitation to journal reflectively, as a technique for practice and evaluation promotes the use of personal narrative in clinical social work and enhances our capacity to hear and capture the stories of our clients.

Elements of the Helping Process can be used for both foundation and advanced clinical practice courses. The many pointers, guidelines, key factors, and practice protocols that organize chapters are particularly helpful for novice social workers, and the inclusion of concepts from self-psychology, object relations, behaviorism, ego-psychology, existentialism, intergenerational family theory, and attachment theory provides rich material for the advanced practitioner."

Howard Robinson, DSW
Assistant Professor,
Fordham University Graduate School
of Social Service,
New York

Elements
of the Helping Process
A Guide for Clinicians
Second Edition

Elements
of the Helping Process
A Guide for Clinicians
Second Edition

Raymond Fox, PhD

Routledge
Taylor & Francis Group
New York   London

Names and circumstances in case studies have been altered to protect confidentiality.

Cover design by Anastasia Litwak.

Library of Congress Cataloging-in-Publication Data

Fox, Raymond,
    Elements of the helping process : a guide for clinicians / Raymond Fox.—2nd. ed.
        p. cm.
    Includes bibliographical references and index.
    ISBN 0-7890-0903-X (alk. paper)—ISBN 0-7890-0904-8 (pbk. : alk. paper)
    1. Psychotherapy. 2. Counseling. 3. Helping behavior. I. Title.
    [DNLM: 1. Physician-Patient Relations. 2. Counseling—methods. W 62 F793e 2000]
RC480 .F654 2000
158'.3—dc21

                                                                        00-065002

To Jeri

I have always felt your love and friendship
As deep as the ocean
As free as the wind
As warm as the sand
As far as a star

ABOUT THE AUTHOR

Dr. Raymond Fox, PhD, received his MSW from Fordham University and his doctorate from the New York University Graduate School of Arts and Sciences with a concentration in individual and organizational behavior. He holds postgraduate certificates in Gestalt, Group, and Sex Therapy, and has studied at the National Training Laboratories, the Jung Institute in Zurich, the Postgraduate Center for Mental Health, and the Self-Psychology Institute.

Dr. Fox's publications, reflecting his professional research interests in mental health, creativity, and teaching, include over thirty articles in professional journals and the first edition of *Elements of the Helping Process: A Guide for Clinicians.* He is currently preparing manuscripts focusing on metaphors, journaling, and film.

Dr. Fox has consulted in a number of private and public organizations and maintains a private practice as a certified individual, marital, family, and sex therapist. He conducts workshops nationally as well as abroad on stress management, clinical practice, creativity, metaphors, and adult learning and development.

CONTENTS

PART II: CONFIGURING A PLAN TO GUIDE THE PROCESS

PART I:
ESTABLISHING THE FOUNDATION
FOR EFFECTIVE INTERVENTION

Chapter 1

To Do Our Work

Experience is the child of thought and thought is the child of action. We cannot learn men from books.

Disraeli

Any beginning, any new understanding in life causes simultaneous feelings of hope and fear.

Ruth Smalley

It takes two to speak the truth—one to speak and another to hear.

Henry David Thoreau

WHAT THIS BOOK HAS TO OFFER

A clinician for the past thirty-five years and a teacher, consultant, and trainer for the past twenty-five years, I have come to appreciate the need for a commonsense and down-to-earth approach to the helping process. Students and colleagues who are learning often ask for direction in finding a practical guide; but what they find—and find wanting—is a literature of long scholarly treatises on theory, extended descriptions of therapeutic technique, and overblown reports on clinical research about effective intervention. Complaining that none of these offers very much usable information about how to work with people on a day-to-day basis, they go on looking for a book to fill the gaps. Theoretical frameworks and findings from research studies provide only limited aid in learning the art and craft of helping. Between the ideas that science provides and the kinds of decisions the clinician must make, there is a gulf that we must bridge before we can take action.

Clients are particular and unique in nature and character. Theory is general. The fit between the two is never perfect; nor is a strong skill base enough, for a creative leap must be made if we are to cross the space between often inapplicable theory and the concrete reality we face every day.

Over and over I have heard clinicians, both new and experienced, ask for practical guidelines, systematic direction, and suggestions for creatively working with their clients. Too often feeling inundated by jargonized and abstract proposals for effectively working with clients, they want help in answering difficult questions, which include: What do I tell clients about myself? How do I divide my focus in the beginning among establishing a relationship, developing a contract, and giving the client something concrete on which to establish a basis of hope? Just how is hope instilled? How can I enhance the process and avoid getting in the way? How do I connect with clients? How do I utilize nonverbal interactions?

This book will help you confront these questions and fill the gap in the literature. It is a practical guide to working clinically with people through the various phases of the helping process. "User-friendly," it describes some familiar tried-and-true techniques but also concentrates on innovative methods of helpgiving. Even though there are computer programs for learning these skills, it seems to me that computers—as valuable as they are—fall short, for they cannot provide human connection, the most essential dimension in the helping process. Even though you "cannot learn men from books," books do serve, next to person-to-person contact, as handy and discriminating means to reflection and introspection. Although there is a tendency to disparage pragmatic tools for clinical practice, what we value most in our work is the application of sound principles. The ultimate test of theory is its usability in actual, direct, face-to-face transactions with clients.

This book, then, differs from other textbooks in several respects. Even though it endeavors to blend theory and practice, it is not typically scholarly and does not emphasize the "science" of our work, although it introduces a variety of objective ideas for evaluating your practice. Nor is it restricted to "left brain" conceptual and statistical elements of the work, even though theory, analysis, and logic are essential ingredients of the mix. The "art" of the work is stressed instead, with "right brain" attributes of synthesis, intuition, and wholeness. No reductionistic formulas or mechanical strategies are offered; but sensible tips, guidelines, rules of thumb, and new ideas for proceeding are given.

Different from other textbooks in that it does not elaborate extensively on any one school of clinical practice, *Elements of the Helping Process: A Guide for Clinicians* is integrative in the kindest sense of the word, describing sundry theories only as they pertain to, illuminate, or explain your more immediate clinical interaction. It seeks to identify theory that fits clients at different points—and under different circumstances—during the work, and focuses especially on finding the most instrumental and relevant interventions. You will notice that what is encouraged is a less rigid and more fluid and personal approach to clinical practice, an approach that, informed by theory and practice, opens the way for *you as you* to respond appropriately, differentially, and effectively to a wide range of clients with a broad array of problems. It will facilitate walking the tightrope between overidentification and excessive detachment, while tailoring your work to your clients rather than expecting them to fit your particular approach.

Using an informal tone, I try to speak directly to "you" rather than addressing myself to some anonymous clinician. This personal style directly reflects my bias about what I believe the work can be.

This book resembles others in the field in drawing from examples from actual practice for clinical illustrations. These are selected to be instructive about intervention and to illuminate the application of theory. I have concentrated on an array of theoretical and practical approaches that characterize each stage of the helping process. A repertoire of varied suggestions and techniques are offered, encouraging you to discover your own style. You will move from the engagement stage to termination, following the progression of the process, with special chapters devoted to creative practice methods. Interventive procedures adapted to clients' discrete needs are identified, discussed, and illustrated. Ways to individualize your clinical practice are suggested.

GENERAL OUTLINE

Elements of the Helping Process: A Guide for Clinicians is divided into four main sections.

Part I: Establishing the Foundation for Effective Intervention

The book's focus and intent are discussed in Chapter 1. The chapter also takes up some of my assumptions about the helping process, along with some basic propositions about the people we call clients. I argue for an integrated approach to clinical practice and conclude with a discussion of the need for you to be an active participant rather than a passive observer in the helping process.

Creating a "safe house" for clients is the theme of the second chapter. The safe house is a powerful metaphor for the helping process that clarifies and unifies such diverse clinician characteristics as empathy, good rapport, neutrality and anonymity, and the real and transferred relationship. Clients' growth and the ability to master internal conflict and external frustration require that you establish a setting that meets their basic needs for security and affirmation. Guidelines are laid out for building such a safe house for clients. I draw upon attachment/separation theory and elaborate upon the concept of the "holding environment."

The third chapter focuses attention on the dynamics of the helping relationship, while stressing the centrality of "relationship" and your own awareness of self. Seven levels of relationship, the seven "I's," as I call them, are discussed: Individualization, Intellectual learning, Imitation, Internalization, Identification, Idealization, and Individuation. The final message of the chapter is that the essence of the helping process may not be the truth that is arrived at as much as it is the manner of arriving at the truth.

Chapter 4 presents some fundamental principles and novel ideas about beginning the helping process and educating clients about the nature of helping, while making possible the deeper purpose of their reviewing their life stories. Phases of preparation for the initial contact are addressed. The chapter underscores the importance of responding to clients' valid need for structure and devotes considerable attention to what you can expect from clients and what clients expect from you. I conclude with a checklist for guiding your reflections on your work.

Part II: Configuring a Plan to Guide the Process

In Chapter 5 I discuss basic philosophy, premises, and principles of goal setting and contracting. An outline for developing a sound contract is followed by an illustration from actual practice. The chapter reviews the benefits of contracting from the perspective of assessment and evaluation.

Chapter 6, "Evaluating Client and Clinician Progress," builds upon Chapter 4 and discusses objective and subjective means for you to consider in evaluating client progress as well as critiquing your own clinical endeavors.

"Learning from a jigsaw puzzle" is the metaphor that rules Chapter 7, where we examine the assessment process. I review what assessment is and is not, while offering guidelines for feedback, and discuss the types and general process of assessment. A section on labeling concludes this chapter.

Chapter 8 amplifies the notion of resiliency as a critical component to consider in the assessment and treatment process. It examines the concepts of will and spirituality as significant ingredients in intensive clinical work with your clients.

Part III: Crafting the Structure for Strength and Support

Chapters 9 and 10 interface with each other, for each uses the same case study to illustrate the benefit of integrating individual and family approaches. Chapter 9 concentrates on individual diagnosis, examining the place of *The Diagnostic and Statistical Manual of Mental Disorders,* Fourth Edition. I review the theoretical underpinnings and various dimensions of individual assessment. Chapter 10 presents various facets of family assessment and proposes the genogram as a useful tool for either individual or family assessment.

Discovering what clients say about effective ways of working with trauma and suicide is the central theme of Chapter 11.

Part IV: Customizing and Culminating the Configuration for Stability and Growth

In Chapter 12, "Creative Ways of Capturing the Life Story," I explain the importance of and guidelines for discovering the client's life story. Two particular methods that I utilize in my own practice are expanded upon: the family tree and the inventory. Both are illustrated with specific examples.

Chapter 13 stresses the written word in the helping process, a seldom discussed but valuable adjunct. The usefulness of several forms of writing is detailed, showing how they crystallize a helping relationship, uncover sources of behavior, and facilitate deepened understanding between you and your clients. The advantages of clients' and your own independent writing are demonstrated, even as the utility of writing as a form of interchange is shown.

"Telling metaphors" is the central theme of Chapter 14. It offers guidelines for discovering and developing metaphors in work with individual and family clients. Extending, enlarging, shaping, and dramatizing metaphors in therapy lead to major alterations in clients' view of themselves, others, and their world.

The final chapter is devoted to the termination process, explaining how termination can be viewed as crisis intervention and suggesting checkpoints for clients' readiness for ending. It elaborates upon the "separation paradox" and upon three distinct but overlapping phases of termination.

A PARADIGM EMPHASIZING CLIENT HEALTH AND STRENGTHS

This book moves away from the typically orthodox methods of help giving with which you may be familiar. A simplified comparison illuminates the differences between the traditional view and my more integrative one:

Traditional Emphasis	Integrative Emphasis
Theory centered	Client centered
One specialized set of orthodox techniques	Combination of approaches and techniques
External direction and rules	Inner listening and attentiveness
Emphasis on intellect and analysis	Fresh appreciation of intuition and imagination
Focus on symptoms or problems	Focus on the whole person
Fixed and rigid	Flexible and adaptable
Clinician neutral and essentially passive	Clinician active, caring, and supportive

Primary intervention is interpretation	Interpretation is combined with a full armamentarium of active techniques
Client is dependent	Client is autonomous
Clinician is authority	Clinician is partner
Change in thinking, feeling or behavior is the goal	Transformation and an experience of deep healing is the goal
Primary reliance on left-brain functioning of both client and clinician	Special reliance on right-brain functioning of both client and clinician
Fit the client to the approach	Customize the approach to the client

Basic Beliefs About People

A humanistic view, coupled with a strong dose of empathy, plays the most significant role in our work. An encounter in which the client is seen as a whole person through the lens of a person-to-person professional relationship underpins the success of the entire helping process.

A dozen beliefs guiding my own practice are as follows:

1. People exist in a continually changing and sometimes incomprehensible world of experience. They struggle constantly to make sense of it and seldom give in or give up.
2. People respond to this world as they perceive it; thus, their "reality" is meaningful and purposeful for them. It is neither totally random nor absurdly ridiculous. They endeavor to find consistency in their thinking, feeling, and behaving.
3. As a result of interaction with the world, and particularly with significant others, a person's "self" is formed. One endeavors to be authentic and self-determining.
4. People want to be active participants in designing their lives and are dissatisfied with settling passively for their "lot in life." They recognize, to a large extent, that self-respect and self-esteem come from accepting responsibility for their lives and earning their way in the world.
5. People strive to create meaningful relationships with respectful and reliable others, whom they try not to deceive, harm, or suck dry.

6. Peoples' selves are distinct and unique and cannot be pigeon-holed.
7. Our strengths and capacities to regenerate our minds, bodies, and emotions prevent us from being just a bundle of defects, deficits, and arrests.
8. People aspire to independence and freshness while welcoming challenge. They do not ruminate repeatedly on "unfinished business" but can search out and achieve difficult objectives.
9. Progress is made in inexplicable circular spirals, for people are not simply the products of static, clear-cut, linear development.
10. People are prospective, not merely retrospective, and can influence the future and redesign their worlds, edit their scripts, and exercise new options, without simply being victims of history.
11. People are actors on the stage of life, not merely an audience. Seeking mastery and self-respect, they face unpleasant and inevitable difficulties.
12. Multimotivational rather than unimotivational, people make what seem to them to be the best choices at any given moment in time and are willing to exert great effort and endure considerable hardship to attain happiness.

From this standpoint, clients are encouraged to accept responsibility for their own lives. Instead of asking only, "What is happening to me?" "What are others doing to me?" "What am I doing to them?" they endeavor to address the question, "What am I doing to myself?" Seeking for such knowledge, coupled with a search for meaning rather than cure, enhances clients' potential for living more fulfilling lives.

The Purpose of Clinical Practice

Our goal, then, is to offer people release from their suffering, encouragement for their striving, and support for their strengths. In the end, such a positive perspective promotes change. Figure 1.1 illustrates the purpose of clinical practice.

Promoting client autonomy and fulfillment is the overarching purpose of clinical practice. Through the integrative power of the helping relationship, you communicate to clients your willingness to understand their unique qualities, and you convey the expectation

FIGURE 1.1. The Purpose of Clinical Practice

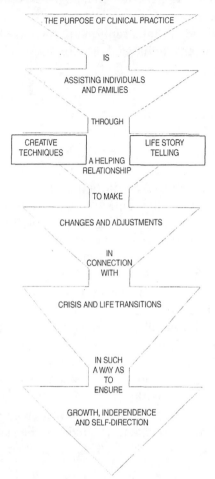

that their troubles can be explored and contained. As the meaning of clients' unique stories and dynamic patterns is grasped, creative interventions lead not only to resolution of problems, but to their continued growth and independence.

The Integrated Approach

Human experience is so rich, complex, and multifaceted that no single theory can explain it. When drawing on many theories and methodologies, we have a greater chance to respond more fully to the range of client behavior. Breadth in viewpoint, greater flexibility in response, and efficacy in intervention are increased.

The helping process includes three dimensions:

1. The helping context
2. The client
3. You, the helper

This book will make it possible to address each dimension with increasing confidence, drawing from a broad array of theories, strategies, and techniques to make you better able to create a climate of trust and to match your intervention to your clients' special needs. It offers ways to keep clients working at tolerable levels of frustration by responding to their desire to be accepted and understood on their own terms. You are encouraged to display maximum empathy and minimum confrontation, while sustaining sufficient anxiety in the client to get to most of the core issues that are raised. You are the significant variable in influencing each of these components: the context, the client, and yourself. You have your own personal style of helping, based on life history and personality. As you absorb new knowledge and experiment with new techniques, you will assimilate them into your own developing style. When we take an active role in genuinely collaborating with clients, we effectively interrupt dysfunctional processes that perpetuate their troublesome behavior, feeling, or thinking. This book examines in detail the aspects of the work, here divided into separate spheres that, in reality, overlap and spiral.

A NOTE ABOUT THEORY, CLIENTS, AND YOU

Theory inevitably guides our work, but theory should not supersede either common sense or the realities in clients' lives. This book, therefore, draws from a broad theoretical base.

We tend to see the world as we are trained to see it; and we rely heavily on certain tenets and generalizations to deal with our lack of knowledge or experience. We also resist contradictory explanations. This often makes change almost impossible. Serious adherence to any one theory runs the risk of producing rigidity or inflexibility.

There is a great gap between how theory explains client behavior and motivation and the way it occurs in actuality. Mine is an invitation for you to free yourself from the constraints of subscribing exclusively to any one theory, to keep your mind and options open, and to generate fresh alternatives and perspectives. I argue here for questioning theories in light of your contact with clients and also questioning yourself and your "certainties."

Clients are faced with complex interactions among variables influencing their lives. You too, as a clinician, confront a variety of competing and conflicting theories and viewpoints that explain both client and therapeutic dynamic. Just as you ask clients to be open and flexible in the way they consider their own variables, you too need to be open and flexible in the way you adopt or adapt theories to the unique characteristics of your clients and their situation.

Do not feel pressured to take sides, to declare allegiance to one particular school of thought. No one has a corner on human experience. Hold open the possibilities that change and integration in clients, as well as in yourself, can occur in a variety of ways.

Be elastic; consider many theories. Attempt to bridge their differences, appreciate their similarities, and weave them into an integrated fabric of what is most apt both for your clients and for you.

Each theory has its own partial truth and its own limited viewpoint. Do not get caught in either/or thinking, but instead, try to achieve a balance by looking at many approaches.

Consider three things:

- What makes sense
- What works for your clients
- What "fits" you

Such a fluid stance captures the essence of a dynamic balance and models the open-mindedness and tolerance of ambiguity that we expect from clients themselves.

Furthermore, various theories may not be as incompatible with each other as they first may appear. Since we lack a generally accepted way to demonstrate the validity and efficacy of the contentions of each of these competing theories, the rational recourse is to remain uncommitted to any one of them. Instead, become familiar with many of them, in order to develop the capacity to describe, explain, or interpret the same phenomena to yourself, your colleagues, and your clients in several different ways, and to inform your ingenuity in assimilating different ways to think about and invent new ways to respond effectively to your clients.

An exclusive investment in any one position, to the exclusion of others, serves to restrict and impair your understanding of your clients as well as yourself.

CLINICIANS' TASKS IN PHASES OF CLINICAL WORK

Tasks in the Beginning Phase

1. Convey a caring attitude and an understanding of clients' pain and distress.
2. Establish and maintain rapport by understanding the dynamics of the helping relationship and the initial phase of clinical work, adjusting yourself to the style, language, tone, and tempo of your clients.
3. Gather information and make accurate individual and family assessments by using verbal, written, nonverbal, and other data sources to identify issues, strengths, and direction.
4. Educate clients about the helping process itself and provide practical information appropriate to their specific needs to relieve them of some of the burden they are carrying alone.
5. Contract to prioritize targets of attention; agree on mutual goals, roles, tasks, and timetable to work toward solutions; set the structure for the working alliance and continually evaluate progress.
6. Motivate clients to be committed to their transformation.

Tasks in the Middle Phase

7. Work "with" rather than "on" clients.
8. Clarify misconceptions and create an ongoing internal and external safe house.

9. Convince clients that you understand their suffering and are capable of helping them.
10. Recognize clients as their own best key resource.
11. Create resources by flexibly providing experiences for mastery, connection with supportive others, and practice in new skills.
12. Create individualized techniques designed to match the clients' style and their situation.
13. Reinforce clients' own competence, strengthen their coping patterns, and increase their ability to solve problems without assistance in the future.

Tasks in the Ending Phase

14. Translate understanding into action that becomes part of ongoing and future experience; generalize changes and new learning so that they automatically become part of clients' repertoire of coping skills.
15. Deal with forces that block learning and create barriers to action; anticipate and plan for both positive and negative consequences of change.
16. Prepare for ending the helping relationship, and advance through the phases of separation.
17. Adjust to irremediable conditions.
18. Terminate the process of analyzing and resolving dependency issues, and help clients to achieve as much independence and assertiveness as possible; stabilize gains and say good-bye.

Tasks Throughout the Entire Helping Endeavor

19. Be patient.
20. Keep a sense of humor.
21. Employ self-disclosure with discretion.
22. Remain compassionate.
23. Stay reality based and pragmatic.
24. Be flexible.
25. Concentrate on strengths—the clients' as well as your own.

Chapter 2

Creating a Safe House

Competent therapists fluctuate between the limits of a scientific
discipline and the infinite possibilities of inspired intuition.

W. Robert Beavers

A sacred space is any space that is set apart from the usual context of life. . . . You really don't have a sacred space, a rescue
land, until you find somewhere to be that's not a wasteland,
some field of action where there is a spring of ambrosia—a joy
that comes from inside, not something external that puts joy into
you—a place that lets you experience your own will and your
own intention . . .

Joseph Campbell

Spy and detective novels, movies, and television shows have made
popular the notion of the safe house, a completely secure location
where inhabitants are free from danger. In novels such as those by
Ludlum, Higgins, and Le Carré, safe houses are places to take shelter
from pursuing enemies for a short time.

Safe houses are not merely a romanticized fictional notion. They
do exist in fact. As far back as biblical times, "the six cities of refuge"
provided security for those who unintentionally killed another person. In the Middle Ages, Abelard established a safe house, the
Paraclete, where he found sanctuary from those conspiring against
him. Today police and justice departments provide safe houses for
key witnesses threatened because of their testimony in criminal
cases. Adversary nations maintain temporary hideaways in hostile
territories to safeguard their agents. While these locations are sup-

posed to be secret, eventually they are found out. But an unwritten code requires that once in the door, the agent remains immune to pursuit.

THE SAFE HOUSE
OF THE HELPING PROCESS

The safe house is a palpable and powerful metaphor for the helping process, clarifying and unifying such diverse characterizations of the helping process as gratification and abstinence, neutrality and anonymity, the real and the transferred relationship. Clients require an anchorage. Here they can literally and figuratively escape for a time from dreadful thrashings. They can find refuge from the dangers and hurts of the external world and from accompanying internal fears. In a safe harbor, they can find calm. They can patch their tears. Just as it does in novels, the safe house for clients provides a respite from painful events and trauma compounded by internal injury. Its climate is warm and accepting.

But respite is not enough. Trauma takes on a private symbolic significance for clients, who interpret trauma according to their own internal psychic realities. In the safe house of the therapist's office, clients not only experience relief from their anxieties but come to understand, meet, and overcome their sense of brokenness. Your office offers a "holding space," in Winnicott's (1986) phrase, for accepting clients' feelings and affirming their strengths. Away from a barrage of abuse, criticism, neglect, and rejection, they can be free to move deeper into themselves.

The important thing to recognize with regard to the safe house is that it is not a return to symbiosis but is a place of structure and transition where communication with you gives clients a growing ability to find themselves.

Because clients come to you at a time when their usual adaptive defenses are weakened, your safe retreat helps them to reinstate familiar and healthy defenses. Here they learn certain strategies to come to terms with the present trauma as well as some dynamics of their internal life that may have made them vulnerable to being overwhelmed or too depleted to find solutions. Success depends upon their revising their view of themselves, others, and the world. The safe house is where you counteract their expectation that they will inevitably fail, that others will be uncaring, and that they will be left to struggle alone. In an atmosphere of positive expectancy and support, clients are restored and better prepared with new skills for returning to face a world that is at times dangerous and violent. In returning, however, because they have been rejuvenated and have discovered previously untapped resources, they are even better able to brave the stress and strain of living.

The "Good Enough" Environment

In the safe house, you supply some of the nurturance that was originally missing from clients' lives. The safe house is a sanctuary, not unlike the one described by Winnicott (1986) as necessary for "good enough" mothering, that which is needed in the present to allow the realization of full potential in the future. In this close, rather than distant, association of warmth, rather than coolness, clients can consolidate themselves. The "good enough" mother is your model for the therapeutic situation. Some children experience being held, cradled, cuddled, and protected from dangerous objects and harmful experiences. Others grow up in an unsafe atmosphere of abuse. Your task is to offer another experience of renewal to those clients who originally experienced it, restoring their balance, and to offer it for the first time to those who never experienced it. In either case, "holding," accepting, and respecting them impels them deeper into themselves so that they learn to "hold" themselves. Eventually, they gain insight into themselves because while you nurture, you also interpret their condition.

In the safe house, clients are not forced to rely solely upon their own already depleted resources. They do not have to "make do" with their lacks and limitations. New possibilities are provided. A temporary shelter where they can find peace and balance in a world askew, the safe house offers a place where change can take place, a space where clients can disarm themselves and lay aside their fearfulness. The painful past can be revealed; unremembered hurts can be reexperienced or experienced as an adult for the first time. Through remembered emotions, a search can be undertaken for a better future.

For some clients, such as Ms. Wall, a better future does not even seem like a remote possibility. Ms. Wall, a twenty-six-year-old single parent of three children, one of them handicapped, had lived in a single room of a welfare hotel in the inner city of a large metropolitan area until they were evicted. She continually abused drugs even while enrolled in a drug treatment program. While there was considerable evidence of child abuse, this situation had never been addressed. Occupying a cardboard shack on the sidewalk of a large conference center, panhandling, struggling to keep her family together, and still dealing with her drug habit, she agreed to move into a shelter to make life easier. The shelter provided a room, a set of rules to follow, and a caseworker who capitalized on Ms. Wall's desire—reluctant though it was—to be clean and sober. Concentrating first on providing food, shelter, clothing, and medical treatment, along with drug rehabilitation, Ms. Wall was encouraged to connect with other women in the facility who supported and encouraged her to "stick with the program." The shelter's stable, structured, and predictable environment, and the worker's persistent attentiveness, contrasted greatly with the disrupted, uprooted, and abusive home that she had known as a child.

Active caring, combined with limit setting and information and proficiency skills needed to care for her children, in a way she herself had not been cared for, improved her parenting behavior, and engendered a sense of mastery and esteem. This change did not occur without the worker first tolerating Ms. Wall's initial hostile verbal assaults, and then helping her to examine them as part of her troubled pattern of relating to others. Exploration increased her understanding of the adverse results of her self-destructive behaviors—drug abuse, angry outbursts, and manipulations.

Establishing the connection between her actions and her feelings when she engaged in self-defeating behavior released painful feelings and helped her to recognize that such behavior was often a defense against further possible physical and emotional injury. Reflecting on feedback about her own negative attitudes and patterns, Ms. Wall became more consistently self-soothing and self-reliant in her behavior toward herself and her children. The shelter, marred by torn flooring, graffiti-marked walls, and musty odors, but furnished by Ms. Wall with her own pictures and decorative plants, became not a palace, but a place of pride.

In the safe house of your relationship, clients pass through a metaphoric version of developmental maturation, as Ms. Wall did. They depend on you for their well-being. This is akin to the developmental process through which we all journey on our way from absolute dependence to autonomy. Recapitulated in the safe house with you is a version of the infant's complete reliance on caretakers. As time passes, the child develops his or her own way, and caretakers have the task of permitting individuality to emerge and separation to take place. This is a multistage process. So it is with your clients in the safe house.

At first, attention is paid to provision of staples necessary for survival and vigor. Focus is then directed toward connection and communication. The third step involves regulating the self, freeing repressed needs, and learning new methods for self-support. Clients learn new ways of thinking and problem solving and come to self-knowledge through the facilitative conditions and interpretations you provide. Knowledge and insight, of course, must be translated into actual change in daily life, through repeated practice to refine change.

The Internal Safe House

Ultimately, clients become sufficiently whole and consolidated to build a more permanent, personal, inner safe house for themselves so they can leave your temporary safe house to venture out on their own with a lasting sense of being at home with themselves.

Make your office a secure base where a client can

> take temporary refuge from the demands and distractions of daily life. . . . He can participate in complex, emotionally charged rituals, suspend his critical faculties, freely express his emotions, indulge in leisurely self-exploration, daydream, or do whatever else the therapy prescribes, secure in the knowledge that no harm will come to him during the session and that he will not be held accountable in his daily life for whatever he says or does during it. (Frank, 1973, p. 325)

A VIEW OF HOME

A profound way of understanding what clients require to get back on course is getting a glimpse of their first home. Although their description of "home" may relate to the past, you will learn from it what constitutes their internal paradigm for present issues of trust, safety, entrapment, hiding, or exposure. In reflecting on and talking about their home, clients present a telescopic view of the significant places and people who fashioned their history. Asking them to draw a floor plan of the home where they grew up, for example, sparks memories and feelings about family, friends, and events. Their simple narrative about home demonstrates the complex relationship between their living space and the nature of their inner lives. Clients create their environments, while the environment affects how they live. Their description of home provides for you a mirror reflecting the world from which they came as well as their inner vision of it, which continues to hold them. The soft and cozy nests, the unassailable castles, and the womblike closets they build and inhabit provide you with an organizing metaphor, capturing not only a picture of their original home, an image of their inner life, but also a guide for establishing the form of your safe house. During the course of your work, changes in their home indicate changes within their perspectives and within themselves.

Carol: Finding Home

The following case illustration demonstrates how one client's view of home influenced the focus and direction of the helping process. Carol's metaphor for her background and for herself was the absence of any safe place in her life. Establishing a safe house made it possible for her to overcome multiple present and past trauma and to find meaning within her current interactions with the world.

Carol, a twenty-eight-year-old graduate nurse, had been seeing me for approximately eight months when she was brutalized, raped, and sodomized in her own apartment. Crawling to her telephone a few hours later, after she regained consciousness, she called the police, who took her to a local hospital. She undressed and waited over an hour for the attending physician, only to be summarily discharged without examination. The hospital had no rape kit. Taken to yet another hospital, she undressed again, for the third time that evening. Unable to reach friends or family, she returned home alone. She had no safe place—now or ever, it seemed. Even the safety of being inside her own body was ended. She had been broken into, violated.

Away at a conference, I received a frantic call from Carol. She was desperate. She did not know where to turn. In contacting a rape hot line, as was recommended by hospital staff and police, she had been counseled not to continue to work with me, a man. Such advice added to her confusion; it further paralyzed her. She had always felt secure with me and stable in our work; but now Carol was getting upsetting advice that contradicted her own instincts. Could she trust me? Could she trust anyone? Could she trust her own instincts? Was there any place where she was safe from harm? Compounding her sense of helplessness, isolation, and despair was the fact that her friends, apparently not knowing how to comfort her, were avoiding her. Shunned by them at the time of her greatest need, she was shamed and devastated; indeed, she started to blame herself for her suffering.

Carol was reassured over the phone by my open caring and concern. For a few hours we sifted through the events that had occurred, her reactions to them, and the choices available to her. She decided to continue working with me. She also decided to start attending a special group for rape victims. Immediately upon my return from the conference, our work resumed.

Originally, Carol had come seeking help after a series of disastrous relationships with men. She was also extremely dissatisfied with her job, her profession, and herself. Early in our work, it became clear that Carol's historical and inner home was troubled. She grew up in an alcoholic household, where she was the oldest of four children and the only female. Her mother worked, frequently leaving Carol to care for everyone else and for the house, which was literally crumbling around them all. She was repeatedly abused physically and berated verbally by her father. Her three brothers continually taunted her. She felt abandoned by her mother. Her recollection of her home and the people in it was grim and sad. She came to believe that men were inevitably cruel and disappointing. She refused to follow in her mother's footsteps, finding her disorganized and unavailable. She recalled her home as being violent and in shambles, an armed camp or a hovel. This image of Carol's home, while certainly relevant in our beginning work, became paramount, along with the rape, as a focal point for reflection, an available and vivid symbol of all her dilemmas about family and self.

Carol had deliberately set up her own apartment to be totally different from her parents' house. It was peaceful, orderly, clean, and free from threats. She designed her home to be a sanctuary, not a prison. After the rape, her home became a fortress, not a castle. The meaning of this central metaphor, representing her past and present state, was continually elaborated and explored.

Our work together was structured to provide an atmosphere of validation and emotional sharing. Feeling "at home" as our work progressed, she found release in catharsis, and support in cognitive interpretation and restructuring of her central metaphor of "no safe place." This structure helped contain and control what she experienced as her inner chaos.

Significant breakthroughs were promoted by Carol's ongoing use of a log, in the form of index cards, on which she recorded memories of the incident, an incident that intensified repressed residual feelings of failure, defeat, and emptiness from her past. On these 5 × 8 cards she also recorded dreams in which she continually relived the pain and humiliation of the rape, but in which she also revealed the emotional process of gradually coming to grips with it. As these cards were sorted, resorted and examined, the story of the rape incident, and its accompanying metaphor, acquired a central role in her deeper deliberations about herself and her family.

All this material led to increasing associations and affective connections. Carol gradually filled the gaps in her understanding not only of the rape, which had precipitated such intensive exploration, but of more buried and previously inscrutable milestones in her life. As she did so, she came to fathom the deeper sources of her pervasive feelings of unimportance, worthlessness, and powerlessness, to make connections to her earlier experiences of deprivation and neglect over which she had no control. She came to recognize that she did not provoke and was not to blame for all that she had suffered. She was able to take control of the events, herself, and the situation.

Finally, Carol came to remember that she did not simply submit to her attacker. She had struggled against him at knifepoint. This discovery resulted in her being able to muster energy and perseverance to press charges against her assailant and to testify against him in court, even though it involved rehashing the details of the trauma. She had gained mastery over it and felt sufficiently strong and revitalized that she asked her father to join her in a few sessions with me to clear the air about the rape, for he had treated her as disgraced, perhaps blameful. We used this time as well to address and seek to resolve the long-hidden issues between them.

Carol did not want to conclude the work, which extended over a period of three years. She wanted to cling to what was safe and sure;

however, she recognized that she had found and could rely upon the safe place within herself.

In the safe house, Carol came to acknowledge the horror of her rape and the horror of her background, but, replenished, she came back able to face them. Not withdrawing, and finding a safe place within herself, she learned to utilize her insights and draw on them to establish an identity and a personal meaning system. Carol currently has a new apartment, is gainfully employed, and is dating.

Relinquishing the Safe House

The safe house is simultaneously timeless and temporary. It is timeless because it does more than merely remove stress or symptoms. It involves a shift in the client's experiential world. It serves as the model and instrument for clients to locate within themselves a safe house to which they can continually turn for succor and growth. The safe house is temporary, insofar as clients cannot stay forever. Ultimately, no care taking is permanent. Clearly, something must happen in the safe house that allows clients to leave it. If they remain, their circumstances would become as unbearable as those they fled. The safe house would become a prison. Just as a nursing mother must wean her baby or stifle its growth, so you must encourage your clients to separate when they are ready. Their readiness is determined by the degree to which they are ready to tolerate separation and have achieved mastery of internal emotions. Separation can bring freedom and exhilaration as attachment can sustain growth. Paradoxically, healthy detachment requires attachment.

ATTACHMENT BEHAVIOR AND EMPATHY

The safe house is a metaphorical way of conveying what the professional literature refers to as attachment behavior, the holding environment, and empathy.

Attachment Behavior

Attachment behavior is viewed by Bowlby (1975) as any form of behavior resulting in an individual attaining or retaining closeness to another differentiated or preferred individual, usually conceived as stronger or wiser. While it begins early in life, attachment behavior continues to be apparent throughout life, especially when a person is sick, upset, or frightened. It is characterized by:

1. Specificity and long duration
2. Emotional arousal
3. A critical period for its development
4. Appearance even in the face of punishment
5. Maintaining proximity to the attachment figure as a secure base
6. Reciprocal behavior by the attachment figure
7. Functioning to protect the individual from danger (Bowlby, 1975, p. 292).

When there is confidence in the availability of attachment figures (in other words, when you are available to clients), they are less prone to either intense or chronic fear. Put simply, they need to count on you in time of need for mutual understanding, giving support, valuing them, and promoting their well-being. Your safe house is the place where clients' inherent capacities for hope and faith, deadened by misfortunes and horrors in the present and in their original home, can be restored.

Empathy and the Holding Environment

The technical name for your attunement to clients in creating a safe house is *empathy*. There is a strong parallel between being a parent and being a professional helper. You do not need to be perfect, but you do need to be good and sensitive enough to your clients' needs to accept and go along with their positive and negative struggles. It is, indeed, reparenting. This is no small order. How is it possible to enter your client's reality to such an extent that you can actually alter the way that he or she perceives and subsequently deals with the world? Empathic listening and understanding form the basis of any effective intervention (Kohut, 1984). We do not make an instantaneous leap of enlightenment but rather engage in a multifaceted process. We show the capacity to project ourselves (while remaining separate) into the inner experience of another.

There is some debate about what empathy is, how important it is, and how it works. Confusion abounds about its definition and significance. This can be expected, for empathy is defined differently by different philosophies and theoretical orientations. Results of research studies based in these theories are certainly not illuminating. It is not fully clear what part empathy plays in producing positive therapeutic outcomes. Questions arise. Is empathy rational or irrational? Does it involve only affect, or cognition as well? Is it only cognition? Is it a mode of observation, or is it projection? Is it a form of identification in which a temporary loss of self occurs? Is it conscious or unconscious? Is it a capacity, a trait, a process, or a form of communication? Is it predictive? Situational? Is it verbal, nonverbal? Neither? Both? Is it experience distant or experience near? Is it the same as sympathy? As love? Does it heal? It should be no surprise that such a complicated phenomenon defies easy explanation.

Regardless of its complexity, empathy is commonly used to refer to your ability to come to know firsthand, so to speak, the experience of your clients. It is considered a necessary, but not sufficient, condition for the helping process. Basch (1983) points out that Freud considered empathy to be indispensable when it came to taking a position regarding another's mental life. The father of psychoanalysis viewed empathy as the process playing the largest part in our understanding of what is inherently foreign to our ego in others. Rogers (1958) sees empathy as including both cognitive and affective elements. *Cognitive empathy* refers to intellectually taking the role or perspective of the client. It means seeing the world as the client does. *Affective empathy* refers to responding to the client's emotion with the same emotion. It means feeling the same way as the client does. Rogers also emphasized the need for the helper to communicate this understanding.

Psychoanalytic writers identify the more subtle aspects of empathy. For example, Greenson (1967, pp. 368-369) stated that

> empathy means to share, to experience the feelings of another human being. One partakes of the quality of the feelings and not the quantity. . . . It is essentially a preconscious phenomenon; it can be consciously instigated or interrupted; and it can occur silently and automatically oscillating with other forms of relating to people.

Kohut (1977) explains empathy as a basic human capacity that not only operates as a therapeutic tool but also defines the field of our observations and interactions by letting us know that there is an inner life. He refers to empathy as "vicarious introspection" and argues that

empathy can only be understood empathically. He explains that a clinician "uses his sensory impressions, of course . . . but these sensory
data would remain meaningless were it not for his ability to recognize
complex psychological configurations that only empathy, the human
echo to human experience, can provide" (Kohut, 1978, p. 700). Kohut
(1977) postulates that the empathic responsiveness of the helper par-
ticipates in the repair of developmental empathic failures caused by
unempathic parents. Empathy, then, is both exploratory and explanatory.

   As I have mentioned earlier, Winnicott (1986), too, emphasizes the
theme that good helping is good mothering. He argues further that
"good enough" mothering is more a matter of who mothers are than
what they do. An essential ingredient is a caring interpersonal relationship that creates an atmosphere of trust (Winnicott, 1986). A
good helper relaxes enough to be vulnerable and perhaps even wrong.
Clients learn then that being vulnerable, being wrong, and stumbling
are okay—a most important lesson.

   Barrett-Lennard (1981) describes the process of empathy as a multistage sequence in which

> empathy is first and foremost an inner experience, a responsive
> experiential resonation in keeping with the responding person's
> set to be this way. For . . . to have an impact . . . its effect will nec-
> essarily depend on qualities of the receiver as well as on the sig-
> nal of the sender (p. 93).

   Hogan (1969), in studying empathy, substantially agreed on the
characteristics of a highly empathic person. These characteristics include (1) skill in imaginative play, pretending, and humor; (2) awareness of the impression one makes on others; (3) ability to evaluate
others' motives; (4) insight into one's own motives and behavior; and
(5) social perception.

   Empathy, then, involves a personal capacity, affective resonance,
and cognitive understanding. All are operative and complementarily
interwoven in interpersonal functioning. Fosshage (1981) suggests
that we are capable of two different modes of mental activity: One visual and sensory with intense affective colorations serving overall integrative and synthetic functions; the other conceptual and logical,
making use of linguistic symbols serving an integrative and synthetic
function. These modes of mentation may be described as different by

complementary modes of apprehending, responding to, and organizing the external and internal world. He emphasizes that despite specialization of function, both hemispheres of the brain process not independently, but complementarily. The degree to which each is utilized in the helping process varies from client to client and from situation to situation.

There is sufficient theoretical clarity and research evidence across the disciplines to indicate that empathy is multifaceted. It is a trait, an emotional and cognitive capacity, that can be activated, and a state manifested in thoughts, feelings, or behavior and demonstrated in a multistage interpersonal process. It involves cognitive understanding of another combined with affective resonance. Both exploratory and explanatory, it comprises vicarious feelings and associations, coupled with correct understanding.

Empathy and You

Put in less theoretical terms, empathy is a spontaneous and temporary experience occurring within you, the helper, having affective and cognitive components whereby you come to know and comprehend what clients might be experiencing. It is a mode of gathering information about clients' internal worlds by attending to your own experience in the presence of clients. It requires an ability to oscillate from observer to participant and back. It is important because it allows you access to clients' inner experience, and in doing so, moves you away from any tendency to objectify clients and view them simply as the repository of symptoms or problems. It also dampens any tendency to treat them as bad, devouring, or manipulative. It is an essential prerequisite for your ability to be empathic—to voice your understanding of clients in such a way that they feel understood and soothed. This feeling of being understood and soothed provides a connectedness that diminishes clients' feelings of aloneness and alienation, and thus strengthens your working alliance with them.

Empathy has the potential to bring the clarity of rational logic to bear upon the profundity of affective experience, a way to synthesize two apparently antithetical figures: the dispassionate and rational scientist and the attuned, resonating artist.

Providing a safe house, then, can be considered as metaphoric shorthand for being empathic.

HOW TO BUILD A SAFE HOUSE

You start to build a safe house for clients by making yourself accessible to them; you actively offer your assistance in helping them design their plan for change, not as a passive participant but as an active collaborator. You do not simply observe your clients but enter into their experience on a fundamental level to get to know parts of them that they may not know. A critical component of drawing the blueprint involves being aware of what you bring into the process yourself; you influence the design. It also involves knowing the strength, shape, and texture of the materials with which you will be working so that they can be employed to maximum advantage.

Digging the cellar and laying the foundation involve getting information that is buried and supports the structure. In the unending relationship between our needs, wants, and wishes and environmental demands and restrictions, we learn ways to react and form patterns that make it easier to adjust to the environment. Some of these patterns are functional and others are not. Identifying them requires immersion in clients' inner lives and experiences; it involves repetitive interactions that sometimes become boring but create shapes, so that old patterns are uncovered and the possibility for creating and altering new ones is enhanced.

You may have to abandon the customary approach of neutrality and aloofness. Enter the experience with them. It is interesting to note that therapist-clients seek in their own therapeutic work a personal relationship, one in which they feel affirmed, appreciated, and respected by another human being whom they like, appreciate, and respect (Grunebaum, 1983). Harmful treatment experiences result from a rigid, distant, and uninvolved interaction. Be highly visible as a facilitator of communication and have a capacity to contain and catalyze behavior and emotions that are denied, projected, and acted out by clients. Providing a containing safe house is a prerequisite for effective work and serves as a basis for change. It has been suggested that you have become a helper partly in search of a safe house of your own. Providing a safe house for your clients serves you as well.

Your role is that of a host who welcomes clients. Be consistent and available. Be generous, receptive, and responsive. Show appreciation and patience. Create an ambiance of trust and support. Face clients squarely. Show that you are present to them. Make your own reactions available for them to study. Impassivity cheats you and clients of your most useful instrument—your own experience and ability to see and to share.

You can make a difference if you are receptive and remember to:

- Delight in the endless variety and unexplored mystery of people
- Be curious, take risks, and be open to challenges
- Experiment, innovate, be original and creative
- Rely on both artistic intuition and scientific intellect
- Know that you do not have total comprehension
- Be humble, vulnerable, and open to discovery
- Be a nondistorting mirror reflecting clients' unknown aspects
- Recognize that your power is based on your ability to face your own inner reality and face it responsibly
- Take time; do not rush to get instant results
- Have the courage to admit your mistakes and failures
- Change what you are doing when it does not work
- Trust and pursue your imagination; daydream
- Endeavor sincerely to get in touch with clients
- Discover your own blind spots and free yourself from excessive anxiety and coldness
- Be generous and kindly

Building a safe house does not mean fusing with your clients. This would be as destructive as a lack of compassion or understanding. It means, rather, opening a dialogue in which clients are expected to help you understand them, rather than your showing superior wisdom. In a safe house there is activity as well as reflection, doing as well as saying, extrospection as well as introspection. Emphasis is placed on the human experience of an active, striving, affirming, and potentiating transaction, on recognizing the continuity of the "there and then" of the distant past with the "here and now" of the immediate present. Both, taken together, establish the conditions for change. The novelty of such integration serves as a catalyst for growth.

If you cannot get yourself into clients' shoes and somehow give them relief as well as resources, the work will dissolve. Have your actions match your words. Clients will progress when they experience your "holding" in an intense way. Kohut (1982) writes: "I must now, unfortunately, add that empathy per se, the mere presence of empathy, has also a beneficial, in a broad sense, a therapeutic effect—both in the clinical setting and in human life, in general" (p. 85). Why "unfortunately"? Kohut feared that such a direct statement would expose him to the suspicion of abandoning scientific sobriety and of entering the land of mysticism or sentimentality. He wanted to maintain his objectivity. But he was on target.

The safe house is more than a symbolic dwelling. It is as much a holding environment for you as it is for clients. When you involve yourself and participate fully with clients, your experiential learning will match theirs.

FOUR PARADOXES

The safe house is poignantly depicted by four paradoxes:

1. For us to be healthily detached and independent requires first being attached and dependent.
2. To "lose" ourselves in a mutually created therapeutic experience is to "find" ourselves anew.
3. Being linked closely together makes us simultaneously vulnerable and powerfully influential.
4. Our means is our end; our end is our means.

Ultimately, clients in the safe house become sufficiently whole and consolidated to build a more permanent, personal, inner sacred space for themselves, so they can leave the temporary safe house of your joint endeavor to venture out on their own with a lasting sense of being at home with themselves. An essential benefit of creating such a safe place for others is that it holds you as well.

Chapter 3

The Helping Relationship

Behold, I do not give lectures or a little charity,
When I give I give myself.

Walt Whitman

The overtones are lost, and what is left are conversations which, in their poverty, cannot hide the lack of real contact. We glide past each other. But why? Why—? We reach out towards the other. In vain—because we have never dared to give ourselves.

Dag Hammarskjöld

In the beginning is the relationship.

Martin Buber

No man is an island. No client, no family, no group, no therapist is an island. We are defined and continually influenced by relationships. The core of our humanity is that we live our lives in relation to other people. Relationship is the essence of our existence.

From the earliest hours of life we are formed and form ourselves on the basis of our experiences with others. Who we are is the result of these interactions. Studies of personality development identify relationships as the dynamic core that makes us human. Elements of each relationship and the ability to accept or reject a relationship contribute to who we are. Without relationships we cease to exist. Babies who are not held and nurtured soon die—often physically, always emotionally. In short, we are creatures who throughout our lives require contact and connection with others.

33

Thus it is true for clients seeking help.

It is within the context of the helping relationship that clients' perceptual distortions, maladaptive behaviors, and paradigms about self, others, and the world not only come under challenge, but are changed. Within the context of the helping relationship, both clients and you deal either explicitly or implicitly with: (1) past experiences that have affected the ability to relate to others; (2) the "here and now" experience of the physical, emotional, and perceptual state of your transaction; and (3) each of your expectations of the other and the process.

Can anything more be said about the helping relationship? Yes. No form of help can succeed unless you first convince clients that you understand them and are concerned for their welfare.

We in the helping professions tend to be increasingly pragmatic. What we like to see is efficiency. What is harder to see is caring, the instrument of change and development. Caring is more elusive, ambiguous, harder to quantify. It requires our participation in pain and our sharing in the experience of suffering. When we continually attempt to refine our understanding of caring in relationship, we are in a better position to offer consolation and hope. Caring does not mean falling into a sentimental trap; rather, it means establishing a vehicle of concern that cultivates the field of intellectual curiosity and exploration. Caring alone cannot resolve problems. However, being cared for gives clients the courage to talk honestly and directly about their troublesome lives.

We tend to run away from painful realities or to try to change them quickly. But cure without care makes us manipulators in the most negative sense and prevents a quality of intimacy that exists when two people are truly present for each other. In this view, you are an active participant in an affective as well as cognitive reciprocal interaction with clients, an interaction in which you both come to understanding and "change" over the course of time. Be ready, willing, and eager to dive into deeper waters even though clients may pull back in terror from such exploration. The very way you attend to them, "be where they are," reduces their fear of facing uncertainty and furthers an ongoing personal dialogue that expresses, shapes, and enriches your immediate experience together. As a consequence, clients are less inclined to slip back into maladaptive functioning.

Even if you accept the phenomenon of transference (implicitly discussed later in this chapter and more explicitly in Chapter 11) as integral to your work, it is unlikely that you will interfere with its occurrence by being open and available. It seems to me that transference is so powerful and ubiquitous that it will manifest itself without special consideration being given to assuming a posture of neutrality and abstinence.

THE DEVELOPMENT
OF THE HELPING RELATIONSHIP

The therapeutic relationship develops in a way similar to other interpersonal relationships. From the initial attraction between clients and you in the first meeting, and from your mutually negotiating contract arrangements, communication opens both to produce further interaction and to enhance cohesion. The relationship is the keystone for the practical, personal, and theoretical elements of your professional helping. When clients feel understood by you, have confidence in you, and contribute to how the work proceeds, positive outcomes result.

The impact of helping resides in how well you use yourself and your sensitivity to guide clients' journeys in understanding themselves. The most important vehicle available to make this happen is your ability in the relationship to model behavior, reflect attitude, and explore thinking and feeling. Change can thus be understood as a process by which clients begin to experience themselves in different ways, so that their previous experience of themselves and others becomes untenable.

Put yourself in your clients' shoes. The process of helping demands that you understand how clients view the world. Empathic understanding means more than mere knowledge of how clients feel. It means the capacity to actually feel what they feel. For clients, having you understand what it is like to be them encourages different ways of experiencing. Clients' attachment to you, combined with your empathic resonance, provides an anchor that allows them to weather emotional storms and is a mainstay to fathom uncharted waters. This corrective experience allows clients to experience themselves differently and thereby make changes. It is a function of the extent to which you can, leaving any preconceived notions aside, get inside them, be where they are, and share their world.

The essence of successful helping is clients' achieving trust in you as a therapeutic instrument. If this cannot be realized, the outcome of the helping process will be thwarted. If it can, stability, identity, and awareness are achieved.

THEORIES
OF THE HELPING RELATIONSHIP

The professional literature speaks of relationship as the vehicle through which help occurs. It emphasizes core conditions in the relationship necessary to inspire change. Rogers (1958) described these as follows:

- Genuineness—your ability to know yourself so as to be fully present to your client while remaining truly yourself
- Accurate empathic understanding—your ability to enter the feeling world of the client
- Unconditional positive regard—your trust in the process of growth and self-actualization

Strupp (1977) identified core relationship conditions as respect, interest, understanding, tact, maturity, and firm belief in the ability to help. Compton and Galaway (1979) conceptualized them as concern for the other, commitment and obligation, acceptance and expectation, empathy, authority and power, and genuineness and congruence. Frank (1973) described these as follows:

- Learning—instillation of new cognitions
- Hope—enhancement of positive expectancies
- Mastery—provision of success experiences
- Sharing—relief of alienation through human contact and arousal and emotional, not merely intellectual, stimulation.

An extensive review of psychotherapy-outcome studies showed that warmth, liking, and acceptance are significant contributors to clients' rating of outcome (Grunebaum, 1986). Other research supports the centrality of these aspects by highlighting what is harmful in the therapeutic process. Part of how we understand what is helpful is to understand what is harmful so as to avoid it. Helpers characterized as distant, cold, unengaged, and lacking in "human quality" were seen as harmful. You can probably add being indifferent, demanding, guilt provoking, judgmental, and dogmatic to the list.

Buber (1970) spoke about two primary types of relationships—"I-It" and "I-Thou." The I-It relationship involves two people viewing and experiencing each other as something that can be objectified, described, and analyzed. The I-Thou relationship depends upon deep empathic contact not attainable by "distance" or by techniques designed to facilitate interaction. He maintained that it is only in the context of a fundamentally equal, reciprocal, and mutual person-to-person relationship that healing occurs.

Marziali and Alexander (1991), in their review of the research literature of the previous decade, demonstrate the relevance of the therapeutic relationship for predicting positive outcome in diverse models of therapy. They assert that the relationship is a potent curative factor in all forms of treatment.

Various approaches to therapy have significantly different perspectives on the significance of the relationship. In the psychodynamic perspective, a "real" relationship between you and the client is downplayed since it interferes with evoking and maintaining a transference relationship, the essential contextual and mutative agent through which change occurs. Existential therapists, on the other hand, actively strive to establish a "real" relationship whose central function is characterized by being "present," open, and honest. Change results from clients' being able to relate deeply to the therapist. Although behavioral therapists once resisted the notion that the therapist is personally involved in the process of treatment, more modern behaviorists view "rapport" as an initial and essential ingredient in the technique of modifying behavior.

To me, the optimum relationship is characterized by one or more of the following: warmth, acceptance, respect, understanding, closeness, interest, maturity, and trust. Your aim is not simply to recapitulate and then supply what was originally missing or repair what was faulty in clients' lives but, rather, to create an atmosphere of responsiveness, expectancy, and hope where new perspectives are possible. You bring, in other words, empathic capacity as well as scientific understanding to your exchange.

Identifying characteristics of the helping relationship as discrete entities is misleading and somewhat artificial because they are so interwoven. Ways of describing one component of the relationship are often the same used to describe another. More important, it is unlikely that you will develop a relationship by focusing on any one relationship characteristic and deciding, for example, "I will be 'accepting.'" Relationship is not built in that way. Relationship is synergistic and includes all the elements mentioned above, in dynamic interdependence. It is more and greater than all its parts.

By way of summary, relationship signifies "agape," in Greek, the highest form of love:

A G A P E

A—Acceptance
G—Genuineness
A—Actuality
P—Positive regard
E—Empathy

Clients absorb and identify with your delicate and immediate facility for emotional exchange and your comfort with such sensitive matters as dependence, conflict, and power. Through the relationship, you help clients more fully understand and effectively use their personality strengths to overcome dysfunctional patterns. You accomplish this by providing an in vivo experience of empathic resonance with them. You offer a firsthand sense of the rich depth of the human mind, an appreciation of the strength of inner or intrapsychic forces, and a grasp of the power of human contact.

Helping is not always positive. Some attempts fail. Clients' uncertainty about themselves, others, and the world can be so powerful that it can have negative consequences. The quality of the experience with you, however, is key to facilitating commitment and change. In an essay entititled "I Tell Homeless Kids, 'Love You, Baby,'" McCall (1988), a social worker for homeless children, expressed the idea that you could never care too much. The essay concludes

My job as a human being is to say "I love you" until my last breath. There are hundreds of thousands of precious and irreplaceable resources in homeless shelters across this land. They are . . . endangered . . . When together we can say "Love you, baby," together we will begin to save our babies. (p. A 19)

SELF-AWARENESS

Unquestionably, the most important constituent in the therapeutic encounter is the therapist himself/herself. This idea is stated most emphatically by Edwards and Bess (1998):

> . . . the application of *what you know as a psychotherapist* (that is,the accumulation of knowledge and techniques from professional education and training) can only be helpful and effective if you are aware of . . . *who you are* as a person in the room with the client . . . (p. 90)

A constant challenge you face, therefore, is understanding the interplay between your personal and professional roles and responses. This is an especially difficult endeavor because helping denotes by its very nature an interrelationship between your life and your work. Yet you are expected to rely upon your experience, personal growth, and training to fathom your own self so as to bring to clients an ability to bear pain, anxiety, and loss, thus enabling them to confront their own. What guides you in doing this is engaging in a systematic inventory of your personal traits and characteristic behaviors that come to you as naturally as breathing, being open to engaging in a process of increasing self-awareness, and being willing to be vulnerable and open to experiencing previously unknown aspects of yourself in order to reach the inner selves of clients (Edwards and Bess, 1998, pp. 97-99).

It has been emphasized that only when you are alert to who you are and what you are doing are you sufficiently relaxed, clear, and open-minded to understand the client. In other words, it is impossible to be attuned to the feelings of others without first being attuned to your own. For example, Helen, who was from a poor family and who was raised in a low-income housing project, had serious trouble working with middle-class clients. She could not fathom why they stopped seeing her shortly after the first interview. She never verbally disparaged them, but tacitly dismissed the problems of economically "better off" clients as being insignificant.

Your personality, values, and sensitivity are the very tools that make you an effective therapeutic instrument. They determine what happens in your interaction with clients. Your *personhood,* in other words, is the essential feature in the establishment and maintenance of the therapeutic alliance. This alliance has been portrayed using other terms, all basically alluding to the same phenomenon: for example, intersubjectivity (Atwood and Stolorow, 1993) and mutuality.

Your own past and present conflicts may interpose themselves on your functioning with clients. They may urge here and restrain there. They may hinder effective work as they compel and censor behavior. They may diminish and distort experience and affect what you selectively perceive. Mark, like many helpers before him, was the oldest child of alcoholic parents and the one charged—precipitously and prematurely—with raising three younger sisters. As a helper, he constantly found himself overinvolved with clients—rescuing them, doing everything for them, not allowing them to undertake the simplest tasks for themselves. His own background had left him unable to trust that anything would be done if he did not do it; that things would ever work out if he did not take charge; that he had value beneath and beyond his caretaking role. As he came to see himself in a new light, his effectiveness as a helper increased.

Unless you know what is going on within yourself, it is tempting to blame clients for a feeling of being stuck. When you come to acknowledge and monitor your own process of denying, distorting, or projecting, when you recognize your inner stirrings, then these processes may, in fact, be called upon as resources to enhance your work.

To be helpful to others, you must understand, rein in, and resolve your own conflicts and problems so that they do not interfere with your ability to understand others'. The loathing that Winetta, a compulsive clinician, inevitably felt for anyone who was late emotionally detached her from clients and undermined her relating to them on any other basis than their lateness. The capacity "to perceive one's behavior as objectively as possible, to have free access to one's own feelings without guilt, embarrassment, or discomfort, is a necessary, if not sufficient, prerequisite for the controlled subjectivity the helping process demands" (Kadushin, 1976, p. 152).

You face a difficult charge. You are expected to be responsive to clients without letting your own feelings intrude or interfere. Yet you are required to draw upon your feelings in the service of clients as a guide to understanding and intervention. This is a delicate balance. Since you can react only from what is within yourself, you must know yourself so that your capacity for being in relationship is increased, your ability to react consciously is intensified, and you are freer to make deliberate choices about how to respond to clients. Only by knowing yourself are you in a position to make active and creative use of feelings, thoughts, intentions, and motives to optimize the helping process. Francisco, for example, found it nearly impossible to nonpunitively tolerate any adult client who abused a child. He would immediately associate this with his own background of being beaten and lose his professional objectivity, stability, and ability to be consistently caring toward the client. Therapeutic errors frequently arise from such countertransference; however, they also can arise from lack of information about the client, lack of adequate training, or even poor timing or utilization of an intervention.

You need to open the way to examine your beliefs and attitudes, to find compatibility between them and feelings and behavior, to expose and to scrutinize your basic assumptions, and to search out who and what you really are. Such awareness leads to more disciplined and clearly directed work. Learn to avoid the pitfalls of omnipotence and countertransference. Touch your own feelings of being able or expected to solve all problems, of being overwhelmed by elusive and unconscious responses to the client, or of being discouraged with reactions that seem uncooperative and ungrateful. All these feelings, when unexamined, lead to unwittingly reinforcing clients' feelings of passivity and helplessness. In honestly facing yourself, you are freed to attend to what is happening with the client.

It may be reassuring to know that in reporting on a study eliciting from seasoned therapists their view of what is most helpful to clients, Coady and Wolgien (1996) found that "the therapist's contributions to the alliance . . . rival the importance of the client's contributions" (p. 312). Furthermore, in that same study the most helpful therapist attitudes and behaviors were listed as being authentic and honest, personally identifying with client issues, attending to impact of self, and using self-disclosure.

If you make mistakes, and you invariably are bound to because you are human, accept them and acknowledge them directly. Recognize, too, that mistakes are not necessarily irreparable; on the contrary, they may be valuable. They can provide lessons to you about the efficacy of your assessments and interventions. Allowing yourself to make mistakes also allows you to participate more fully in the relationship. Furthermore, it enables clients to accept their own mistakes.

In brief, do what you expect clients to do. Take a hard look at yourself. Through self-examination, discover, acknowledge, and accept yourself for who and what you are, alter what is possible, and you will be better able to accept clients for who they are. Develop a realistic understanding of your world. Assume responsibility for your actions and reactions.

Some Important Questions for Self-Reflection

Being a therapist, then, starts within oneself. It is up to you to decide if you are willing to invest in other people. What should you consider in making this decision? First, think about people who have helped you. What were they like? How did they help? How did they share themselves with you? Try to picture how you felt during those phases—the awkwardness and confusion, the desire to do well, to feel better, the fear of failure. Consider the ways you were guided through difficult times.

Think about your role. How would you act differently as a therapist? What do you bring in terms of self-awareness, knowledge, skills, special talents, and insights? Visualize specific, positive change in how you present yourself and how you behave in times of both stability and crisis. Images such as these enhance your capacity to tune into clients and provide a framework for therapy.

Are you accessible and open to yourself? To others? Again, as a therapist you can offer only yourself. Can you talk about yourself openly, yet selectively? Can you share your memories of past struggles and fears as they pertain to your clients'? If so, clients will not only see you as more human, but also as someone who can understand how they feel, as someone who has faced obstacles and managed to learn and succeed, as someone who can help.

SEVEN LEVELS OF THE RELATIONSHIP

The effectiveness and success of the helping endeavor depends largely upon your ability to institute and sustain a helping alliance with clients. This alliance is usually described in two ways: (1) as a means to sustain clients as they work on problems, or (2) as a prototype of the problems they may have in other relationships. The relationship is not just a way to manipulate clients to accept help. It is integral, therefore, when clients act toward you in ways that are inappropriate or self-defeating, that you comment on these behaviors. This provides clients with an opportunity to change their behavior with you and others in the world. These constructive changes in behavior can then become integrated into clients' regular patterns of behavior.

Although there is general unanimity about the importance of human relationship in promoting growth and change, understanding about just how relationships promote such development is less common. I characterize the "how" in terms of seven "I's" in dynamic interrelationship. They are in rank order (a) with the later processes contingent upon the quality of the preceding ones and (b) of decreasing client awareness. The "I's" are: Individualization, Intellectual learning, Imitation, Internalization, Identification, Idealization, and Individuation. Each "I" is defined and described below and then illustrated with a case example based on the following vignette.

> Marta's two children, Jesus, three, and Sonia, two, were placed in foster care in a large metropolitan agency because of their father's repeated and brutal physical abuse. Marta was committed to doing all she could to have her children returned to her care now that Carlos, her partner, had died of AIDS.
>
> Marta, nineteen years old, had lived in foster care most of her own childhood because of her mother's mental illness and father's desertion. She loved her children and was highly motivated to reach her goal.
>
> Marta, Jesus, and Sonia all test HIV positive although none have symptoms.

Individualization

Individualization is the process of individualizing the client, focusing upon this particular person rather than on his or her problem or on this person as representing a whole class of people. It involves recognizing and affirming clients and building upon their unique qualities while ironically and simultaneously conveying the message that they are not alone with their troubles. Others have suffered and overcome similar adversity, and you are available to join them.

Bear in mind that many of your clients are demoralized. They have been emotionally if not physically battered. They have been browbeaten, rejected, mocked, and humiliated—even by people who called themselves helpers. Often, in the name of "help," clients have been labeled crazy, weak, stupid, selfish, or evil. Why should they believe that you will treat them differently? Why should they believe that you will try to see them for who they truly are? Respect the diversity and variety of individuals; do not stereotype them.

Individualization means accepting and appreciating the uniqueness and dignity of clients as separate and autonomous beings. Marta was responsive to help because she felt that for the first time a professional did not "speak down" to her, "like other caseworkers, as being some sort of worthless jerk," or cower for fear of contracting AIDS, or stereotype her as an unfit mother.

Intellectual Learning

Intellectual learning entails encouraging clients to consolidate and apply in the conduct of their daily lives new knowledge and skills developed in the helping process. Every action between you and the client creates structures and patterns of learning and awareness.

At this level, the relationship involves the cognitive processes of learning and teaching. Its object is knowledge and skill enhancement. Within the context of the relationship, clients' perceptions about themselves, others, and their environment come under challenge. This challenge is cognitive in the sense that their ideas are questioned and they are encouraged to consider new ideas. At this level you appeal to their cognitive and conscious processes. You involve them in a dialogue in which they become aware of untapped knowledge, ideas, and strengths. Information is given, concrete suggestions and advice are provided, and direct guidance is offered. You provide a realistic view of the client's ongoing interactions with others and with the environment. The purpose is to nourish a sense of mastery over the rational and tangible aspects of their situation. A further purpose is to alert them to habitual patterns of self-loathing and self-blame that cause still further self-defeating reactions to life.

In your role of teacher and coach, you provide technical assistance for developing and improving skills in problem solving and decision making and assisting clients to recognize the impact of their "self" on that process. You do this by asking key questions, providing new experiences, highlighting inconsistencies, suggesting modifications, reframing (i.e., helping clients to see their situation in a different way), focusing, and contracting. Ask clients to look at and talk about themselves and their dilemmas. Intellectual understanding is a necessary component. It bolsters decision-making and problem-solving skills but focuses on increased self-appraisal. Marta, for example, listened attentively to my direct instructions about legal steps and parental skills necessary to ensure her children's return. She acted on each one of them, closely following the suggestions offered. Each step she made, to assure medical screening, to find adequate housing, and to enroll in a parenting workshop, reinforced a sense of accomplishment.

Imitation

Imitation is a process in which clients deliberately emulate or simulate what they perceive as positive in your interactions with them. At this third level of relationship, you continually demonstrate your competence to clients. This involves clients directly observing if you practice what you preach. They closely observe your dealings with them, other clients, staff, and colleagues. Inevitably appraising your ability to facilitate communication, manage anxiety, encourage mutuality, and foster cooperation in working together, they ask themselves, "Are you a person who will hear me?" "Will you help me feel trust, encourage me to open up?" "Are you sensitive and aware of nuances?" "Do you deal with tension and conflict openly?" "Are you warm, accepting, respectful, understanding?" "Do you show interest, tact, maturity?" "Do you believe in your own ability to help?"

Your role at this level is that of a model. When clients sense your expertise, coupled with an intellectual understanding of the process, they are motivated toward imitation. They shape themselves to "take on" parts of you. Clients do not become clones; rather, they imitate your effective decision making, calmness, actions, and attitudes by adopting and adapting your compatible and favorable qualities into their own behavioral repertoire.

Imitation is reinforced when you share with clients how they themselves, as well as what is happening, affects you. Inquire about your impact on them. You model a way of operating that can effectively change clients' perspective and behavior. For example, quietly studying my nonpunitive interaction with Jesus and Sonia during interviews with the family, Marta adopted as her own my style of selecting alternative nonverbal activities for Jesus and Sonia, of nonphysically disciplining the children, and of rewarding their "good" behavior. Awkward and stilted at first in the way she copied me, practice and the positive results she got made it easier to make it more naturally her own.

Internalization

Internalization, the fourth interconnected level, involves clients making the goals, attitudes, and behaviors you reflect toward them in the relationship an integral part of themselves. It pertains, in other words, to your management of the relationship itself. This involves mutual reflection on your exchange with clients and how you handle the dynamics of this encounter.

Reduce anxiety and convey an atmosphere of trust. Invite clients to share their reflections and introspections about themselves, but, more important, about this immediate relationship. Encourage clients to experience, examine, and ultimately talk about the problems, strains, and tensions in your relationship with them. Open discussion creates an atmosphere of mutuality and collegiality. It promotes reflection about the meaning and the mechanics of establishing and maintaining functional relationships. Through this kind of dialogue you assist clients in liberating themselves from rigid or stereotyped responses that limit them. In a climate of acceptance and honesty, you open channels to explore together such questions as, "What can we gain from this experience together?" and "What can we give to each other?" Building a warm, supportive environment with a sense of security leads you to an alliance that eventually permits the expression of clients' doubts and apprehensions without fear of harsh judgment.

Clients' habitual ways of relating to others and their ingrained ways of looking at themselves in relation to others are reenacted in their relationship with you. They can experience you in the same way in which they experience others in the present and have experienced others in the past. Most significantly, they can experience you in ways in which they have never experienced anyone before. Likewise, they can experience themselves in relationship to you in ways with which they are familiar and, at the same time, in ways in which they are not.

Understand clients' repetition of the past in the present, but provide a special interpersonal experience and environment in which change can take place. Illumination occurs in the context of this new and uniquely experienced relationship. It results in clients losing the attraction of old ways and the concomitant development of a more adaptive stance.

No significant human relationship proceeds without conflict, stress, and stalemates. These are interspersed as well, with periods of both rapid and barely discernible change and times of confidence and of doubt. Moderate these shifts to prevent them from constituting a threat or arousing intolerable uncertainty. By doing so, your clients learn to tolerate and integrate them reasonably well as essential to the overall harmonious functioning of this, as well as all, relationships.

In this relationship, anger can be expressed and responded to without overwhelming anxiety. It can be reasonably resolved collaboratively. Encourage mutuality and reciprocity so that barriers become foci for examination and growth rather than impenetrable walls.

Throughout life, we all need to interchange our observations with others in order to sustain our level of functioning. Clients achieve the capacity to integrate new experiences with you into a meaningful system by practicing the sharing of perceptions with you. It helps them develop what has traditionally been referred to as an observing ego.

Your role is that of medium—a channel of deep expression and responsiveness. Immediacy and self-disclosure about your reactions to them enhances understanding of the therapeutic process. It fortifies clients' recognition of triggers of their own intensive emotional reactions in this as well as in other relationships. In a way, clients, without conscious plan or cognizance, "take in" a part of you. This firsthand experience of rapport leads clients to a more relevant inquiry and critical analysis of their own contribution to the helping procedure. The very process of gaining this relationship with you inducts them into perceiving and understanding better who they are. They discover and then develop control of their own responses.

Immersion in the evolution and consolidation of the relationship propels clients toward arriving at a heightened understanding of themselves and the forces that operate in their lives. They assimilate and integrate your manner, which alters the way they interact with others. Encouraged to verbalize her introspections about herself as she participated in the helping relationship, Marta became aware that her way of interacting with me and with others had altered. She became less suspicious of others' motives and more willing to trust that their assistance in various concrete ways—accompanying her to welfare centers, giving her clothing, and baby-sitting—arose from good intentions, not necessarily from ulterior motives. She recognized that the helping relationship had corrected her usual perception of herself and others in relationship. Clients' more satisfying and healthy relationship with you becomes internalized, that is to say, it counters and, in some cases, actually substitutes for past internalized dysfunctional relationships.

Identification

Identification involves clients taking in as a permanent part of their personality structures the attributes, characteristics, and values they detect in you as you interact with them. The fifth significant level of relationship, it is less conscious than the four others already discussed. Identification involves the way you establish an alliance, stay optimally in touch with the clients' experiences, and handle their vulnerability within it. It entails clients' exquisite sensitivity to your empathic resonance, your response to their subjective experience, and the way you convey understanding of their feelings, attitudes, and ideas. Clients experience, absorb, or "soak up" the way in which you empathize with them and establish the core conditions for change.

For many clients, suitable objects for identification have been unavailable. For others, there have been impairments or interruptions in their relationships, making the necessary identifications impossible to achieve. You are in a position to correct this privation. Provide a positive outlook and a less self-critical attitude along with an opportunity for introspection and reflection.

You serve as a mentor for clients. What cannot be conveyed in direct ways is incorporated by association. The way you manage your complex mixture of roles, tasks, and emotions instructs them, but, more important, it impels them toward greater compassion for and acceptance of their own. How you relate to clients exposes them to a broader array of adaptable and acceptable behaviors to practice for themselves.

Clients are exquisitely aware of your communications and your mistakes. The way in which you tune in to them, and to yourself, reflects back their emotional and intellectual state, tracks the process of change, and shapes the organization of clients' selves. At a conscious and unconscious level, clients recognize your mode of interrelating, which becomes an internal part of their own identity and structure. Over time their identifications become increasingly discriminate and focus on features and qualities that are compatible with and enhance their own. Your attributes and qualities are integrated and become transformed into the nucleus of their own being. Responding to Marta, for example, with gentle warmth and acceptance of her deeply rooted self-doubts and with empathy for her anguish associated with having abandoned her children the way she herself had been, allowed her to come to forgive herself. In a protected environment, as I expressed my sympathy for her pain and sense of desperation, validating her experience, while conveying a matter-of-fact attitude about current and previous self-destructive behaviors, she eventually risked treating herself with the kindness, nonjudgment, and respect she experienced from me.

To a significant degree, identification is a sine qua non for eventual individuation (see pp. 51-53), in the process of growth and development. Clients transform interactions with you and characteristics of you into inner regulations so that what is internalized becomes part of the structure of self and is integrated.

Idealization and Mirroring

Idealization and mirroring are interconnected processes. Idealization comprises your welcoming clients' admiration of and identification with you for strength and security and for confirming their own positive sense of self. Mirroring involves recognizing, approving, and admiring clients' ability to become independent and create something of value. This dimension of relationship is thoroughly unconscious. It emerges from your willingness to immerse yourself in their experience and your accessibility to and utilization of your own vulnerability within the context of the relationship. In addition to experiencing trust, warmth, and empathy, clients "feel into" your conscious and disciplined attention. They experience the way you use your vulnerability and sensitivity in guiding them. As you transform your own vulnerability into awareness and creativity, you provide a mirror for them. Clients need to feel understood and affirmed for who they are, to feel safe and comfortable, to feel some degree of sameness or likeness with you and others. Some of these needs for validation and affirmation are met to a limited degree through your exposing them to challenging experiences, which, when faced, produce a deep sense of accomplishment and mastery. The relationship fulfills more of these through the process of mirroring.

Kohut has pointed out that the healthy adult needs the mirroring of the self by others and needs targets for idealization (Kohut, 1973). Clients internalize the function provided by the new self-object, you. They see you draw freely on your inner life, which reinforces and corroborates their personhood. As you share your perceptions and subjective reactions, you free clients to expose theirs. You allow them to merge temporarily with you. In so doing, they receive an infusion of certainty and confidence. Provide clients with a vehicle to develop an internal means for maintaining esteem and for tolerating mistakes and failures. When clients become more certain of themselves, they require your support less and feel increasingly confident without your affirmation. Clients thus come to reach into themselves for the validation you initially provided.

In terms of idealization, clients intercept and respond to your emotional accessibility to your own self as well as your availability to them. They wonder, "Are you a genuine and caring person?" and "Are you free enough of your own 'stuff' to be available to me?" They are sensitive to your ability to engage in a deep interpersonal relationship without losing integrity or autonomy, allowing them to become less rigid and protective. They take into their self-structure the qualities you evidence and utilize them for inner regulation. Marta became severely depressed at the loss of her children and suffered from intense panic attacks, doubting every decision she made. Building on Marta's intellectual and nurturing capacity, I helped her view the surrender of her children as a temporary and creative way to become a better mother. This intervention provided her with a new positive identity as a "succeeding" rather than a "failing" mother. Viewing herself as smart and loving, rather than stupid and unfeeling, relieved her anxiety and depression. Invited to participate in a group of mothers where she was dubbed the "expert," the gratification from her role as model augmented that from her new identity as "good" mother. Marta had merged with my belief in and validation of her, making it her own.

Individuation

Individuation results in clients separating from you as a consequence of their gaining, through the relationship, mastery over their own lives and concomitant higher self-esteem, the freedom to confront life's challenges on their own. Draw upon your capacity for empathic introspection as you attend to data that clients present. It will not only enable you to connect various elements of clients' current problems to the pattern of their life experience, but will intensify your fathoming their essence. In doing this, generally applicable explanations may elude you, but you will grasp the core of what makes them individually and uniquely themselves.

With this kind of responsiveness in the relationship, clients discover a new awareness of anxiety and a greater ability for self-control. They learn how to acknowledge and accept themselves and to understand and alter maladaptive behavioral patterns. More significantly, and perhaps ironically, through the relationship they come to increase their basic level of differentiation. The stabilization of your unique way of relating to each other in this special alliance forms and reforms their sense of autonomy and separateness. When you interact with clients flexibly, without fully gratifying or fully frustrating them, when you encourage, recognize, and reinforce their facing and mastering difficult internal impulses and external stresses increasingly on their own, you nurture integration and individuation. When you honor their taking increasing charge of their lives, and they accept their own role in their progress and your gradual withdrawal from involvement with them, they gain an increased security in their own identity and autonomy and the capacity to preserve the distinction and separation between themselves and others. Improvement, therefore, does not depend on maintaining the relationship, but on your encouraging their accepting separation from it.

Marta succeeded in getting adequate public housing, arranging medical attention for herself, Jesus, and Sonia, enrolling in training to become a legal secretary, having her children returned to her care, and ending her work at the agency. Her progress dramatizes the power of the relationship for revising the image of oneself—Marta came to reject the picture of herself as insensitive, depriving, or malevolent toward her children. She freed herself from self-defeating means of survival, no longer desperately clinging to familiar but destructive behaviors. Through the reliability, consistency, constancy, and emotional resonance supplied by the relationship, she overcame her false "toughness" arising from premature maturity, and let down the facade of being "street smart" to take pride in herself as being a self-governing, expert survivor.

Developing an adequate and autonomous sense of self, then, requires your suspending judgment and supplying the following:

1. A holding environment or safe house that allows for maximum emotional comfort and trust for clients
2. Empathic resonance and response
3. Sensitivity to clients' suffering
4. A stable and steady structure for self-exploration and practicing new behaviors
5. A balance of serious attentiveness and spontaneity in mutually searching for self-definition and healthier functioning
6. Opportunity for identification with you
7. Adequate experiences of caring, approval, and achievement
8. Tolerating clients' hostility and outbursts
9. Support for clients' increasing independence of thinking and action

A short article titled "To Be a Mental Patient" (Unzicker, 1988) touched me greatly because it described in powerful terms what happens when these basics are ignored or forgotten. It concludes

To be a mental patient is not to die—even if you want to—and not cry, and not hurt, and not be scared, and not be angry, and not be vulnerable, and not laugh too loud. . . . Because if you do you prove that you are a mental patient . . . even if you are not.

And so you become a no-thing, in a no-world, and you are not. (p. 89)

The helping relationship is a unique construction created by the mutual interaction between you and clients. Clients progress when you treat them in ways that substantially parallel the ways you encourage them to employ with others—family, friends, colleagues. Self-development and personal individuation are inextricably intertwined processes.

RELATIONSHIP: KEYSTONE OF HELPING

The relationship is the keystone of the helping process. Help involves two important components: (1) what is given, and (2) how it is given. "What" is discussed in other chapters. "How" is the very experiencing of the relationship. It is the quintessential learning experience. The immediacy of your presence and attitudes, rather than your skills or techniques, is the heart of helping. The relationship enables clients to learn how to observe themselves and their capacity to integrate experiences into a meaningful system. The building and maintenance of the relationship not only facilitates clients' capacity for change. It *is* the change.

Relationship: Simply Stated

Beyond all the jargon, elaborate concepts, professional requirements, and injunctions, what constitutes a helpful relationship? The following statement, ironically enough, is taken from an advertisement by Lord and Taylor in the Christmas Eve, 1991 edition of *The New York Times*. It's sentimental, but simple and accurate:

Give a smile
rare, sweet and sunny
A moment of friendship
in a chaotic world.

Give an ear
to someone's hurt
and anguish.
The gift of comfort
is beyond price.

Give yourself
to the beliefs
you hold dearest.
Mere money cannot
move mountains
like an hour of your talent and toil.

Give love
to someone who is
difficult to love.
Give hate to no one.

Give thought
to a season too brief
and beautiful to give
anything less than
your entire heart.

Chapter 4

When You Begin,
Begin at the Beginning

To let a beginning be a beginning, to further its being a beginning in all its tentativeness and awkwardness, rather than to rush to solve all the problems in the first interview calls for knowledge and disciplined skills in a process that is truly professional.

Ruth Smalley

He did not start forward to seize on my slightest pause, to assert an understanding of something before the thought was finished, or to argue with a swift irresistible impulse—the things which often make dialogue impossible.

Anne Rice

Why are initial interviews so important? A simple answer is that there is no second chance to make a first impression. Although a first impression may not be lasting, it certainly influences whatever follows and is critical because it prefigures the entire helping experience.

Poorly planned and hastily conducted first contacts frequently result in failure. This makes sense: when clients do not feel understood, they do not return. When they do feel attended to and accepted, they do come back, with even more motivation to be involved.

Take time. Listen actively. Observe selectively. Being present and available, you show your understanding and make possible a successful engagement.

Identify clients' strengths as well as problems. Recognize contextual factors in addition to internal dynamics. If you do, clients will likely return, having already sampled an effective model for your ongoing work together.

The initial interview lays the foundation for the total helping process. You and your client advance through a series of interactions, forming a microcosmic model of what is ultimately to be built. Together you design what follows and structure the basic framework of the relationship. You participate in a time-limited, exploratory partnership that clarifies two situations: the one troubling the client, for which the client is seeking help; and the one in which you discover whether you can work as a team.

In the initial interview you offer the client a chance to present hurts, defeats, and problems. Different clients, of course, act differently: various behaviors are highlighted. Some clients minimize problems; some act helpless; some become blustery and aggressive; some present themselves as wronged. Their unique ways of behaving and reacting both to you and to the interview give you a sample of how they handle themselves, their feelings, and their problems. This previews the way they will undertake the bigger job. Each feature and each reaction to you and to the interview foreshadow how they will react in the future. In other words, the first interview offers you a chance to learn firsthand about your clients' prospects for partnership. How capable are they? How do they handle themselves in this trial run? What personality characteristics, patterns of behavior, and decision-making abilities do they display as they explain themselves to you?

This initial encounter naturally offers clients an opportunity to assess you and determines whether you understand their suffering and whether your tools will be useful for what they want fixed or want to build. Do not forget that clients are measuring you as well as your work with them for this short time. They try to get a sense of how apt a partner you would be in helping them repair or reconstruct their lives. How do you react to them? How comfortable do you feel with them? Do you have the equipment it will take to assist them? Can they work with you? Can you work with them?

While initial interviews are geared to identifying clients' problems, making problems less confusing, and enabling clients to assume responsibility for resolving them, they also have a deeper purpose. This purpose is to provide clients with an emotionally corrective, nonjudgmental experience of true acceptance, respect, and hope; a collaborative experience of being heard and understood in a way that leads to purposeful and goal-directed activity.

This is a large order. Is it possible to accomplish this in a few contacts? It is, when time and thought and compassion are present.

The remainder of this chapter proposes, in not-so-poetic ways— some tried and true, some new and creative—to make initial interviews more successful. It attempts to answer some questions you might have about initial interactions with clients. These common-sense questions are: Should I sit close or at a distance from the client? Should I touch the client? Should I sit behind a desk? Do I accept at face value what the client says, or do I look for deeper meanings? To what should I direct attention—content, interaction, details of appearance? What should receive priority? How do I expand on minimal information? Should I ask questions or make comments? Should I keep quiet and wait for the client to begin, or should I make some opening remarks?

PREPARING FOR FIRST CONTACTS

Prepare for your clients. It is worth the effort. Preparation occurs in phases—tuning in, setting the stage, warming up, and deciding to listen.

Tuning In

Before actually meeting the client, review whatever information you have available about him or her. Read reports from phone contacts, from intake interviews with other people, or from other collateral sources. Talk to those who know your client. Reflect on all the information. Shelve it for a short while.

It has been argued that it is better to see a client without being swayed beforehand by the possibly biased opinions of others. A critical look at available information, however, provides a counterpoint for reflection. The more knowledge you have, the greater your chance of being able to address the client responsibly. The more knowledge you have, the better able you are to consult, consider, and confront your own and others' impressions and interpretations. On one hand, you can take stock of your own prejudices and preconceived ideas about the problem or the person. On the other, you have an opportu-

nity to evaluate and contain stereotypes and to forestall premature
conclusions or snap judgments.

Intelligent understanding allows you to be free beforehand to enter
the rhythm of the exchange, to be more fully present to the client. Advance information also furnishes you with an opportunity for antici-
patory empathy, a chance to walk a mile, as it were, in the client's
shoes.

Advance information helps you to clarify the purpose of the initial
interview. It also helps you to formulate a focus. Then, too, a little
preliminary research helps you to get a clear sense of what you know,
what you do not know, and what you should find out. It enables you to
gear up to select the best approach to making a difference. It gives
you an opportunity to determine what you can offer and ascertain the
limits of what you can provide.

Setting the Stage

If you can do so, provide a private, quiet, and comfortable place to
sit alone with your client; physical space is a central component in
creating a helping environment. Avoid interruptions for either the client or yourself. Abrupt breaks in the flow of serious dialogue, such as
a telephone's nonstop ringing or an incessant pounding on the door,
are distracting. Picking up the phone or opening the door is worse.
Beyond being an annoyance, it disrupts any meaningful exchange between you and the client and short-circuits the natural flow of communication. Endeavor to minimize the intrusions. Post a "Do not
disturb!" sign on your doorknob. Have your calls relayed. Turn off
the bell on the phone. Intrusions steal precious time, depriving the client of your full and undivided attention.

Warming Up

The initial contact really begins well in advance of actually sitting
down with the client. Preliminary arrangements such as appointment-
setting or brief preinterview telephone conversations are stepping
stones toward building a solid foundation. Lay the groundwork for
optimizing the initial face-to-face contact. When you make an appointment, do your utmost to keep it; if you cannot keep it, call the
client promptly. Be punctual for the appointment. Cordial preliminary exchanges, all too often neglected, set a tone. Greet the client.

Treat him or her receptively. Shake hands and give your name. Invite the client into your office. Observe the common courtesies. Do not treat the client in a stilted "hands-off" manner: this is simply callous. Show the reasonable human response that any person inevitably expects from another. The client is a *person* first. Particularly because this *person* happens to be a *client* in the context of a professional relationship, kind and civilized amenities ought to be observed. Treating the client in this way will put him or her at ease. More important, the client's sense of worth and dignity will be enhanced. This is an exceptionally productive way to begin.

Take an active role in initiating and maintaining the interaction. Seek to reduce emotional distance. Endeavor to reduce physical distance created by barriers to easy conversation. Keep in mind that people continually respond to and are influenced by aspects of their physical settings. Endeavor to take this into consideration in the way you set up your office or cubicle. For example, position your desk and the client's chair less than five feet apart. Making such suitable accommodations is important and reflects your attunement with your clients, since we all respond to both the concrete and symbolic aspects of our physical settings: the concrete conditions affecting people in similar ways and the symbolic meanings attributed to them varying (Gutheil, 1992).

Induct the client into the process. Reduce ambiguity. Let clients know how much time they will be spending with you and how much time remains in the interview as you proceed. Let them know how frequently you might be seeing them. Reduce embarrassment, irritation, and suspicion. Take nothing for granted. Prepare for the extent to which the client is experienced or knows what you expect of him or her and what he or she may expect of you. Acquaint the client with regular procedures and simple routines, such as being announced, confirming appointments, and filling out forms. Taking the time to explain the reasons for all these practices (second nature to you but foreign to your client) reduces unnecessary anxiety and elicits cooperation.

Deciding to Listen

Listen attentively. It is time to be, as the saying goes, "all ears." Probably the most common problem in communication is the failure to attend fully to what is being said, causing you to miss the core message. Every communication needs some degree of clarification because it is so complex. Recognize that what clients hear may not be what you say, and that what clients think they hear may be distorted. Remember that what they mean as they respond may be different from what they actually say, and that what you hear them say may differ from what they have actually said.

Listening is an active and selective process, the major component of your job. Listening is more than just listening. By your selection of words and actions, you inspire telling. To listen is to observe and sometimes to encourage. To listen is to highlight latent material for yourself and perhaps for your client. To listen requires coming to terms with and seeking to eliminate blocks to communication for the client, for yourself, and for your mutual transactions. Barriers to communication hurt the relationship, producing resentment and defensiveness. These barriers include ordering, threatening, criticizing, lecturing, blaming, and shaming. Briefly stated then, to listen is to assemble and integrate a comprehensive picture of the forces at work within the client, within yourself, and within the interaction. Your commitment to listen is primary.

Manners

It is difficult to imagine how a seemingly old-fashioned concept such as manners can improve your practice. Actually, returning phone calls and saying "thank you" and "please" is basic to human communication. They reveal how you consider the other person. It is an attitude that is expressed in concrete and practical action. Being mannerly is a simple but direct way of showing clients your respect for them. Start on the right foot by keeping in mind the little things such as saying "hello" and shaking their hands. These gestures mean a lot. Attention to such "little" details makes a big difference in how clients will respond to you and to the work.

Be flexible in your preparations. Once the session begins, the interaction and attentiveness to who the client is and what he or she says take precedence over whatever plans you made. Ironically, preparation makes such flexibility possible because structure encourages spontaneity.

WHAT YOU CAN EXPECT FROM CLIENTS
IN THE FIRST CONTACT

At first clients are uncertain, ambivalent, and reluctant. Why shouldn't they be? Many people may have told the client that they "only wanted to help," but instead have ended by criticizing, teasing, deceiving, tricking, bullying, threatening, taunting, degrading, or manipulating. Parents may have humiliated, neglected, or abused them, only for "their own good." Teachers shamed or flunked them, thinking they were helpful. Caseworkers abandoned them. I recently spoke to a foster child who had been in seven foster homes over the previous two years, all arranged by eight different caseworkers. There are countless horror stories (I fear many of them are true) of how different "therapists"—psychiatrists, psychologists, social workers—all in the name of "help," became instead "the rapists" who further devalued and even molested their clients. Indeed, a social work student recently came to see me for a "consultation." He reported how his therapist dusted her office during the interview. In "only trying to help," she would slap his hand if he wept.

It is not so hard to comprehend, then, that even though they are hurting, even though they need help, clients alternate between seeking help and rejecting it. Their reserve is seldom revealed in a direct manner. Clients need and deserve your patience and perseverance.

Clients are initially wary, fearful, not ready to acknowledge openly their emotional unrest and turmoil. It is difficult enough for them to acknowledge the need for help to themselves, let alone to a stranger. Furthermore, there are cultural injunctions against allowing these feelings to be internally recognized or expressed to others (e.g., "Keep a stiff upper lip!"; "Pull yourself up by your bootstraps"). The common belief, still prevalent, is that people should be independent. Asking for help is equated with weakness, perhaps even with being "bad." Clients need your assurance and support.

In the beginning, clients may expect you to direct them. They want answers. They want quick results. Who does not? We live in an age of instants—coffee, soup, advice. Why not expect instant relief? They do not see the helping process as a joint exploration. Much has been imposed; they have been repeatedly told when to think, what to feel, how to behave. Clients need your partnership. Without theirs, you cannot proceed. You have to tell them that. Your office is not the traditional "fix-it shop." They cannot leave their psyches behind and come back another day to pick them up. Clients fear rejection; they fear loss of autonomy; they dread others knowing their disgrace. Recall a time when you yourself had to face rejection, admit failure, or hide shame. Recall a time when you could not resolve your problem alone, when you broke down and had to ask for help. What was it like to request help? Were you frightened? Humiliated? Lucid? Overwhelmed? Trusting? Did you want instant relief or introspective reflection? Could you talk easily to the other person? Or did you test the other first to measure if he or she was genuinely interested and could be trusted? Did you consciously distort some of the facts? Unconsciously censor some? Looking back, did you succeed in deceiving yourself and perhaps the helper?

Clients seek help because something has gone wrong. They are frightened, in need of your interest and compassion. When you show these, they more easily disclose their troubles and more willingly recount their life story.

Clients' hesitancy and wariness, often dubbed "resistance," are predictable and revealing responses that hint at their life story. Do not treat their reactions as resistance. When you do, you will usually alienate them further, and in many instances, "blame the victim."

Endeavor to get past complaints. Yes, something has gone miserably wrong. But if you get stuck in resultant conditions—symptoms, if you will—although these are relevant, little will change. Clients have a story to tell, one that is integrally connected to their problems. Encourage them to tell it.

Do not define your clients simply by the sum total of their problems, deficiencies, and injuries. Your work, at its most effective, goes beyond a strict focus upon their bundle of problems. Rather, it encompasses some attempt at fathoming their life story. Clients have enormous anxiety, however, about telling it. Recognize that they want to protect themselves against even their own recognition, to present themselves to you in the best possible light, to defend against your labels and anticipated denouncement, and to preserve some sense of integrity and dignity. Recognize all this and respect them for it.

Clients come to the initial session with a variety of attitudes and behaviors. Some clients appear too "comfortable" (e.g., clients who repeatedly return to talk to you about their problems as a substitute for self-reliant action or outside relationships). Some clients act "cool"; others behave angrily. Expect diversity in the way clients respond during first interviews. Always keep in mind, however, that it is hard to ask for help—sometimes even harder to receive it.

It is hard to open up to an intimate associate—even harder to open up to a stranger.

It is hard to view yourself honestly and clearly—even harder when you are exhausted, overwhelmed, guilty, or ashamed.

It is hard to be composed when under internal stress—even harder when external pressure is relentless.

It always takes courage to confront who you are and where you came from—whether voluntarily or not.

It takes plain guts to review, edit, and attempt to rewrite your life story.

If you respect who clients are and hear them thoroughly, you will achieve the goal of the first interview. They will return for the second.

WHAT CLIENTS EXPECT FROM YOU

One of the most common errors you can make is to rush the process along without giving clients ample opportunity to reveal their story and have a chance to assimilate the experience of being in a new kind of relationship. An old adage, "Fools rush in where angels fear to tread," is apropos here. Try not to leap to conclusions without first appreciating the client's perceptions and feelings.

Clients have certain reasonable expectations for you during the first contacts. These include expectations of initiating and maintaining communication between them and yourself, of being sensitive to their tension and discomfort, and of structuring interviews.

Open the door to communication. Clients are on your "turf." They need to be invited in and given the opening for talking. Consciously decide to allow clients to express themselves by guiding conversation along paths that let them determine whether and to what degree they are going to be able to express troubled feelings and thoughts. You can enhance a sense of welcome by being there "for" the client in a caring but nonsentimental way. Assign importance to what they present and avoid any temptation to pressure for what they are not able or willing to say. You will not be able to convince them that you are trustworthy or expert unless you behave in a way that shows that you are. No matter how often you assure them you can be trusted, it means nothing unless your demeanor matches your words.

When clients begin to open up, be silent for a while to see where the spontaneous flow goes without letting them get lost. Provide verbal (e.g., "Please explain that last point further," "Tell me which of these issues you find to be most frustrating," "Come back to your feelings about your oldest daughter") and nonverbal (e.g., nodding your head, extending your open palm, smiling) encouragement so that they know what to focus on. To begin where they are is to communicate in an array of ways that you are with them—which is precisely what they should expect of you. Check and correct your perception as you move along. For example, "Is what I hear you saying . . . ?" "Am I correct in thinking that you feel confident about yourself when you are able to confront your wife?" "At this moment, you seem sad to me—am I seeing you accurately?" In this way you develop a model of reciprocity. Convey, "I want to know who you are. I want to know as much as possible about you so that I can tailor our work to your unique situation and strengths." Customize your approach to clients' discrete and individual styles.

"Being with" clients is shown by active involvement with them in the process—setting a climate of acceptance and concern, clarifying, suggesting new perspectives, and being sensitive to boundaries and limitations. It involves encouraging them to see that even if, up to this point, they have done the best they could, there might be the possibility to do more in the future. It is not helpful, particularly in this beginning stage, to behave as a neutral, impersonal observer or commentator. This makes them more anxious and perhaps confused. Be an active participant and reveal your desire to help. You facilitate their sharing openly and honestly and motivate them toward increased reflection and introspection.

At times, especially when starting work, clients need direction and structure during interviews. Begin at the surface. Gradually proceed into greater depth, step by step. Clients expect you to give ample attention to their presenting problem or complaint. Try not to get totally caught up in it. Understand the immediate concern that brings them in and allow it to direct your learning about who they are. When you devote almost exclusive attention to the "problem," you compromise the "person." Clients expect, indeed need, you to consider them as people with problems, not the reverse.

Let them know that they will be doing most of the talking. Let them know that things sometimes seem to get worse before they get better. It takes time for a problem to develop, and more time for it to be remedied. Remind them that their range of choices is greater in the present than it was in the past. Let them know that their range of choices in the future will be that much greater as they come to terms with themselves and their history. Let them know, therefore, that you might explore their past with them in order to expand present and future choices.

Notice and build on what they do well. Enable them to recognize that they can be their own best resource. Proceed cautiously from the outside, from the skin, to the inside, toward the viscera, as does a skilled surgeon. In so doing, you not only show caring but learn a great deal about clients from witnessing their adaptation and integration—all displayed in the way they present themselves and behave in relation to this new situation with you.

Clients perceive you as possessing special skills and abilities, as planful in your actions. They may also distort you in a variety of ways—see you as a lover, an ally against a hostile world, or a miracle worker. You are obliged, at some level, to accept the status and authority with which they invest you while you create mechanisms for correcting distorted images. Because expectations are a central force in stimulating behavior, be alert to what is expected and how you assimilate this into your conduct.

Double-check that you provide a sense of direction without being restrictive. Stimulate and guide without bias and pressure. Be conscious always of the ultimate purpose of meeting clients' needs. Convey a sense of hope. You can do this by making explicit to clients the way in which information they provide will be used, what is expected of them, and what they can expect. For example, explain how the financial data that they are reluctant to offer may enable you to obtain health services they require but cannot afford. Honestly note exceptions to confidentiality. When it is necessary to confer with your supervisor about specific concerns posed by clients, inform them of this course of action and identify the selected details you intend to share. These are some fundamental ways of letting clients know that you are with them and that you are available to assist them in making new discoveries about themselves and their situation.

Empathic Responses

Particularly during the beginning phase of your work with clients, but certainly throughout your contact with them, display your empathy. Following are some ideas for phrasing your comments, ques tions, or interpretations. Abstracted from Hammond, Hepworth, and Smith (1978), they may put your clients at ease. They may also facilitate the sharing of even their innermost private thoughts and feelings.

- So, as you see it . . .
- As I get it, you feel that . . .
- It sounds as if you're indicating . . .
- If I'm hearing you correctly . . .
- You seem to be saying . . .
- Your message seems to be . . .
- Listening to you it seems as if . . .
- Sometimes you . . .
- It appears to you . . .
- I gather . . .

HOW TO APPROACH THE INITIAL PHASE

During your first and early contacts with clients, you will see them under stress. They probably will displace feelings from other relationships and situations onto you and this contact. Recognizing this about them can be very illuminating. Their basic characteristics and patterns will be manifested, indeed exaggerated. Because of this, you will have a sharper portrayal of them. This clearer image, taken in concert with whatever content clients relay in words about themselves and their problems, enhances your ability to do the following:

- Understand how clients see themselves in relation to their problems
- Identify reasons for seeking help
- Specify attempts at resolution
- Evaluate internal stresses
- Define external pressures
- Assess and correct expectations
- Break global issues into smaller problems
- Formulate preliminary goals
- Establish limits

- Ascertain commitment and motivation
- Establish ground rules and procedures
- Glean clues to major themes
- Estimate obstacles to progress

You are attempting to achieve a comprehensive overview of the behavioral, affective, and cognitive characteristics of your client. Since you must move ahead very often on the basis of limited knowledge, structure is essential to set a climate conducive to observation and interaction. You translate the general purpose of the interview into a series of specific objectives or requirements that affect the range, depth, and transitions of the exchange. Although the interaction is reciprocal, your influence on the client is greater than the client's influence on you. Figure 4.1 seeks to capture the spiral process of proceeding during these first contacts.

Continually ask clients to help you understand what is troubling them and what is happening to them as you interact. Let them know what information you already have and its sources, and get their reaction to it. Pace and lead the discussion. If you can, convert questions into statements; if you must ask questions, break big questions into smaller ones and, when possible, leave the questions open-ended. Make yours an inquiry, not an interrogation. Avoid feeding clients the answers you want them to give. Try not to bury the answer you expect within the body of your question. Be sure to request feedback by paraphrasing and restating what you hear clients say. Ask for their comments, giving them a chance to correct your understanding or repeat what they mean. As you develop ideas or hypotheses about clients, check them out directly. Ensure that you and your clients are aware that you are going somewhere.

Some Hints for Beginnings

There is no formula for effective help giving because it is a dynamic and organic process, not a static entity. Although there is no standardized format to follow, you need to have in mind some definite ideas, some considerations about how to initiate and maintain the flow.

It is especially important to strike a balance in the first contacts between being too much or not enough help. "Size things up" so that you do not interfere where you are not needed.

FIGURE 4.1. The Flow of the Process

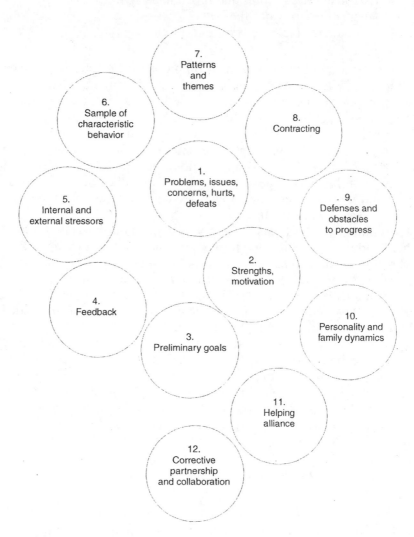

- Be curious, not nosy, to stimulate wonder.
- Be definite, not rigid, to enhance self-determination.
- Be caring, not sloppy or sentimental, to sustain trust.
- Be compassionate, not judgmental, to open communication.
- Be collaborative, not authoritative, to build bridges.

- Be respectful, not paternalistic, to enhance esteem.
- Use ordinary words, not jargon; they clarify perception.
- Be candid, not oblique, to encourage participation and direction.
- Explain all along what you are doing, to foster cooperation and continuity.
- Respond to feelings, not only to ideas, to provide relief.
- Be creative, not complacent, to free imagination.
- Be daring, not safe, to offer challenges.
- Be readily accessible, to reduce irritation and suspicion.

Explain along the way what you are doing and why you are doing it. For example, preface questions with the remark, "I'm going to ask you a question about . . ." combining it with an explanation of why you want the information. Use language that matches and reflects that of your client. Exercise clients' drive and capacity to face themselves and their situation more fully, competently, and independently. Enable clients to explore their own life spaces because of your presence, not despite it. Recognize and reinforce progress, and reflect specifically on success. Provide opportunity to practice new behaviors. Give guidance and direction without pressure. Do not hesitate to offer sound advice; no one ever suffered from good advice. When selectively suggested and not imposed, advice can stimulate thinking and decision making. There may be times when it is helpful to say simply, "At this point, just forgive yourself. You may have erred in the past, but you are unlikely to behave that way again."

Sequentially order your interventions. They are absorbed more fully when progressively built upon. Strengthen linkage with other people. You may not always be the best available helper. State honestly when you cannot help or do not know how to proceed.

Increasing client autonomy results from reciprocity in your transactions. You should both have responsibilities. How these are distributed has to do with the goals toward which you are working, clients' capacities, the conditions under which they live and under which you work, and the dynamics of this particular relationship.

Be sensitive to sequence, progression, and timing. Observe and respect clients' "space" and "style." What you convey by doing so is that you find what they say and how they say it meaningful and that you want to hear more. What you say is, "I have time for you and I care about you." I also find it helpful to suggest to clients that they re-call positive memories. These can be drawn upon subsequently for self-soothing during the process of difficult or painful work in ther-apy as well as when they experience hard times in their lives.

Adjust your methods of working to meet clients' needs, personal-ity, and style. This is the premier professional stance. Clients should not be expected to adapt to one particular method of help giving; rather, you should have the knowledge, skill, and experience to find the most effective approach to help them.

Where Do I Go from Here?

Toward the end of the initial interview, summarize the session. Consolidate gains. Recapitulate what has transpired. Explain the next steps. Ask clients if they have any specific questions that you can help with now. Your clients have been vulnerable and are probably raw at this moment. Walking out into the real world again might seem frightening. They may feel that they have given part of themselves away. Soothe the rough spots. Give them something to take away. This may be something as palpable as an appointment card or a hand-shake, or as intangible as a compassionate glance. It is important for clients to leave with something from you which conveys understand-ing and belief that change is possible. This sustains them. Assign homework, reading, or other activities and make sure that your next interview time is scheduled. Tell them what will happen next and that you are willing and available to them.

It is helpful always to focus on the positive, to build on their strengths, to support their healthy accomplishments, and to validate their experiences.

WHEN A REFERRAL IS NEEDED

Complex issues arise during initial interviews, and sometimes dur-ing the course of an ongoing therapy, that require your involving other professionals or services. It is your responsibility to make ap-propriate connections to other resources when you continue your work with clients and even when you cannot provide service. Consid-eration for a referral arises when:

- You cannot meet clients' needs.
- Clients are not willing to accept the service you offer.
- There is the possibility of a dual relationship.
- Their problems are beyond your competence.
- Clients request, need, or require additional help.
- You want additional support and backup.
- A second opinion is critical.
- Clients are not eligible for the service you offer.
- Your work is finished, but clients require more and different intervention.
- There is a language barrier.
- There are financial limitations and concerns.
- There is a long waiting list.

Arranging a referral involves helping clients to see the need and relevance of such a step and subsequently involving them in developing a plan to follow. Make sure clients understand the reason for the referral, be it for a one-time consultation or a permanent transfer of service. In either case, elicit their feelings and reactions to the change. Provide clients with a brief profile of the person or service that you are considering. Help them make decisions about which one of you will more appropriately initiate the contact and when and under what circumstances it will be made. Develop with clients a clear and concise summary of the condition or situation for which the referral is being made. For example, if medication is indicated, identify the symptoms, etc. Explain any obstacles they may encounter in both the short and long run. Offer support and stay in close touch with them throughout the transition period, and follow up to make sure that connection has been made. Reassure them of your continued interest and availability and perhaps rehearse with them how to present themselves in the new site.

Knowing your resources is crucial. What are the qualifications of the professional or agency? Have you gotten any feedback about them from others? What is the specialty? What information is required for a referral to be considered? Are there eligibility or financial requirements? What is expected of you? Of the client? Will you receive reports, either written or oral? How can pressure be exerted if service is denied or inadequate?

A CHECKLIST TO GUIDE YOU IN ASSESSING FIRST CONTACTS

The following is a checklist to consider in relation to yourself, your clients, and the process of interaction during the initial stage of help giving.

Preparing

_____ Unclutter your mind and direct thoughts only to your client.
_____ Clear your desk and office.
_____ Create a warm space.
_____ Collect notes, lists, and papers, and have them accessible.
_____ Minimize the chance of interruptions.
_____ Reserve this time exclusively for your client.
_____ Anticipate specific questions or concerns.
_____ Review available information.
_____ Suspend your biases.
_____ Walk a mile in your client's shoes.

Setting the Stage

_____ Greet the client cordially.
_____ Initiate the dialogue.
_____ Use words that convey welcome and intent to help.
_____ Use gestures to demonstrate interest and attentiveness.
_____ Use gentle and frequent eye contact.
_____ Lean forward.
_____ Show that you are listening by nodding and perhaps smiling, if appropriate.
_____ Inquire rather than interrogate.
_____ Note themes and patterns.
_____ Focus on what the client says and conveys.
_____ Do not put words into the client's mouth.
_____ Do not use canned responses.
_____ Reflect back to the client what you hear him or her say.
_____ Listen to the client's reactions to your feedback.
_____ Check the accuracy of your understanding.

Enabling Participation

_____ Start at the surface and gradually work inward.
_____ Explain your need for information.
_____ Explain your role and the client's.
_____ Be selective in your questioning styles and types.
_____ Be clear and concise, and avoid jargon.
_____ Approach exchanges from several points of view.
_____ Be aware of your own nonverbal behavior.
_____ Structure the interview.
_____ Repeat important information.
_____ Ascertain the client's strengths.
_____ Be generous with support and guidance.
_____ Convert questions into statements.
_____ Customize your style to your client's.

Closing

_____ Reach for clear, open agreement with the client.
_____ Clarify what is likely to happen.
_____ Pull things together.
_____ Ask your client to recap the interview.
_____ Ask if there is something else you ought to know.
_____ Use polite gestures in closing.
_____ Plan next steps.
_____ Schedule another appointment.
_____ Explain how the process is to proceed.

If you were to do it over again, what would you change? What would you keep the same? What did you learn about yourself from this contact?

PART II:
CONFIGURING A PLAN
TO GUIDE THE PROCESS

Chapter 5

Contracting Through Goal Setting

If you have no goals you have nothing to reach for.

Farmer's Almanac

The illusion that one can unilaterally control other people underlies many problems that bring clients to therapy. My dilemma as a therapist is how to free people from this illusion without buying into it myself.

Lynn Hoffman

The helping process should be one of mutual influence between clients and you. A contract based upon goals provides you with a powerful helping tool for proceeding in this direction. Incorporated directly into the helping process, goal-oriented contracting promotes genuine collaboration in exploring needs and identifying goals. It goes beyond a client's request, "tell me what to do," to mobilize the resources of clients in self-directed activity, and enlists their cooperation in identifying and determining to a significant degree the shape of the helping process. Furthermore, goal-oriented contracting provides a concrete and objective means for measuring and documenting progress and growth.

Following are the three most significant characteristics of contracting:

1. Contracting demands active participation of both clients and you in the helping process. When you work together to identify

goals, participate in achieving them, and help shape the direction of your work together, it is difficult to remain detached from the process.

2. Contracting bridges the gulf between clients and you; it creates a sense of empowerment. There is often a sharp distinction between those who deliver service and those who receive it. It is doubtful whether this sharp distinction benefits either party in the helping process. It is more likely that it impedes progress. When you collaborate with clients, the power line is crossed, and they can assume responsibility for themselves in a fundamental way.

3. Contracting means that change is an interactive endeavor, not a process in which you "pour" answers into clients as if they were receptacles to be filled. Contracting encourages clients to see their task as making change for themselves and their lives; at the same time, it encourages you to see yourself as creating avenues for change.

COLLABORATIVE CONTRACTS

Contracts structure intervention around observable, measurable, and mutually acceptable goals that clients themselves state in terms of favorable outcomes. Contracting emphasizes clients' active part in finding their own solutions. When clients are fully involved in outlining the direction of the process, you are more likely to avoid any possibility of inadvertently maintaining or exacerbating their problems. Contracting provides a step-by-step account of how clients think and feel; it also offers a sample of their typical behavior patterns. Such information helps both of you to work in tandem to tackle problems.

A contract is an agreement between clients, the consumers of service, and you, the provider. It specifies purpose, issues, goals and objectives, procedures and constraints, roles, and a time for your work together. Such a dynamic tool reduces anxiety, provides clarity of direction, and verifies success, since clients are maximally involved at every juncture in defining and examining their own needs, problems, and strengths. They are, subsequently, more ready to participate in the process, because every effort is made to start where clients are. Involving them fully reduces resistance and motivates them to participate in the change effort.

This chapter presents a model of contracting and gives practical answers to frequently asked questions about contracting: What kind of information should be included in the contract? How can it be used in a systematic way throughout the helping process? Can a contract be modified? Should it be written? What are its disadvantages as well as advantages? Are there times when contracts are contraindicated? How does a contract affect client expectations?

BASIC ASSUMPTIONS ABOUT GOALS, CLIENTS, AND CONTRACTING

Goals

Goals provide a common ground for your joint venture; they do the following:

- Assure that both of you agree about what is to be achieved
- Provide direction for the helping process and prevent aimless wandering
- Foster clients' self-determination and self-directed activity
- Facilitate collaboration in selecting appropriate strategies for intervention
- Assist clients and you to monitor and document progress
- Promote focus on what realistically can be changed
- Open avenues of communication
- Correct distorted perceptions

An anagram summarizes the function of goals:

> G—Galvanize therapy by generating graphic guidelines gauging the work.
>
> O—Operate with an orientation to observable outcomes organized around options and objectives.
>
> A—Attend to action and achievement.
>
> L—Launch and lead work through the leverage of listing and labeling.
>
> S—Structure the corrective situation by selecting strategies, skills, and sequence of intervention. (Fox, 1987)

Clients

Undergirding this approach is an optimistic and positivistic view that clients:

1. Can and should make informed choices
2. Know much about themselves that can be stated in easily understandable terms
3. Can share in the responsibility for the helping endeavor
4. Have the capacity to consider and evaluate the accuracy of their needs and wants, which can be expressed in the form of goals
5. Know how much they are willing to invest in the therapeutic endeavor and can articulate this
6. Already possess strengths and capacities that can be enlisted and extended in the helping process

Clients know much about what ails them and have valid ideas about resolution. Rather than limiting attention to problems, contracting builds upon clients' available strengths and resources so that the helping process becomes construction rather than simply repair or restoration.

Contracting

Contracting is a philosophy of intervention relying on clients' cooperation in designing the helping process. It emphasizes participation and involvement in a deliberate, genuine, and voluntary partnership with you in which mutual assessment and exploration about common grounds for action are encouraged. Creating a contract facilitates communication and activates commitment to the difficult process of change. Open acknowledgment of and respect for clients' input fosters autonomy and self-determination; it also reduces any sense of helplessness by providing some level of control over what happens in your work together. An atmosphere of acceptance and involvement promotes flexibility in the therapeutic endeavor. Clients lead the work; they do not have to fit into your preconceived notion of helping. The process is tailored to clients' expressed and unique needs and special concerns (Fox, 1987).

Contracts take different forms—preliminary contracts, which establish the parameters of the relationship at the initial stage as it acquires focus and purpose; primary working contracts, which are formal agreements about goals, procedures, and responsibilities; and minicontracts, which focus on particular tasks or special needs within the framework of the guiding contract. With each new client I see, I propose a preliminary eight- to ten-week contract to enable both of us to determine if the work "fits." During this time, not only do clients have the opportunity to experience how I work, but I have the opportunity to observe firsthand how they function. In addition to regularly scheduled face-to-face interviews, clients are asked to complete an inventory, described fully in Chapter 12, and to keep a log, described in Chapter 13. After experiencing this preliminary contract, each of us, having sampled what ongoing work might involve, can more knowledgeably and freely decide whether and how to proceed. Sometimes, no further contact is needed, because the preliminary contract resolves the problems presented. More frequently, the preliminary contract paves the way to a primary contract; the R family contract, described in detail later in this chapter, is an example of a primary contract.

The usefulness of a minicontract is illustrated by work with John.

John, a forty-four-year-old recovering alcoholic who had, during eleven months of intensive work at a men's shelter, moved from "skid row" to his "own place," was warned that his chain smoking was hazardous to his heart and lungs. He had considerable difficulty in quitting, continually reverting to approaches that did not work—exercising willpower, going "cold turkey," and puffing on cigarette substitutes. We devised a minicontract to stop smoking, within the context of the established primary contract, to meet John's acute and special need.

Carrying around a small piece of paper in the cellophane of his cigarette pack, John recorded the frequency, specific times, circumstances of lighting up, and feelings that accompanied this ritual. The exaggerated attention paid to lighting up, coupled with the task of writing, spotlighted for John striking aspects of his behavior of which he was unaware. More important, guided by our discussions, he began to recognize specific types of anxiety that smoking relieved and realized that these were associated with his former drinking binges.

Concomitantly, he obtained positive reinforcement for his achievement by graphing, at my suggestion, the frequency of smoking when he started this regimen and its decline over time. The effect was cumulative and improvement was progressive because change was visual and could be attributed to his own efforts. He stopped smoking. John also came to better understand sources of and responses to his anxiety, which continued as the focus in our primary contract.

Whatever form contracts take—preliminary, primary, or mini— they draw upon the same principles (alliteratively stated) that contracting is a central concern for both clients and clinicians; it promotes cooperation, fostering choice and collaboration about concrete and concisely stated behavioral goals and considers consequences of change in a consistent climate that encourages compromise, clarity, and commitment to commonly shared goals.

A bonus of contracting in any form is that its various procedures, detailed later, are themselves guidelines for clients to follow in their day-to-day problem solving. When coupled with close attention to the current life context and to rehearsal, clients are able to transfer new skills learned in your office to real-life situations. The process of contracting also educates clients about what it is reasonable to expect from the entire helping process.

Keep in mind that contracts are not chiseled in stone; they are open to alteration and renegotiation. They can and should be revised whenever emergencies arise, new data are presented, or contingencies of the immediate situation require it.

WHY GOALS?

By positively stating concerns in terms of favorable outcomes and by emphasizing a desired state, goals propel your work with clients in a positive direction. Goals are not simply a vehicle for assessment but are an integral part of the total intervention process and provide criteria against which to measure progress and performance. Clients reasonably wonder, "Are your goals the same as mine?" and "Are you confident we will be able to achieve them jointly?" Getting affirmative answers to these questions, through observing the very way you interact with clients, motivates them to proceed.

Setting goals is not a static or isolated activity; neither is it restricted to the helping process. It is a necessary and recurring process faced daily by clients. Goal setting within the helping process is a natural and felicitous activity because it transfers directly to day-to-day life by focusing attention on achieving desired states rather than on eliminating negative conditions.

Goal setting is ego enhancing because clients realize that what they think and feel is taken seriously as an integral part of the helping process. They build the foundation for the work. When you place demands on clients, believing that they are capable of fulfilling them, you create hopeful expectations. Remember, the greater the importance of the goals and the greater the expectation of achieving them, the more likely clients will act in ways to attain them (Fox, 1987). Sometimes, achieving goals is sufficient reward for clients. It is possible, however, to add incentives directly to the contract for accomplishing named tasks.

The benefit of establishing what the "end" should look like at the outset of the helping process is that it defines and directs present interaction. Highlighting possibilities rather than problems accelerates change because strengths are mobilized and barriers anticipated before they occur. Explicit, observable, and measurable, goals provide tangible evidence of accomplishment. Since results of helping are often elusive and hard to define, goals, as they are achieved, afford a sense of gratification, furnishing an identifiable marker of success.

The three types of goals are final, facilitative, and functional.

Final goals are statements of "ends," of terminal conditions or results, naming what is hoped to be ultimately achieved—for example, "Harry will stop physically beating Lowella," "Carmen will move out of the shelter into public housing," "Seth will get better grades in school and be promoted," "The foster family will adopt Maria."

Facilitative goals are statements of "means," of action and/or incremental steps, stepping stones, describing how the ends are to be accomplished, including both clients' and your activities—for example, "Harry will be taught how to express demands and argue using words," "The worker will accompany Carmen to perspective apartments," "A twice weekly tutoring program in math at the agency has begun," "Forms are being completed jointly by the Judds and the worker."

Functional goals are statements of operating arrangements, conditions, and ground rules for involvement, including time, place, duration, and participation—"Weekly, one-hour counseling sessions are scheduled," "Carmen will phone housing projects to set up visits for herself and the worker," "The worker will confer with Seth's teachers every second week," "The paperwork must be completed within two months."

Optimum use of goal setting occurs when goal setting is guided by the ten steps shown in Figure 5.1.

Goals should be specific, making a concrete, definite, and precise statement of intent in simple, understandable language. Explicate the goals; do not assume that clients understand fully what you have agreed upon until you both openly and directly restate the goals. If you sense some reluctance or discomfort in discussing a particular portion of the contract, take it as a cue to spend more time assisting clients to more plainly state what they want.

Goals need to be feasible, particularly in regard to clients' capacities. They should also be realistic and attainable in terms of whatever time is available. The goals, methods, roles, and tasks set forth in the contract should be within your or the client's reach. Do not promise more than you can deliver and do not expect from clients more than they can give. Be sure that clients do not agree to actions that they cannot carry out.

A major purpose of the contract is to keep clients moving at a steady pace, not to shame or punish breaches. Not all contracts go smoothly. When there are significant differences between you and your clients, work them out early. Do not avoid conflict. When contracting goes too smoothly, it is often a sign that one side is selling out to the other; furthermore, an agreement between worker and client not to pursue service because of recognized differences or conflict is, in fact, a good contract (Seabury, 1979).

Contracts are not immutable; modify them in the light of existing constraints, events outside clients' or your control, that may hamper progress. New and different problems might emerge as you move along. If the progression of the work leads you to a new level of commitment, or to explore yet uncharted territory, review and change goals accordingly. Approaching goals in the order of priority for clients makes movement more readily apparent, and stating goals in measurable terms allows documentation of change over time.

FIGURE 5.1. Ten Steps in Goal Formation

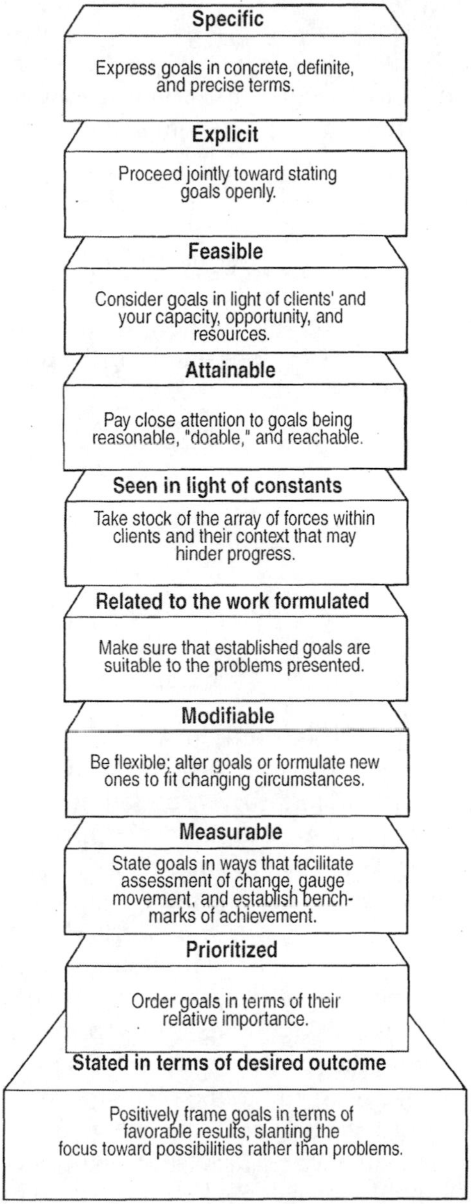

Specific

Express goals in concrete, definite, and precise terms.

Explicit

Proceed jointly toward stating goals openly.

Feasible

Consider goals in light of clients' and your capacity, opportunity, and resources.

Attainable

Pay close attention to goals being reasonable, "doable," and reachable.

Seen in light of constants

Take stock of the array of forces within clients and their context that may hinder progress.

Related to the work formulated

Make sure that established goals are suitable to the problems presented.

Modifiable

Be flexible; alter goals or formulate new ones to fit changing circumstances.

Measurable

State goals in ways that facilitate assessment of change, gauge movement, and establish benchmarks of achievement.

Prioritized

Order goals in terms of their relative importance.

Stated in terms of desired outcome

Positively frame goals in terms of favorable results, slanting the focus toward possibilities rather than problems.

PROCEDURE FOR CONTRACTING

Your ability to find and respond to patterns in clients' behavior rests on the adequacy of your methods; in other words, the kind of answers you get are limited to the kinds of questions you ask. Although, in the end, the effort to change must come from clients, you have a key role in assisting them in shaping change through identifying clear goals.

In the initial phase of work, jointly examine and assess clients' initial expectations, capacities, and goals. Identify, at the same time, your own areas of expertise in terms of approach and resources. When needs and goals are explicated and agreed upon, confusion diminishes about the direction and content of the work (Fox, 1987). The following questions guide your matching the unique needs of clients with the requirements of the therapeutic task:

1. What specifically needs to be done?
2. On what do we agree?
3. What is required?
4. What do we expect from each other?
5. Who will do what?
6. In what sequence?
7. What constraints exist?
8. How will we know when we have achieved our goals? (Fox, 1987)

Answering these questions jointly not only moves clients and you toward establishing a genuinely reciprocal and collaborative relationship, but builds a clear-cut and firm foundation for change. Work is clearly defined and steps are delineated for corrective measures. Concentrate at first on the issues that are most important to the client, but, over time, feel freer to spread efforts over the range of concerns clients may introduce during the course of work.

Goals can be developed for change in thoughts and feelings as well as in behavior. Whichever the focus, the very process of systematically attending to goals moves clients away from irrational and self-limiting thinking about themselves, others, or their situation. Clients also come to recognize what cannot be changed. When setting goals, specify an end result for each goal. Translate goals into statements of behavior clients will display or tasks they will accomplish after a specified time. Doing this makes make it easier for both your clients and you to recognize incremental steps while enroute to achieving goals.

Contracting usually occurs in four stages:

1. Selection of goals
2. Delineation of what is to be changed
3. Planning action
4. Feedback for evaluation

The first stage involves clarifying competencies—clients' and your own. It also institutes communication and collaborative arrangements. Mutual determination of purpose and limits leads to mutual investment and commitment. The second phase involves the actual collection and analysis of data, identification of the range of options and decisions needed, and consideration of alternatives. The third stage actually mobilizes you and your clients toward establishing a workable structure. The final stage balances the goals with the plan of action so that ongoing correction and modification can be made as you move toward achieving the identified results.

OUTLINE FOR THE GOAL-ORIENTED CONTRACT

In this section you will find an outline for the goal-oriented contract. Although for illustrative purposes it traces an actual contract with a family, the process and procedure are equally applicable to work with individuals or groups. Its eight points are not discrete entities and usually overlap. The outline exemplifies an actual written contract with the R family, employing their actual language and style. The family consisted of four members: Mr. R, a thirty-eight-year-old draftsman; Mrs. R, a thirty-six-year-old part-time nurse's aide; John, their twelve-year-old intellectually gifted son, and Sally, their nine-year-old daughter. The Rs had come for family therapy as a last resort after a series of unsuccessful attempts at individual work for John. John, with a superior IQ, was not achieving his potential in school. Indeed, he was not attending school at all much of the time. His sister Sally, with average grades, was a model student and daughter. For purposes of clear illustration this example traces only one of five goals the family identified, namely, to improve the relationship between Mr. R and John. Other goals included: to improve school performance, measured by more frequent attendance and completion of homework; to reduce Mrs. R's overinvolvement with John and Sally, measured by her transporting them to fewer activities by car and hiring a baby-sitter when she shopped or ate out rather than always bringing them along; and to develop a better relationship between Mr. and Mrs. R in terms of their spending more time alone, increasing the frequency and duration of sexual relations, and building on common intellectual and sporting interests.

1. *Clients and you generate baseline information.* This is contextual data describing clients, their situation, and their needs and concerns as the work begins. It enables clients and you to capture a "before" picture of the initial level of functioning against which change "after" the contract can be measured. The baseline information addresses the question, "What is the original level of functioning?" An example of a statement from the actual contract with the R family reads, "Mr. R and John spend little 'good' time alone together. The only time they relate is when Mr. R punishes John for not doing his homework. Mr. R wanted John to play baseball and signed him up for the Little League, but never goes to watch the games. All he does is criticize John for what he doesn't do right."

2. *Clients and you then specify your focus and expectations.* You discuss explicitly what you want ultimately to achieve and record it. I use newsprint and keep goals posted at all meetings. At the same time, identify proximate and incremental goals. These are stated in concrete terms so that it will be possible to know when they have been achieved. This procedure helps determine what kind of approach is necessary and narrows down possible strategies while discovering additional information. It answers the question, "What is to be accomplished?" A statement of expectation from the actual contract was, "Mr. R and John agree that they want to like each other better and spend time together in an enjoyable way. They agree that for one month Mr. R would relinquish the responsibility of John's homework to John. Mr. R will take John to one baseball practice and one baseball game each week. As a fresh start, they will together begin the tree house that John has wanted and Mr. R has promised to help him build."

3. *Clients and you proceed to set priorities for goals.* Goals, after being considered in relation to their feasibility and clarity, and

after being stated in a terse fashion, are ordered in terms of their importance. The question guiding this part of the contract is, "What is the relative importance of each goal?" Attention is directed at the central or most important one first. The R family agreed that the "awful" relationship between Mr. R and John was the most pressing issue and needed immediate attention.

4. *After establishing the conditions to be changed, clients and you identify observable behavioral characteristics and describe how changes will be exhibited by them.* This segment of the contract is crucial since it establishes a tangible sign of achievement for clients and you. It answers the question, "How will improvement be recognized?" The actual contract statement read as follows: "For one month Mr. R and John will spend at least four hours each week with each other. Mr. R will note how much time they spend together without arguing. John will keep a record of how many homework assignments he completes each week. Mr. R will note each time he was tempted to criticize John's homework, baseball, or building skill but refrains."

5. *Clients and you delineate your respective roles and explain your responsibilities.* Here you elaborate on the requirements for participation, by each answering the question, "What are we willing to offer?" For example, "Mr. R and John are willing to carve out six hours to spend with each other each week in selected activity. They each will keep records suggested by Dr. F, and will honestly report weekly results. Dr. F will read the reports, continue to coach and offer suggestions, and work out a reward system with Mr. R and John."

6. *Clients and you develop a plan that includes alternative solutions.* You devise a method for reviewing work. The guiding question for this portion of the contract is, "What is the most effective way to tackle the problem?" A sample statement from the contract is, "It's good to gradually stop some of the negative criticism. More important is doing some new 'good' things together. The progress will be examined week to week but also more thoroughly after the first month."

7. *Clients and you agree on a time frame.* Included are such factors as duration of the contract, length of sessions, and progression sequence. The guideline questions are: "How much time will it

take to achieve the goals?" "How much time must be put into preparation?" "How much time will be devoted to each meeting and to each task?" and "In what sequence will the contract be implemented?" The actual contract read, "For the first goal we will put aside one month, meeting each week for one and a half hours. Time outside the session devoted to this goal will be six hours, as described earlier in the contract."

8. *Clients and you build in and specify criteria for step-by-step evaluation of the achievement of goals and transferability into actual life at home.* The method for the measurement of change is agreed upon, with the question being, "How will progress be measured?" or "How will achievement be demonstrated?" For example, "by the end of one month, John will be doing his homework alone each night; Mr. R will be attending practices and games without criticizing; and the tree house will be half completed . . ."

PROGRESSIVE STEPS
IN THE CONTRACTING PROCESS

When developing contracts, be sure that the following steps are taken:

- The problem is clearly defined.
- The goals are spelled out.
- The work that needs doing is delineated.
- The alternatives are considered.
- The work is organized into clear jobs.
- The tasks are related to each other.
- Decisions are made about sequence, method, etc.
- Feedback is elicited.
- Progress is evaluated.
- Necessary revisions and alterations are made.

These steps break down into four process stages, which are built on the basis of the goals. The first stage involves establishing a therapeutic relationship (Chapter 3). The second requires reframing, with your clients, problems into possibilities (Chapter 5). In the third stage, clients are guided to consolidate and integrate their new realities (Chapters 9 and 10). Finally, you emphasize the gains the clients have achieved, stress their resources, both external and internal, and actively explain the process you have mutually undergone to have successfully gotten where you now are.

LIFE-PRESERVING CONTRACTS

Being faced with a suicidal client is an awesome responsibility. It requires being totally available, being alert, and having the highest degree of knowledge, compassion, sensitivity, and energy. It was said to me by a colleague, metaphorically, that dealing with either a threat or a suicide attempt requires all the stamina, attention, focus, and introspection that is required to survive driving through an ice storm. What do you do when you face such a challenge as preserving life? What do you need to recognize? What do you say? What active steps do you need to made to formulate a life-preserving plan? Considering all these factors constitutes a very special type of contract.

Since a client's suicidality is perhaps the most important, if not the most difficult, challenge you will ever confront as a therapist, and since no single formula exists for therapists to follow in facing a suicidal client, practical guidelines for assessing lethality, ideation, and risk factors, as well as strategies for managing suicidal clients, are essential.

A client's suicide is profoundly troubling for any therapist. One of ten clients who makes a suicide attempt will die, and of those who die, most will have previously threatened or attempted suicide. To respond most effectively to clients and, simultaneously, to avoid feelings of guilt at having neglected the client, guilt over your failure to hear the intensity of your client's distress, or shame that you have failed, or to avoid the devastating conclusion that an effected suicide proves your incompetence or irresponsibility, take the necessary precautions and steps.

Do an extensive and explicit evaluation with clients to ascertain the urgency of their suicidal inclinations, the extent to which specific plans have been made definite and acted upon, and the availability of any means of suicide (pills, gun, rope, etc.). Include a discussion of the availability of the means, how lethal those means are, and the urgency to commit suicide. Explore with them any drug use or delusions. It is extremely important to identify any history of suicidal thoughts or attempts of their own as well as in their family. Ask about supportive people in their lives—friends, siblings, co-workers. Directly ask such questions as: "Are you so upset that you're thinking of hurting or killing yourself? What are you thinking of doing?"

Since research has indicated that suicide is a response of a person with a vulnerability to act on powerful feelings, encourage the expression of these feelings as you proceed to develop a life-preserving contract. This contract, which may be oral although it is better written and signed, should include notations about the frequency of contact and, usually, arrangements to increase contact. Spell out ways clients agree to contact you if their urges increase. Provide auxiliary resources, phone numbers of other professional personnel, hotlines, and agencies to whom they can speak should you not be able to be reached quickly. Make sure that clients recognize the need for additional support—professional, familial, medical—as they work with you to avert suicide. Although it is not specified in the contract, know that you, too, need extra support, from supervisors, colleagues, or consultants, during this time of stress. Try to fathom the significance of clients' wish to die—appeal for help, escape, challenge to the fates, reunion with a lost loved one, rebellion, penalty for failure, an attempt at ultimate control? Better understanding their motives better fashions your interventions. Convey to clients, as best you can, a sense of hope that pathways of meaning can be found by living, appeal to the healthy parts of their personality, and entreat them to furnish themselves and you with a fair chance at helping them see their lives as worth keeping. Make a copy for each of you to have readily at hand.

In making such a contract you become an ombudsman for clients, promoting their welfare, doing everything possible to sustain their lives. The contract creates direction. Doing it reminds them that life is the best choice among lousy alternatives.

WRITTEN OR ORAL CONTRACTS

An implicit contract always exists between you and the client when you start working. Written contracts, however, are better than oral ones because they reduce ambiguity and avoid misunderstanding. If it is not written, it should be thoroughly verbalized and discussed. A written contract is an immediate and tangible reminder of agreements that conceptualize problems, give form to the chaotic nature of initial requests, and also provide a visual document that makes it possible to get back on track easily when resistance or obstacles have led you astray. Neither written in stone nor as binding as a legal document, the "spirit" of the contract, mutuality, is most important.

When I work with clients, I record and revise the wording on newsprint as goals are stated and changed. This newsprint, posted at every session, serves as our written contract. As each goal is achieved, it is crossed out, accentuating success; as new goals are identified, they are listed. My clients' participation and cooperation is continually enlisted in the development of the contract. Not as inflexible as it may sound, the contract does not preclude but rather encourages you to deal more spontaneously with crisis and other pressing issues that invariably arise during the course of the work; structure frees you for spontaneous interaction.

BARRIERS TO CONTRACTING

There are several roadblocks to effective contracting. To begin with, excessive attention to problems limits involvement, as does inordinately focusing on obvious information or irrelevant details. Attend rather to clients' strengths—these must be enlisted anyway to grapple with problems. Too, when clients look for some concrete help for specific problems, and you look for major personality change through introspective techniques, impasses and conflict are bound to occur, opening the way to disappointment on both sides and, often, premature termination. If agreement is too easily reached, it may mean that someone is holding back or attempting to avoid confrontation for fear that the conflict will be unresolvable and work will terminate. It is very likely that attempts to avoid conflict eventually will lead to unresolvable differences later on. Other barriers include unrecognized fears, rigid behaviors, and persistent thought patterns that defend clients from facing change. In families and couples, deeply entrenched dysfunctional patterns of interaction, which protect them from facing themselves and which preserve the status quo, forestall contracting. What can you do about these powerful blocks to change?

Take account of what *can* be accomplished. This means avoiding both excessive expectations about what can be accomplished and doing too much for the client in terms of formulating the contract and in carrying out its tasks. By doing too much for clients, you support their own beliefs that they are inadequate and unable to plan or care for themselves. It may be quicker and easier to do it for clients, but, in the end, it is more helpful to encourage them to take responsibility themselves. Know when to step back and allow clients to take increasingly active roles. Let them know (and remember yourself) that the contract is one aspect of a larger helping process. Do not ignore issues as they arise during the course of your contact. Restricting your attention only to what has been agreed upon originally is a mistake. Also, use precise language to identify what is to be changed, to determine goals you are working toward, and to evaluate progress.

ADVANTAGES AND LIMITATIONS OF CONTRACTING

Goal-oriented contracting takes three important principles of growth into consideration: clients progress most effectively when they (1) see a need, (2) know how, and (3) are involved.

The exchange between the clients and you during contracting involves the dimension of mutual decision making and agreement. In coming to look at and formulate a plan, you develop a viable system together that defines and nurtures the helping process.

Advantages

A major feature of goal-oriented contracting is that it introduces genuine collaboration into the helping process. It is fluid. It makes possible individualized work and mobilizes ingenuity and energy to perform tasks. The contract has many other advantages. Explicit, it is a source of motivation and involvement. Time limited, it eliminates a protracted and indefinite time frame. The limit is established in direct relation to client needs.

Contracting promotes focus and avoids ambiguity by clearly explicating problems and goals. It avoids games and hidden agendas that frequently accompany the helping process and thereby minimizes control and manipulation. Commitment to carry it out is enhanced.

Stating goals clearly at the beginning gives guidance and direction to both clients and you and sets criteria for evaluating the undertaking. Initial success, symbolized by the very existence of a contract, gives impetus for continued expectation of resolution and confidence that continuing effort will lead to success and positive results.

A seldom-mentioned issue is your need to see that you make a difference, that you make an impact on clients' problems. Goal-oriented contracting allows for such gratification because it provides you with tangible signs that something is being accomplished (Fox, 1987).

The advantages of goal-oriented contracting in terms of assessment, treatment, and evaluation are described in the following sections.

Assessment

The goal-oriented contract permits earlier, quicker, and more accurate assessment. Directly observing clients as they undertake the process of identifying goals in the session illuminates how they characteristically interact in their home environment. It provides data immediately about roles, hidden bonds, and strengths that may not be otherwise available. As the client is observed undergoing self-reflection and analysis, knowledge is gained about existing capacity for reality testing and flexibility in adaptation. Precision in identifying themes and issues is enhanced, and any impact of intervention is seen immediately. Clients' capacity for reality appraisal and flexibility in dealing with tasks and altering patterns becomes evident, as does their unique emotional, cultural, and social context.

Process

The contract encourages precision in describing and designing interventive methods for resolution, thus keeping you and clients more attuned to the stated purpose and conduct of the work. Tension is relieved because abstract global concerns are broken down into manageable concrete terms and logical frames. Immediate modification of dysfunctional communication patterns and support for productive ones are an added advantage of contracting. Distorted perceptions are corrected and mutual exchange and examination are encouraged.

Because goal setting is central to the entire helping endeavor, contracting complements and facilitates, rather than intrudes. New avenues of communication are opened and unhealthy patterns are revealed as clients observe themselves involved in planning change in their lives through mutual exploration and compromise. Immediate feedback about how the work is progressing allows for modification.

Even when clients are involuntary, see no problems, or have reduced capacity to abstract or visualize outcomes, goal-oriented contracting is possible because it invites them to choose an outcome they desire. Clients are more inclined to "own" what they have designed and not see it as imposed and therefore oppose or rail against it.

Evaluation

As is clear from the contracts with the R family, previously presented, the goal-oriented contract provides systematic data about the effect of intervention for clinicians, but more important, for clients. Comparing initial and subsequent statements on the contract, or any portion of it, provides tangible evidence of progress. Contracting makes evaluation possible, indeed easy, because it employs a practical methodology that integrates criteria for single-system research into the clinical procedure: specifying problems; measuring them; collecting information about them over time, both before and during intervention; using a planned format or design; and specifying an intervention program (Blythe and Briar, 1985).

DISADVANTAGES OF CONTRACTING

Despite its many advantages, contracting has some limitations. In the first place, it may be seen as oversimplifying a very complex process. Because contracting is a relatively formal process, it may be viewed as static and binding. The contract is not intended to be rigidly or blindly followed; rather, its very intention is to promote flexibility. Problems occur when it is inappropriately used to address routine matters that are by definition not negotiable. For example, a limitation arises from misperception of the contract. It is not a cure-all. It is not a prescription. It cannot do more than enable clients and you to deal with a few well-defined and circumscribed issues that are capable of being worked on within a defined time frame. Finally, it is limited by reality. The contract is only as good as the people who formulate it. It cannot be expected to accomplish more than the resources, expertise, and investment that clients and you bring to it.

Goal-oriented contracting can be described as much by what it is not as by what it is. Not intended for particular types of clients, as a compromise or a substitute for other types of work, or as a device to be employed to be expedient, it is a deliberate and effective treatment of choice for a gamut of client situations. Its use is not limited to certain practice agencies or fields of practice. It has relevance for all types of human services: mental health, child welfare, and medical.

A FINAL NOTE ABOUT CONTRACTING

Goal-oriented contracting structures intervention around observable, measurable, and mutually acceptable goals. This chapter describes the rationale, principles, and procedures for undertaking such an approach. It is illustrated with a case example of a family contract. Goal-oriented contracting encourages individuals and families to function independently, making more possible the transfer of change from the therapeutic situation to real life. It is based on the operational principle of "starting where the client is." It is an approach that demonstrates to clients the relationship between their interaction and the problem; it examines and then establishes and reinforces appropriate vehicles for client development, growth, and stability. It makes it possible to adapt the helping process to different types of clients. It teaches clients to observe their own process and establish new and better modes of communication and support, and encourages higher levels of differentiation.

I believe that contracting intrinsically contains possibilities for confronting the fullest and deepest range of your clients' experiences. Clients initially come to work on identified "symptoms" or problems. These are genuine problems for which they ought to receive help. Once in the helping situation, as clients formulate the contract and begin to work on the problem, the depth, breadth, and quality of your presence, sensibility, and courage encourages them to fathom, ever more completely, the fullness of their life story.

Chapter 6

Evaluating Client and Clinician Progress

Before beginning a long journey, it is wise to know where you are going, that way you will know that you've arrived once you get there.

A. A. Milne

The journey of a thousand miles begins and ends with one step.

Lao-tzu

In the present climate of increased accountability, managed care, and briefer forms of treatment, with increased pressure on you to demonstrate evidence of progress, it is crucial for you to develop a variety of means to evaluate your practice, promoting what Bloom, Fischer, and Orme (1995) refer to as "scientific practice" (p. 7). Sound clinical wisdom suggests that interventive activities need to be linked closely to clients' goals and objectives. As a clinician, therefore, you will benefit from procedures that enable you to examine your practice in ways that link your interventions to outcomes associated with clients' goals. This chapter takes the idea of emphasizing the importance of goals to a more advanced level.

What forms of evaluation are feasible for clinicians? What steps can be taken to make practice evaluation an integral part of your practice? Are there evaluation methods that can be built directly into your therapeutic encounters without being intrusive? Is it possible to utilize methods of evaluation that reflect the interface between the "art" and the "science" of clinical practice?

This chapter describes a variety of methods for evaluating practice and highlights the literature related to practice evaluation. It concen-

trates on two distinctively different frameworks; two for objectively
or quantitatively appraising client progress in treatment and one other
for you to use in subjectively, qualitatively assessing your headway in
managing your own work.

CLINICAL EVALUATION

You probably have heard it argued that practice evaluation is "impossible, never really objective, politically incorrect, meaningless,
and culture-biased" (Gabor, Unrau, and Grinnell, 1997, p. 3). There
is a tendency to dichotomize the art and the science of treatment. This
leads to an impasse where as a clinician you must consider yourself to
be either an artist or scientist but not both, and certainly not both at
the same time. The art of the work requires sensitivity and intuition,
which do not lend themselves to objective scientific scrutiny or evaluation. The science of the work demands rationality and analytic precision.

Evaluating your practice has multiple advantages—to refine diagnosis and assessment, to facilitate treatment planning and task as-
signment, to show improvement to the client and to yourself, and to
facilitate meeting the rigorous demands by managed care organizations for quality assurance reviews. Evaluation improves the quality
of your treatment. It also guides your decision making, assures accountability to the client, and enables you to examine critically your own
work. It helps ensure that clients get what they need and that clinicians
meet the standard of being conscious and disciplined in their practice.

Evaluation can cut across diverse theoretically based practice
models. Theoretical diversity is a hallmark of contemporary practice.
It is plausible to expect that clinicians' practice models will influence
not only their assessment techniques and choice of intervention strategies, but also their evaluation processes. Several theoretical orientations lend themselves to greater use of empirical evaluation methods.
Some of these are the cognitive-behavioral, family systems, and solu-
tion-focused models of intervention. The psychoanalytic orientations, on the other hand, rely more fully on self-evaluation methods.

FORMS OF CLINICAL EVALUATION

Evaluation is not new. It has always been with us. As clinicians we
are continually challenged to find ways to demonstrate outcome ef-

fectiveness of treatments that are cost-effective but do not compromise quality. Evaluation has traditionally taken a more informal stance. Self-reflection, for example, as one form of evaluation, is almost axiomatic. Supervision is another form of evaluation. Case conferences and consultation are also types of quality control and evaluation. These approaches, however, have relied heavily and perhaps solely upon subjective, qualitative assessment. These methods are not insubstantial and, indeed, are encouraged and developed further in this chapter. They can be enhanced and refined through the addition of objective forms of evaluation.

Although, over time, clinicians' acceptance of the relevance of evaluation has seemed to increase, the actual methods or means to employ continued to be argued. I believe that evaluation is a fundamental clinical activity rather than a research activity, even though research methods are frequently employed. Clinical evaluation refers to the means that practitioners use to assess the effectiveness of their interventions with clients. These means can be both qualitative and quantitative, pragmatic and empirical. Both methods can effectively estimate clinical effectiveness. Qualitative methods, historically arising from "practice wisdom," have been employed at first. Quantitative methods, on the other hand, have arisen from empirically based practice models that have gained considerable attention over the past two decades.

The key features for achieving skills in practice evaluation are flexibility and balance. The advantage of a multimethod approach is that it provides a range of evaluation methods that parallels the range of experiential exposure you may encounter in your practice. Your theoretical orientation will certainly influence which methods you adopt or adapt, to the exclusion of others. You may use a variety of intervention strategies (technical eclecticism) in your work with clients that may require different evaluation methods at different phases of the work or junctures in the progress. Including different sources of information (e.g., client, family member, teacher, supervisors, and students' own observations) enhances the reliability of your assessment. Remember that the method you choose is only as good as it is appropriate for the particular client and purpose of your intervention. The special and discrete purpose of evaluation should guide your selection of relevant methods to use. Just as your treatment strategies are tailored to meet the particular needs of individual clients, so too should your evaluation methods be selected with care.

The original impetus for clinical evaluation came not merely from researchers but from practitioners themselves, who viewed practice evaluation as a necessity, albeit an impressionistic and imprecise one. Interest in promoting clinical evaluation is even stronger now for reasons stated previously. The various perspectives that have influenced the development of practice evaluation have tended to polarize a qualitative/quantitative distinction into a schism, dogmatized methodology over practice realities, and resulted in unwarranted tension between practitioners and researchers. Tyson (1995), who favors a "naturalistic" approach to practice evaluation, acknowledges that a chasm has developed between the practitioner and researcher based on their different perspectives and methods. Practitioners see the researcher's methods as artificial and intrusive on the therapeutic aims. The researchers see the practitioner's "practice wisdom" as subjective and unscientific.

OBJECTIVE DESIGNS
FOR CLIENT EVALUATION

Continuing observations of a client over time, before, during, and/or after your treatment, constitute what is called a single-subject or single-system design for evaluation (Bloom, Fischer, and Orme, 1995). All quantitative designs require that client behaviors or events be specified in measurable terms in order to make evaluation meaningful. This was the basic focus of the previous chapter on goals. These goals provide a reference point or baseline measurement against which changes can be compared. They also suggest that measures be taken at several points in time. This allows for a control against which change during the treatment regimen can be compared. They emphasize (1) specifying target behaviors, (2) setting realistic goals, (3) identifying a suitable measure, (4) employing it systematically, (5) analyzing observations over time, and (6) charting change. The following two methods for objectively evaluating your work emphasize establishing a clear and quantifiable "before-after" picture of your practice. They allow you to examine and assess progress at various intervals during the therapeutic process as well as upon its completion. These methods are adaptations of the Single Subject/System

Design (SSD) (Bloom, Fischer, and Orme, 1995) and Practice Outcome Inventory (POI) (Ho, 1976). No attempt is made here to provide a detailed description of either the range of sophisticated variations or elaborate statistical approaches within each model; rather, an appeal is made to you to seriously consider incorporating some structured type of evaluation into your practice. The models presented, even in their most simple form, are offered as illustrative examples, not as hard and fast authoritative paradigms.

Single-Subject Design

Single-subject design is presented here not strictly as a research activity, but rather as one means of evaluating clinical practice. As in other forms of objective evaluation design, following a clear identification of relevant issues or problems, initial targets or goals are stated, and on a regular basis the same measures are used to monitor client progress toward the achievement of their goals. These baseline data are important because they allow you to infer that your intervention is effective, that it is possible to attribute change in your clients to your interventions rather than to other factors (Rubin and Babbie, 1997). Systematic means are introduced for monitoring change and assessing progress in treatment.

A particularly novel and easily understood idea for single-subject design involves the use of a chart or graph to track client progress. This makes it possible to individualize the evaluation process to the unique characteristics, needs, and dilemmas of your clients. Charts and graphs provide ready visual gauges for both you and the client to monitor progress. As interventions are guided by a specific theory or principle, decisions can be made as to whether or not there is significant change in a desired direction, thus meeting the expressed purpose of the treatment. Corresponding adjustments, therefore, can then be made in the approach.

A number of easy-to-use prepackaged scales, many reliable and valid, are available for you to incorporate into your work. No matter what your professional orientation, you can draw upon them to assist you in evaluating your practice. From an analysis of the information you glean over a series of time periods, you are able to draw reasonable conclusions about your treatment's success, options for continuing or discontinuing treatment based on these results, altering interventions, making a referral, or terminating therapy. When such methods are incorporated directly into treatment, they can actually propel as well as enhance the therapeutic work.

In the following example of work with Mr. H, a forty-six-year-old man suffering from depression, measures were taken at weekly intervals over a twelve-week period. Using the Beck Depression Inventory (Beck, 1979), three independent sources for measurement of depression were utilized—client self-report, spouse report, and clinician assessment. Each of these separate measures was juxtaposed onto a single graph that tracked Mr. H's headway. The treatment model employed was cognitive-behavioral therapy.

Cognitive Therapy

Cognitive therapy concentrates mainly on thoughts. It emphasizes clients' situation at the present time. Clients are actively taught self-help techniques and given homework to offer them control over their symptoms and life events. Usually brief and time limited, it fosters a collaborative effort between you and the client within a structured format to address problems. Beliefs and thinking are closely examined. Cognitively oriented therapists believe that distortions in thinking lead to inappropriate conclusions about oneself, others, and the world—and that these distortions guide behavior. Treatment, therefore, focuses upon correcting clients' negatively distorted thoughts and helping them to think more realistically. In the depressive cycle, as in the case of Mr. H, his loss of employment activated dysfunctional automatic thoughts such as "I am never able to do anything right," accompanied by feelings of dejection and devaluation. As a consequence of accepting these skewed thoughts as a foregone conclusion, a depressive cycle occurred whereupon Mr. H stopped trying to do well and displayed a poor attitude. This not only worsened his situation but deepened his depression. In other words, in a cognitive framework, depression is viewed as an induced emotional state triggered by an event. Negative meaning is ascribed to this circumstance or event. Utilizing the cognitive model, the therapist, applying principles of logic and evidence gathering, enables clients systematically to identify and to confront distorted thoughts causing these negative emotions and behaviors and to analyze these thoughts in light of their validity and usefulness. Attempts are made to shift clients' attention away from thoughts or beliefs that are unrealistic and harmful to those that are more rational and useful.

Mr. H's Situation

Mr. H sought therapy after being "excised" from a middle management position in a large urban retail store. His wife, upset at his increased lethargy, "blueness," and trouble sleeping, insisted that he seek counseling. Mr. H initially refused but, pushed hard by his wife, relented and called for an appointment. At the initial interview, Mr. H reported that he was sad, disgruntled, and almost paralyzed with the fear of never working again. A number of ancillary problems were identified, but he readily agreed to focus on reducing his depression as a primary object for our attention. Believing strongly that "nothing could really help him," he nonetheless reluctantly agreed to participate in a cognitively oriented approach, once it was explained in detail to him and once a time limit was established. To meet his need for recognizing progress, as well as to monitor the success of selected cognitive interventions, he agreed to complete the Beck Depression Inventory each evening while in treatment for a period of three months. This scale was chosen because of its clarity and ease of administration by oneself or another. Clear-cut and adaptable, it takes but a couple of minutes to complete. An advantage of the Beck Inventory is its empirically proven validity and reliability. Although it is intended for a clinician to administer, it is so clearly user-friendly that I regularly encourage clients and select others (family, friends, other involved professionals) to complete it along with the clients themselves after obtaining instruction and gaining practice in its application. Mr. H completed one copy of the inventory each day. A weekly composite score of his level of depression was calculated by averaging his daily ratings. Mr. H's wife agreed to complete the inventory once each week for the same period of twelve weeks. Mr. H. also kept a log describing his mood each day, which he gave to me each week at our scheduled session. Perusing his journal, I arrived at a separate third score, a composite weekly score, by averaging the daily entries. Such a procedure created three independent comparative measures of his level of depression over the three-month course of treatment. These three separate indices were captured on a graph. Not refined, but certainly serviceable and practical, a copy of the graph tracking Mr. H's progress appears in Figure 6.1.

Although no arbitrary score can be used for all purposes to classify different degrees of depression, the following guidelines are suggested to interpret the scale (Beck, 1979).

0 to 9	Normal depression
10 to 15	Mild depression
16 to 19	Mild-moderate depression
20 to 29	Moderate-severe depression
30 to 63	Severe depression

These scores are reflected in Figure 6.1.

Interestingly, there is remarkable correspondence among the separate scores—his own, his wife's, and mine—for Mr. H's level of depression over time studied. For the first nine weeks of therapy, Mr. H's level remained severe; nevertheless, it was steadily declining. Between the tenth and twelfth week, there was a marked decrease in the level of depression. Everyone took this to mean that Mr. H was recovering from a major depression and making healthier adaptations in his life. Most important, it demonstrated to him that it was possible to overcome feelings of despair even though he initially believed that

FIGURE 6.1. The Single-Subject Graph

SCORE	Week 1	2	3	4	5	6	7	8	9	10	11	12
65												
60	@%	@%										
55	#	#	@#									
50			%	@%#	@%#							
45						@	@%					
40						%#	#	@				
35								%#	@%#			
30												
25										@%#		
20											@%#	
15												@
10												%#
05												

Key: @, Client; #, Clinician; %, Spouse

"nothing could really help." For me it affirmed that the chosen inter-ventions, journal keeping, homework, maintaining the Beck Inventory, confronting cognitive distortions, and so forth, were having a beneficial effect.

As you can see, the graph makes it immediately evident by three separate indices that Mr. H made substantial headway over the twelve weeks toward overcoming his depression. There are added diagnostic and clinical advantages of using such a visual method for tracking progress. Beyond being a tangible sign for all concerned that progress was being made and at what rate, it became a catalyst for further intensive discussion about other adjustments Mr. H needed to make in his treatment as well as in his life. These discussions, in turn, led to identifying supplementary goals for treatment, including the development of strategies for finding employment.

Goal Achievement

A similar method for assessing effectiveness of treatment and client progress is charting goal achievement. More subjective than the previous one, in that it relies more heavily upon client self-report, POI is one of many models that focus on attainment of goals. Using the POI method, you initially list the goals clients state that they want to achieve, giving special attention to being as specific as possible in terms of actual behavioral outcomes for each of these goals. You proceed to help clients rank each of these in terms of importance for them on a scale from 10 down to 1, 10 being the most important goal, 1 being the least important. Clients are then asked to refine these goals by stating them in specific behavioral terms or anchors for each. They proceed to rate each of the goals named in terms of how characteristic each one is at the present time. To do this, they ascribe to each goal a weight from -5, not at all descriptive, to $+5$, very descriptive. A summary score is computed by totaling the collective individual scores at the initial session and the last session, providing a "before" and "after" picture of the family against which to measure progress. This procedure allows clients to develop a measurable indicator for overall goals as well as for each of the behavioral anchors. The change from one time to a subsequent point in time is measured by computing the difference in scores at the two points in time. The following example depicts this procedure as it related to the L family's goals over a six-month period of family therapy. The example shows two overall goals and five behavioral anchors, plus the rank, weight, and score at two points in time, six months apart.

The L Family

The L family, of Irish-Italian ancestry, consisted of a thirty-two-year-old mother, Mrs. L; a thirteen-year-old retarded daughter, Mary; a twelve-year-old son, Steven; and a ten-year-old daughter, Susan. The Ls lived in a two-family dwelling above the maternal grandparents, both of whom were deaf-mutes. They survived on public assistance, supplemented by "gifts" from Mrs. L's parents. Unemployed for over three years, Mr. L made no financial contribution to the family. At the point of contact, he had been forced to leave the home by his wife because of his total lack of support, alcoholism, and physical abuse of the entire family. Mr. L had already moved to a one-room furnished apartment eight doors down from the original family residence. Although he was maintaining contact with the children, Mr. L declined, upon invitation, to participate in the treatment.

Mrs. L and her children started family therapy because she was totally overwhelmed by confusion and uncertainty about her situation, by the management of her three children, and by their conflicted reactions to Mr. L's absence. She had at first seriously considered requesting foster care placement for the children. She was adamant that she "desperately needed help" for herself and the children in adjusting to their troubled situation.

While conducting a goal attainment interview during our first session, Mrs. L's foremost and pressing desire to place her children was thoroughly explored. After discussion, she decided to postpone placing them in foster care, instead choosing to engage the children and herself in treatment. As seeking placement was set aside, other goals, aimed at improving the relationship and communication between Mrs. L and her children, were identified and targeted for attention. Two overall goals were stated: (1) "understanding each other" and (2) "expressing feelings." These rather global goals were subsequently honed down, specified more concretely into five subunits: devoting time for family discussions, talking about problems, doing things together, controlling children's bickering, and learning the cause for the bickering. All five of these foci were ranked and weighted as described in the section above. Figure 6.2 shows the ratings both for these goals and for the anchored specifiers as scaled at

FIGURE 6.2. Goal Achievement Chart

GOALS	Time 1 (initial session) (May)				Time 2 (final session) (November)		
	Rank	Weight		Score	Rank	Weight	Score
Understand one another	.5	× 10	=	5	2	× 10 =	20
Express feelings	-3	× 9	=	-27	2	× 9 =	18
Concretizations						=	
Time for family discussion	-2	× 8	=	-16	0	× 8 =	0
Talk about problems	1	× 7	=	7	1	× 7 =	7
Do things together	-1	× 6	=	-60	0	× 6 =	0
1. Play games	0	× 5	=	0	0	× 5 =	0
2. Take trips	-5	× 4	=	-20	-4	× 4 =	-16
Control children's bickering	-5	× 3	=	-15	-2.3	× 3 =	-6.9
Learn cause of bickering	-4	× 2	=	-8	-4.3	× 2 =	-8.6
	Composite scores			-80			13.5

two points in time, six months apart. Undergoing this goal identification process not only revealed definitive data for problem identification and treatment planning, but unveiled the family's patterns, themes, interactions, and problem-solving procedures to which I might not have access otherwise.

Comparing the goal attainments at Time 1 (the initial session) and Time 2 (the final session), you can detect quite certainly Mrs. L's perception of change for each goal and behavioral unit identified originally. As is evident, the movement was considerable, and it occurred in a positive direction for all but one goal—finding out the cause of the bickering. Reviewing the procedure provided tangible evidence for Mrs. L and her family, as well for myself, that progress was made. At the last session, when the outcome of the goal attainment process

was examined, the Ls could have opted to terminate treatment, hav
ing accomplished much of what they had set out to do. Instead, examination and discussion of the goal attainment chart by the entire
family and myself served as the basis for the formulation of yet another goal attainment contract. This time we concentrated on areas in
which there had been only slight improvement or no marked improvement on the previous one. The particular goals constituting the
new contract, which were even more specifically stated than previously, included talking about problems and differences the moment
they arose, playing games together at least three evenings a week, and
finding the cause of the bickering. The Ls succeeded, at the conclusion of three additional months of therapy, in meeting the first two of
these reestablished goals. Still unable to identify the cause of bickering, they agreed that this was acceptable to them, perhaps even no
longer important, since their lives had become so much more manageable and pleasant. Placement of any of the children in foster care
was averted.

Advantages of Objective Forms of Evaluation

Neither of the two examples of evaluation presented here are well
polished or elegant. That is not the point here. The point is that both
offer you a utilitarian and hands-on means to more effectively assess
client progress and the efficacy of your own interventions. Clearly,
from these two examples, the first involving individual treatment
with Mr. H, the second involving family therapy with the Ls, there are
significant evaluative and clinical advantages for using more objective forms of evaluation. Clients are encouraged to partialize their issues, articulate them in plain and explicit terms, assess their relative
importance, and ultimately have documentation in black and white of
the fruits of their efforts to improve their situation. You, the therapist,
are immediately alerted to your clients' progress as well as to the efficacy of your interventions. Four major advantages of objective forms
of evaluation, as adapted from Proctor (1990), are that it: (1) facilitates the assessment of each situation and monitors changes over
time; (2) indicates whether positive or negative changes have occurred in targeted problem areas; (3) assesses whether interventions

are causally linked with these changes, and (4) enables comparison of effectiveness among interventions.

SUBJECTIVE DESIGNS
FOR SELF-EVALUATION

An array of means exists for self-evaluation of your clinical practice. Among them are ongoing practice logs (see Chapter 13), intensive case studies (see Chapter 12), and critical incident analysis. Process recording is yet another method of self-reflection. It greatly assists you in better understanding, assessing, and critiquing your practice. Process recording has long been one of the most prominent and most utilized ways for clinicians to conceptualize and evaluate their treatment. It is so difficult to truly know whether or not you are being effective; the form for process recording discussed here addresses this dilemma because it serves as both a *product* and a *process*. It offers a structured format for recording, analyzing, and evaluating contacts with your clients.

A process recording enables you to conceptualize your work at all stages of interaction—preparation, assessment, intervention, hypothesis testing, outcome—in whatever arena of clinical work you are engaged. It is an efficient way to document your work. It can be reviewed quickly. With the clinician-client interaction laid out in written form, it is easy to quickly pinpoint specific sequences of exchange for review or comparison. The exercise of reconsidering, reflecting, and reconstructing your contact with clients results in obtaining a better hold of their themes, patterns, and blockages. In addition, writing demands that you rethink, and reconsider, from a distance as it were, the interchange in a way that allows you to recognize client concerns that you may have missed or interventions that were off target during the actual encounter. It allows you to reach beyond literal reporting of information, events, or transactions toward a fuller analysis and conceptualization of your helping endeavor.

This form of recording reflects what Elks and Kirkhart (1993, p. 557) refer to as a "pragmatic-professional model." It truly enhances your ability to discern your effectiveness. Pragmatic and down-to-earth, its major benefit is that it includes four of five components identified by Elks and Kirkhart (1993) as integral elements in self-evaluation—

intuition and experience, personal and professional values, client change, and the clinician-client relationship.

Prototypes of Process Recording

The model of recording proposed in this chapter is adapted from a recent paper (Fox and Gutheil, 2000) and from two earlier ones by other authors (Cohen, 1988; Urbanowski and Dwyer, 1988) that focus on process recording as it is intended for educational purposes. Although each of these was originally designed for one-to-one interaction, the form described here is intended for use with an array of varying client systems in a range of settings.

Cohen (1988) advanced a five-step format for process recording, including the following dimensions:

1. Preengagement—recording affective and cognitive preparation for the interview
2. Narrative—describing the details of what transpired during the interview (not a verbatim reconstruction, but a summary of verbal interaction that will help the clinician recall the interview)
3. Assessment—evaluating what transpired
4. Plans—describing the agreed-upon next steps
5. Questions—recording any questions about the content or process of the interaction

Urbanowski and Dwyer (1988) offer a six-part structured approach to process recording. This method outlines the following content:

1. Purpose of client contact—formulating a concise, clear, and specific statement of purpose of interview or encounter, bridging contact with the previous contact and reflecting the clinician's awareness of the particular function of the agency and the clients' capacity and motivation.
2. Observations—describing general impressions of the physical and emotional climate of the meeting and the specific impact on the clients, noting significant changes in the client's appearance or surroundings.
3. Content—presenting a picture of the interaction between the client and the clinician during the planned contact and describing

how the interview or activity began. Discusses the responses of both client and clinician. It also includes facts and feelings revealed by both client and clinician and what preparation is made for the next contact, along with a statement of how the contact ended.

4. Impressions—statement of impressions based on facts, with analytical thinking demonstrated as the clinician integrates theory and comes to better understand the interaction between himself or herself and clients.
5. Worker's role—this section highlights the clinician's activity with clients, reflecting roles, skills, and techniques, along with an evaluation of one's effectiveness as a helping person.
6. Plan—brief statement of plans for the next contact and recording of thoughts about long-range goals for the client.

Although these models evolved from different assumptive bases about what constitutes process recording and, therefore, what content is prioritized, their similarities are the focal point of this new proposed model. Their differences are less substantive and more formative, that is, they stress parallel content but suggest different formats for capturing it. Two similarities are key: (1) emphasizing your critical thinking and conceptualization of the interaction between clinicians and clients rather than mere literal replay of dialogue; and (2) concentrating on your awareness of yourself as a professional helper who selectively employs knowledge, techniques, and theory in your work.

Doubtless, the following five-part framework requires time; however, it is time devoted more to advancing your critical thinking, reflecting, and conceptualizing than to actual writing. There is little danger that this framework will either straitjacket you or stereotype clients. Although the outline may be standardized and structured, uniqueness emerges from the individualized way you use it, with emphasis on your own as well as clients' special features and characteristics.

FRAMEWORK FOR SELF-EVALUATION

This framework captures the "process" or conversation between you and your clients. It condenses into a structured format the collection of facts with added attention to critical thinking and analysis. It is

a flexible as well as a substantive guideline for recording. Not intended to be a rigid format, its five components can be adapted to fit
your particular interests, discrete needs, and theoretical bases. Depending upon the unique features of your practice, your recording
may be discursive or narrative in form. At other times it can be brief
and anecdotal, in shorthand, or quite elaborate. At no time should you
employ excessive detail or include extraneous information. As with
most other types of evaluation, it documents service, identifies goals
and needs, forms a basis either for referral or for continuity in service, and presents a vehicle for tracking progress and sharing information with colleagues. Its principle feature, however, is that it
places special emphasis on you as a consequential variable in the
helping process.

As mentioned earlier in the chapter, the unique feature of this
framework is that it is both process and product oriented. It provides
an instrument to focus and direct your critical abstract thinking (process) about your interaction (process, again) with clients. In this regard it offers a framework for higher-level conceptualization. Also,
since you are the person involved so closely with the client, it allows
you to determine the effectiveness of your interventions. It is simultaneously an outline for crisply and coherently writing a document
(product) that is vital for evaluating and documenting client progress.
The framework, furthermore, integrates previous models into a single
generic framework for an ongoing consideration of the helping process across an array of practice settings—mental health, forensics,
family service, child welfare, etc. At the same time, it provides a flexible vehicle for differential application among a range of different
practice roles and methods.

The recording provides vital feedback on what you need to know
or do or alter in order to customize your interventions to help clients
achieve positive outcomes, and for them to capitalize on what the
helping process has to offer. It offers an inductive approach. Included
in it are your observations, gathering of data, analysis, and interpretation, among other things. It provides a sound means to connect your
work to research findings and theory, to foster your own hypotheses,
and to discern clients' patterns.

The proposed five-part framework, offered as an outline of questions, follows. Its components are not truly discrete entities, but they
are presented as such for heuristic purposes. You may integrate the

components into one narrative, or divide them into separate headings. Five critical elements of clinical practice are accentuated—preparation, observation, knowledge, skills, and planning.

I. Preparation and Purpose (Preparation)

You should complete the *preparation* component, capturing baseline information, prior to or at the time of the initial contact with your clients. State the reason for your contact, relevant identifying information, key thoughts, prospective agenda, aims, and plans for the contact as well as any potential obstacles or pitfalls you anticipate. Include collateral information that is pertinent to the situation presented. Incorporate methods you are considering, data to be obtained, preliminary assessment formulations, issues for focused attention, and possible barriers to be overcome. If you are working on a continuing basis, include the current situation, issues being addressed, and any material from the last meeting or intake with the clients that should be revisited. Spell out goals for both you and your clients. Some guideline questions include: What are my goals for this contact? For me? For clients? What are some key elements to look for? Am I clear about what my role is? Is my role clear to the clients? What would the preferred outcome be? Do I have sufficient information and resources? What preliminary arrangements need to be made to enhance the exchange? (For example, should furniture be arranged in a particular way? Should mother and child be seen together at first? Is there a need for special physical accommodations, e.g., ramp?)

II. Process and Relevant Information (Observation)

Here you describe the ebb and flow of the contact, including the verbal and nonverbal activity. It may be verbatim or a paraphrased and summarized description of what occurred interpersonally during the contact, noting the responses and activity of both you and the client. In this section you compile your *observations*. Begin with factual information such as who was present, description of the clients, unique and unusual factors, and cultural variables. When the interaction is presented in summary form, include direct quotes, where appropriate, to individualize and highlight significant elements. Some guideline questions are: How did the contact begin and end? Who was present? What changed during the contact? What changed since the last contact?

What decisions were made? What tasks were accomplished? What was the structure and direction of the meeting? What homework was suggested? What strengths did the client manifest?

III. Thoughts and Analyses (Knowledge)

Articulate your unspoken thoughts and reactions to clients and examine your own and clients' functioning. You might jot down some hypotheses about the problem and its possible solution. Denote client strengths, capacity, and motivation, as well as impressions regarding the nature and quality of the helping endeavor. Assessment refinements and evaluation of the climate of the exchange are also included here. Special attention is given to the identification of significant patterns and themes that emerge. Also appraise the power of your own relationship with clients and theirs with you. In brief, critically evaluate your activity and clients' progress toward goals, drawing upon both your intuition and *knowledge* base. Important questions include: What did I learn about myself and my knowledge and skill application? What do I need to know more about in terms of the clients and ways of interacting with them? What went particularly well? What was particularly difficult for me or the clients? If I were to do it over again, what would I do differently? What alternatives are available to me? Was agreement achieved? Why? Why not?

IV. Interventions (Skills)

Identify the *skills,* methods, and distinct techniques you used to reach the stated purpose, to tailor the interaction to clients' expressed and special needs. Reflect on and assess how appropriate, realistic, and effective your strategies for intervention were, with singular attention to goals, feedback, and contracting. Some guideline questions are: How effective was I in joining my method of intervention to the needs of the clients? What interventions were successful? Which ones did not work? Why? How do I build on what has been accomplished? What other methods may be appropriate? Are auxiliary modalities appropriate? Family therapy? Group?

V. Next Steps (Planning)

Consider the direction for your work with clients in the future. The focus here is on *planning.* Where are the clients heading? Is it where they want to go? What homework for myself would be helpful in better understanding and connecting with the clients? Where am I heading? Is the direction sound? Should I be doing something more? Something different? Is a referral necessary? To whom? What homework would be instrumental for clients? Are concrete services needed? Auxiliary services? What are the short- and long-range plans? Are the short- and long-range plans in need of revision? Are collateral contacts indicated? With whom? How soon? How is follow-up to be handled?

The recording can be supplemented with other written material (genograms, sociograms, ecomaps, etc.), other supplemental and illuminating material (diagrams, graphs, charts), and other technological material (audiotapes, videotapes, etc.). With this in mind, the outline can be utilized, expanded, modified; various parts can be emphasized more than others.

WAYS TO USE SELF-EVALUATION

Although generally associated with encounters with clients, recording can be used for a variety of purposes to enable you to take a critical look at your work. In addition to recording work with individuals, families, groups, and collateral contacts, you can use this outline to examine task groups such as teams and planning committees, in order to gain a greater understanding of the dynamics of a meeting. Recording that requires increasing assessment, self-reflection, and analysis as you proceed can help you track your own professional growth and development. You can use your analysis of process to prepare for supervisory conferences by raising issues, concerns, or questions for your supervisor or consultant.

The framework parallels the components, process, and sequence of the steps you follow with clients to evaluate their progress. Although it has been argued that such a self-evaluation may have nothing to do with changes in client behavior, such a process is a lifelong, ongoing professional career requirement based on practice wisdom and ethical considerations. A major feature of this framework is that it requires focusing. It necessitates an explicit identification of goals and processes. It gives guidance and cogent direction to you and provides concrete means for measuring and documenting performance. Flexible in its utilization, it provides a robust method for examining and evaluating your own performance as a professional helper.

Chapter 7

Assessment:
Learning from a Jigsaw Puzzle

We never see only what we see; we always see something else with it and through it! Seeing creates, seeing unites and above all seeing goes beyond itself.

Paul Tillich

Not everything that is faced can be changed; but nothing can be changed until it is faced.

James Baldwin

Clients are complex and multifaceted. Seldom, if ever, will you be able to pin one label on them that either completely satisfies you or fully describes them: that is a tribute to both of you. Clients, like you, are composed of many varied parts, like jigsaw puzzles. Some of these were cut long ago; some continue to be shaped day by day; some have jagged edges; and some are smooth and curved. All of us continually try to figure out who we are and how we can fit the pieces of our lives together.

Think about your clients in ways that include a consideration of the multiple features of their life experience. As you endeavor to understand their stories, recognize that clients' life experiences are reenacted with you. Take account, then, of the stock from which they were cut and how well their facets interface as you undertake "putting it all together." In a way, figuring out clients is much like solving a jigsaw puzzle. Seeking coherence needs to be your nagging preoccupation. Through assessment, you bring all the seemingly disparate pieces together into a coherent whole.

WHY IS ASSESSMENT IMPORTANT?

Accuracy and sensitivity in assessment, to a large degree, contribute to your therapeutic effectiveness. They guide inquiry into the fullness of clients' lives and help you to select and continually monitor your interventions. They guide you in the immediate and delicate interactions with clients. They are integral to the entire helping process.

Assessment is ongoing. It is not merely a formal statement, an end product after a prescribed period of time. It requires time taken together with clients that allows both of you to pause, reflect, and reevaluate. Certainly, at the end of each encounter and at preset and spontaneous intervals along the way, you summarize progress and take stock once again of where you are going; but, in truth, you are assessing from moment to moment.

Why is assessment important? It enables you to avoid the mistake of assuming that only you are in charge of the change effort. Both you and clients work hard and do independent thinking. In the end, the soundness of assessment depends upon how well your thinking meshes.

Assessment focuses on clients, their problems, the helping situation, and you. Events do not move in a straight line from cause to effect. Problems result from complicated interactions among numerous variables. Clients are influenced by many things, and are neither determined nor cured by any one thing. To seek a single cause dooms you to failure.

Determining what is to be avoided and what is to be supported, what is to be strengthened and what is to be altered, are all vital functions of assessment. In clearly identifying sources of pain and anxiety, assessment prevents you from having things go from bad to worse by rushing in to fix them too quickly without full awareness of what you are dealing with. Often, in the rush to make things better, you may reinforce clients' old patterns and encourage them to carry forward unresolved issues, which then further overwhelm them. Assessment is vital because it locates attributes and capabilities to be tapped in enhancing clients' potential.

If all these reasons are not enough, assessment is important because it helps do the following:

- Ascertain the nature of the person
- Specify the nature of the problem
- Differentiate attitudes toward self, family, and environment

- Name motivational forces
- Describe the reality of their experience
- Identify what is normal, healthy, and positive
- Select what is possible and practical
- Locate barriers to change
- Detect resources available for overcoming barriers
- Characterize resistant factors
- Determine prognosis
- Determine the frequency of appointments
- Estimate the duration of the helping process
- Set the tempo of the work
- Decide the modality and method of intervention
- Match your methods to the discrete needs of clients
- Select appropriate points for different techniques
- Discern the relationship to you
- Predict the consequences of any change that might come later
- Evaluate the efficacy of the intervention

Obviously, assessment is simultaneously a process of elimination and exclusion, of ruling things out, as well as a process of pulling things in.

Assessment provides an overall picture, not just a classification, that permits clients and you to evaluate the extent to which goals have been reached and the degree to which change is enduring. It is an opportunity for you to assemble and order pieces together and, ultimately, to make decisions about terminating your work together.

WHAT ASSESSMENT IS NOT

Consider, for a moment, what assessment is not. It is neither a reductionistic pigeonholing of pathology or problems nor a labeling from some typology or classification system, although that might be one step in it. Assessment is, rather, a humble attempt at comprehensive discernment of the overall nature of clients. It is an appreciative, holistic look at human beings in all their complexity, singularity, and dignity.

Assessment is not a one-sided abstract opinion delivered by you, the expert. Rather, it involves interactional collaboration in which clients participate actively in a feedback process that does the following:

F—Focuses on what is changeable
E—Extends and shares parts of each of you
E—Elicits feelings, reactions, suggestions, and questions
D—Describes rather than confines, judges, or interprets
B—Builds on honesty and openness
A—Allows time and space for thorough consideration
C—Concentrates on and reinforces strengths and observable changes
K—Knits secure relationships

Assessment is not a restrictive intellectual exercise arriving at an analytical inventory or list of problems but is an inclusive, discriminating depiction of a whole that is not fixed or static. It is a flexible and dynamic process that changes as clients grow and change.

Not simply a retrospective account of what happened long ago and far away, assessment incorporates a prospective view of what is hoped for. A view from the past juxtaposed against a view of the future rounds out the picture of clients' present life situation. When assessing clients, respect the continuity of their lives.

DOING THE JIGSAW PUZZLE

Doing an assessment is much like doing a jigsaw puzzle. The end result is finding unity in the face of apparent fragmentation. The challenge is to bring the pieces together into a coherent whole. Your task, in brief, is to put it all together. Figure 7.1 illustrates some of the components of a finished puzzle.

Imagine the pieces of a jigsaw puzzle as if it were dumped haphazardly, scattered on a table. An accurate analogue of clients' lives in crisis, to begin putting it together demands a creative mentality, enthusiasm, and patience. As with clients, clarity about your own role, values, and intentions as well as confidence that there is some solution, that it can be put together, encourages success. Assessment also requires the confidence that clients have the capacity to change and to

FIGURE 7.1. A Human Jigsaw Puzzle

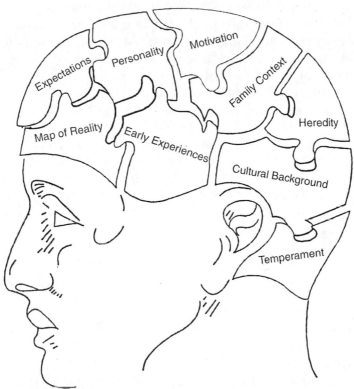

grow. It also requires your engrossment in the process. At first, you might recognize isolated bits, but rarely an amalgamated whole. How can the puzzle best be solved?

Puzzles are usually solved using a combination of intellect (science) and intuition (art). A sprinkling of inspiration (spirit), enthusiasm, and creativity also help. Working from the left brain, you draw upon logic in reasoning how various pieces might fit together, and you calculate next steps using a linear, sequential, and inductive approach. Simultaneously, working from the right brain, you draw upon intuition.

Select a starting point. Take a cursory overview to locate similar pieces and then collect and assemble them. These pieces are combined into piles of like size, shape, color, and impression. The next step involves finding pieces with clear boundaries, usually straight edges, which, joined together, give the outer border. It is extraordinarily difficult, if not impossible, to put it all together without first discovering the outer framework. These edges make it possible to direct attention inward. Such a frame makes the puzzle less elusive, clarifies the broad outline of the basic pattern, and allows you to visualize how the whole might finally appear. You cannot solve the puzzle without first accepting the limitations imposed by the framework.

With clients too, assessment involves sizing up their external reality and situational, social, and cultural factors. Develop a structure and an organized strategy for determining what to look for next.

As you proceed with the sometimes boring and time-consuming task of actually piling similar pieces together, you begin to discover a basic pattern, the relationship of parts to each other and to the whole. You begin to recognize how the parts intertwine and interrelate and sometimes converge. It is seldom as simple as it seems.

Take your time. Hurrying, scrambling to put pieces together, only increases frustration. Examine what is before you. Clarify and reformulate the information. Make a continuous endeavor to look for the internal continuum, the interface, the link between discrete pieces.

Take close account of negative space. In other words, infer what probably is missing by studying the gaps in the puzzle. Look for them. Take stock of what pieces are missing, so you have a clue about what might fit. As with a jigsaw puzzle that you work on without benefit of the finished likeness, you may at first know only where to explore, not what you will find. Even when a piece is missing from the image, it is still possible to have a rather accurate, though incomplete, representation of the whole. Very often, patience with this sequence gives you a clearer hypothesis or sense of the whole. Step away from it for a while; put the puzzle aside.

When you return to the puzzle, get more information, gather more pieces, and rearrange them based on fresh impressions. Be open to serendipitous discoveries. You may discover, by accident, that some fit. Do not force pieces together that do not interlock easily or smoothly; they were not meant to fit. You will fail to capture the puzzle's unique design. Although some areas of the puzzle will come together almost spontaneously, for the most part, success in completing it depends upon tolerance of uncertainty and persistent hard work.

You will not triumph over the chaos until you discover the basic relationships among pieces. Progress may at first be uneven. Indeed, along the way, you may face what seem to be insuperable barriers posed by clients, circumstances, or you. Pieces may be misplaced. The table may be jarred. You may lose interest or be distracted. Stay with it. As you relate parts to the whole, a more congruent picture emerges, giving you increased confidence that it is coming together.

Gradually you will discern the context and character of the larger picture. This informs your next move and makes it easier to fill in the inner core. The final solution unifies what at first seemed to be disjointed details.

There is a point at which the puzzle metaphor breaks down. With clients, you do not have an image of the final picture in front of you. The puzzle is fixed and static, with but one solution: clients, on the other hand, are in constant flux, and there is always the potential for new elements. The continuous circular movement of exchange between clients and you influences not only each of you reciprocally, but the end result as well. Clients are not completely determined by their context and actively contribute to determining their characteristics and movement.

The puzzle analogy breaks down further when you consider that total success with a jigsaw puzzle requires restoring it to its original prescribed form. Success with clients, on the other hand, often means the construction of a new reality, a redefinition of self, or an expansion of boundaries. With clients you act as a catalyst in the search for new connections, deeper meanings, and unexpected answers.

As with any puzzle, time, experience, practice, and experimentation help make it possible to absorb and code information faster, bringing solutions more quickly into awareness.

Here, in summary, are tips for approaching client assessments or puzzles:

1. Because you cannot know how much you do not know, begin with a sense of not knowing, being open to discovery.
2. Get as many perspectives on the puzzle as possible; recognize all the various combinations, because you cannot imagine what you may find.
3. For each combination, formulate alternate views; feel bold about looking.

4. Consider the function of each piece in relation to those around it.
5. Think of assessment as involving phases or intermittent bursts of work, so that factors that elude you at first can be successfully discovered and explored later.

THE GENERAL PROCESS
OF ASSESSMENT

Assessment is a process with constant interplay and interdependence between you and your clients. See Figure 7.2 as an example.
There are many types of assessment—popular and informal, professional and formal, reliable and unreliable.

FIGURE 7.2. The Process of Assessment

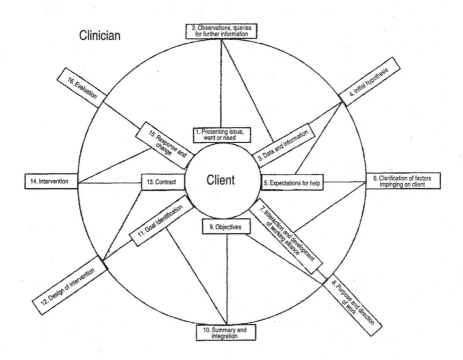

Popular and Informal Instruments and Techniques

Some of the more popular types of assessment appear regularly in self-help books, magazines, and newspapers; sometimes they even appear in professional journals. They take the form of self-reporting questionnaires, indexes, profiles, and forms. Various procedures attempt to assess personality based on unusual and unexpected factors. For example, the Luscher Color Test attempts to analyze personality using information on color likes and dislikes. It has even been argued that "you are what you laugh at."

While some of these may have some measure of validity and may indeed provide an accurate portrait of one aspect of clients, beware! For the most part they are mechanistic and simplistic and can, in and of themselves, reveal little. Their danger is that little may be taken as a lot. They can, however, be fun, even revealing. Engaging your clients in them can be enjoyable for both of you. What they say about assessment and the way clients respond to them provide invaluable clues for augmenting your face-to-face assessment.

. Games too, such as the Ungame, can offer incisive information about clients. Do not hesitate to use these, discriminatingly, recognizing their limitations. You are more likely to use them successfully, however, when you know their shortcomings and fallacies, and when you leave yourself open to the unexpected. Games can be rich sources of information. When you deliberately and knowingly suspend rules, clients sometimes reformulate established ways of behaving and rediscover truths already known or discover new ones. Variety, seeing clients from as many angles and under as many circumstances as possible, can help you get a more complete and well-rounded image of them. Avoiding conventional and stereotyped methods generates more distinct portraits of clients. Creative viewpoints and solutions often come from unexpected juxtapositions, strange combinations, and odd connections. Playing the game Monopoly, for example, helped to put José into sharper focus and helped him to see his own behavior as others saw it.

> José was an exceptionally bright twelve-year-old who was not liked at all by his peers. It had reached the point that they were making their dislike very clear to him by continually teasing and taunting him. At a time when peer acceptance was paramount, he seemed to do things that only intensified his rejection.

As part of our work, we began an ongoing game of Monopoly. Diagnostically, it provided a look at José's behavior both when things were going his way and when they were not. It allowed us to examine his behavior in response to his feelings. As I mirrored his behavior and modeled my own, he was able to see what others might feel in response to his gloating, crowing, bullying, whining, cheating, and insulting behavior. It allowed him to come to terms with his competitiveness. It provided impetus to talk philosophically about winning in the short run and losing in the long run.

Professional and Formal Instruments and Techniques

You are probably familiar with some of the more common forms of psychological testing for personality and intelligence. Just peruse a psychological assessment catalog. The tests, profiles, and scales mirror every theory (Freudian, Jungian, Adlerian); reflect every modality (individual, group, family); and trace every approach (cognitive, affective, behavioral). Examine them closely. Each captures one element of truth.

Tests are available to measure intelligence, attitude, achievement, developmental patterns, aptitude, adaptive behavior, and even suicidal ideation. Some are pencil and paper, others electronically scored. Some are objective, others projective. Some are taken in isolation, others in groups. Some require an observer; others are self-administered. Some are self-scored; others are scored by computer. Some use no words, but utilize drawings or blocks instead; others are verbal. Assessment and diagnostic tests come in a wonderful and endless variety. Some are named for their developers, for places where they were developed, or for the rating technique used to score them. Others use acronyms.

The following litany is but a small sample of assessment instruments that are widely available: Rorschach, TAT, MMPI, Wexler, Myers-Briggs Type Indicator, Q-Sort Technique, Stanford-Binet, Wechsler-Bellevue, WAIS-R, Cognitive Abilities Test, California Achievement Tests, Iowa Tests of Basic Skills, and Person/Tree/House. These can be of considerable value in refining your understanding of clients. In Chapter 6, you read about how one standardized instrument, the Beck Depression Inventory, was incorporated directly into the treatment process with Mr. H as a means for improving diagnosis and evaluation. The limitation of such instruments, however, is that they are usually extrinsic to your actual work. In other words, they are "applied to" clients, independent of your exchange.

Do not mistake a unidimensional profile for a full picture. All these instruments are of assistance in more completely understanding clients. They amplify understanding, but they are not substitutes for your immediate clinical observations.

Because these instruments can be intrusive, use them selectively. Employ them when you need to answer questions or fill in important gaps that cannot be obtained in more direct and interactive ways. You may notice over time that these tests very often will confirm some of your own impressions. Take that as a sign of your clinical acuity.

Secondhand reports are another source of qualitative data. Reports from other professionals from the same or other disciplines can be of great value. Take them as suggestive and instructive, rather than definitive. Consider them for what they are: auxiliary sources of information. Consider them in a serious light, but do not allow them to prejudice your judgment or predispose you toward a particular stance that overshadows your own.

Use what is of benefit from all forms of assessment, but not at the expense of participating with clients as they unfold their life stories. When you include all relevant data, direct and inferential, in perspective, you will generate a more complete and accurate assessment. Employ a range of data sources—those already mentioned, combined with autobiography (described and illustrated in Chapter 12), drawings and logs (described with case illustrations in Chapter 13), family trees (described at length in Chapter 10), and inventories (described with examples in Chapter 12).

No one method of assessment can measure or interpret the whole person. Each, taken alone, can diminish clients by reductionistically mistaking a narrow view for the wider panorama. Taken together, they provide a balanced, integrated, and comprehensive picture of the whole person. This comprehensive look at clients helps to ensure that you do not see the problem presented merely as a reflection of a client's personality deficiency.

Person-to-person collaboration gives you a formidable portrait of the underlying themes and repeating issues in clients' lives. In many

ways, your best tactic is to learn the tools of a good investigative re-
porter who asks, "Who, what, why, when, and where?" This hands-
on approach has a definite advantage. It adds freshness and immediacy to the work. Assessment is integral and incorporated into rather
than separate from the ongoing transactions between you and your
client. Furthermore, it can be fun. You will learn and appreciate what
makes clients laugh as well as cry. Seeing them from as many vantage
points as possible will make them more real and make the work lively
for both of you. It will motivate and possibly strengthen clients' self-
healing potential. That is quite an accomplishment.

WHAT'S IN A LABEL?

Considerable controversy exists among helping professionals about
the appropriateness of diagnostic labeling. Although there seems to
be general agreement that effective treatment depends upon accurate
evaluation of clients and their life situations, concerns are expressed
about the degree to which categorizing and labeling clients—as
schizophrenic, borderline, developmentally disabled, delinquent, or
unemployable—actually creates stigma and limits opportunities. Other
criticisms of assessment and diagnostic labeling approaches are that
they unintentionally or intentionally distort facts or dynamics; over-
emphasize pathology and overlook attributes; ignore multidimensional contextual information and lack theoretical integration. All
these challenge the viability of ensuring comprehensive treatment
and planning based on accurate assessment and diagnosis. Clearly,
there is no consensus about the critical focus and means of labeling.

Although a label can be limiting, respect its value for what it does
tell you. Appreciate, as well, that a label pinned on a client shapes or
alters your relationship.

A label helps you to name things, gives you some sense of control.
There are, however, some dangers in labeling. A label poses a risk of
reification—that is, treating an abstraction as if it actually exists. A
label may also give you a false sense of comfort or security that simply by knowing the label you understand all that you are dealing with.
Once a label is affixed, it is extremely difficult to remove it, and it can
stigmatize when it no longer applies. The danger, too, is that a label
may stereotype and thereby shape, rather than reflect, the client's per-

sonality or situation. In other words, it can create a self-fulfilling prophecy.

When you purchase a sweater, for example, the label will give you quite a bit of information: its size and place of origin; whether the fabric is hand or machine woven; whether the material is new or processed. However, it fails to tell you about texture, pattern, and quality. Like a sweater label, a client label tells you facts but fails to capture essence, resilience, integrity, and, again, quality. These can be determined and appreciated only by careful observation and handling. Such features are not identified on the label; nor can they be, for they are subtle yet substantive elements that defy easy depiction. Yet they are precisely the factors that, to a large measure, determine whether the sweater will wear well.

Some people never look at a label. They believe that it reveals nothing of true value and is intended only to placate an easily fooled consumer. But the label gives instructions about care that cannot be discovered in any other way. Do not hesitate to look at a label. Get a feel for the material. Try it on to see if it fits. Turn it inside out to scrutinize its construction.

What has a sweater label to do with client assessment? The comparison is quite appropriate, with an important exception. Sweater labels, even though deficient, characterize garments better than client labels characterize people. People labels tend to emphasize what is wrong rather than what is right. They are distillations of clinicians' conceptions, reworkings of clients' accounts rendered in jargon. The jargon, however, constrains and trivializes clients. When we stray so far from sources and reduce complex phenomena to shorthand, communication certainly becomes more efficient; but the essence of clients is compromised, perhaps lost. People labels are superficial and cannot give instructions for care. They reveal what is on the surface— and often mask clients' subjective experience of their distress and the way they cope with it. If you take labels to be more than they are, your perception will be distorted and limited; the way you interact with clients will be slanted and incomplete.

Do not settle for a label. Do not ignore or discard it either. A label reveals something relevant. It tells one part of a larger story. It helps you to make sense out of the information you have. Be mindful, however, that in using it, you are always dealing with a version of reality and not absolute truth. When combined with other labels and viewpoints, especially your own, it can have a further benefit. Your clients deserve your most thorough, inclusive, and far-reaching assessment. As with any procedure, labeling can be used positively or negatively—it is the care you take in its use that determines whether the outcome is helpful or hurtful to clients.

THE STANDPOINT OF STRENGTHS

Spheres of Strength

So much of what constitutes professional writing about mental health actually concentrates on disease. Such a stance invariably raises questions, then, about what constitutes health. Is it simply the absence of disease? Is it the adjustment or conformity to established social norms? Is it an attitude? Is it self-actualization? In grappling with trying to elucidate the concept of health, I have approached it in terms of spheres of strengths—self, social and societal, and spiritual.

Self

Intellectual health involves the degree to which we engage our minds in creative, stimulating activity; our ability to see beyond the present to what the future holds; capitalizing on available internal and external resources to expand our knowledge and skills; sharing these with others; and being goal directed, productive, at ease with ourselves, and striving for insight.

Emotional health includes our awareness and understanding of our feelings; feeling positive and enthusiastic about ourselves, others, and our lives; having the capacity to control our feelings and related behaviors; having a sense of humor; and acknowledging and accepting who we are as well as our gifts and limitations.

Social and Societal

Social health entails our comfort with other people, including our ability to form and sustain intimate relationships; elasticity and spontaneity in these relationships; and appropriate restraint of our aggressive and hostile reactions.

Societal strengths encompass our interdependence with others and a level of satisfaction gained from being productive in a career and contributing to the community.

Spiritual

Spiritual health denotes our ongoing search for meaning and purpose in our lives and embodies a deep appreciation for the depth and dignity of both humankind and nature.

More plainly stated, mental health, as captured in the Serenity Prayer, may be the art of living in peace with what you cannot change, having the courage to change what you know you should change, and having the wisdom to know the difference.

Pointers for Making Strengths Assessments

Keep these pointers in mind when undertaking an assessment:

- Refinement ascribes primacy to clients' uniqueness.
- Your clients' cultural and environmental contexts are crucial.
- The process should benefit your clients in some way.
- Actively drawing and building upon their strengths is as important as recognizing them.
- The very manner in which you conduct the assessment and the data you glean sets the stage for effective intervention.

Practical Guidelines for Assessment of Strengths

The following guidelines for generating a strengths-focused assessment are extrapolated from Cowger (1994).

1. Give preeminence to your clients' understanding of the facts.
2. Believe your clients.
3. Discover what your clients want.
4. Move the assessment toward personal and environmental strengths.
5. Make the assessment of strengths multidimensional.
6. Use the assessment to discover your clients' uniqueness.
7. Use language your clients use and understand.
8. Make assessment a joint activity with your client.

9. Reach a mutual agreement on the assessment.
10. Avoid blame and blaming.
11. Avoid cause-and-effect thinking.
12. Assess; do not simply diagnose.

Chapter 8 explores the notion of resiliency in depth. Chapters 9 and 10 interface with each other, using the same case study, to illustrate inclusion of a strengths perspective as well as the benefit of combining individual and family approaches to assessment and intervention. Chapter 9 concentrates on individual assessment, examining the place of the *Diagnostic and Statistical Manual of Mental Disorders*, Fourth Edition, and reviewing the theoretical underpinnings and dimensions of individual assessment. Chapter 10 presents various facets of family assessment and proposes the genogram as a useful tool for both individual and family assessment.

Chapter 8

Resiliency:
"Who Says I Can't?"

The people who get on in this world are the people who get up and look for the circumstances they want, and, if they can't find them, make them.

George Bernard Shaw

We are healed of our suffering only by experiencing it to the full.

Marcel Proust

These quotations, selected by my friend Sylvia for this chapter, epitomize what she believed guided her life. She also instructed me to use her actual name.

Sylvia was a quadriplegic who triumphed over adversity, and is a perfect example of the way resiliency can transform one's life. Her experiences with the harshness of her disability and the brutality of some of its consequences, and her long-term psychological reaction to both, are central to an understanding of resiliency. Fathoming some explanation for such resiliency, beyond what the professional literature identifies as its central components, is this chapter's focus.

Sylvia died in an accident as I was finishing a draft of this manuscript. In special tribute to her, therefore, her story is told as though she were still living, as it was originally written. At the time of her death, we had already scheduled a meeting for her to review and comment on this material.

As irony would have it, while walking across a busy city intersection the day after Sylvia's funeral, a car felled my daughter and me. In the subsequent days in the hospital, I was a prisoner in my own body, requiring me to rely on other people to attend to every need. During this period I believe that I experienced in a profound way a shadow of what Sylvia lived with hour by hour, day after day, for some twenty years—a talent and a mind captive to a stilled body, a fiercely independent woman chained into dependency.

But she prevailed! How did she do it?

Sometimes, as a therapist, I shake my head and wonder how people find the will to continue in this life. Sylvia had that effect on me. Each time I saw her, I left filled with awe, wonder, and curiosity.

As she was not a client of mine, I came to know Sylvia in a unique way. Two years ago, Sylvia approached me after a workshop I co-led and asked me to mentor the writing of her life story. I was reluctant. She was determined. Sylvia wanted to write a book to inspire and encourage others, beyond and different from what Christopher Reeve's book did. A hopeful book. A message celebrating will and spirit.

How did Sylvia prevail? What explains her transcendence? What explains the constant struggle of a woman to make her world significant even as her disability became more virulent and disabling? What allowed her to invent meaning when facing what first appeared to be a ruined life?

After hours of talking together, I came to explain Sylvia's fortitude in three ways—deliberation, determination, and decisiveness. Deliberation denotes her supreme consciousness, awareness, thoughtfulness, and ability to choose living above all. Determination explains her resolve, perseverance, stamina, energy, and willfulness—the powerful internal force that propelled her forward. Decisiveness indicates her lack of ambivalence, her firmness, her absence of doubt, and her courage in assuming responsibility for herself. All signal the most important message of her life—the ever-present potential for exercising greater control over one's life.

Sylvia agreed with my "academic" explanation. But she explained it differently, said it better.

Truly a phoenix, when her life was torn to ashes she found something inside herself that gave her the strength to contribute, to make a difference not only in her own life but for others as well. Sylvia had a knack for generating excitement and for sniffing out artistic openings. She transformed meaninglessness into meaning; personal adversity into a springboard. What did she see as enabling her to make such a leap? Her message is simple, but it is a testimony to her. It is emblematic of her ongoing commitment to live, examine, and improve her life to the fullest. It epitomizes the resiliency of human spirit:

> Be clear about what you want, what is your heart's desire
> Be stubborn, fight for what you believe
> Get real about mistakes as well as accomplishments
> Be self-reliant and resolute
> Endure
> Accept necessary losses
> Know that nothing can hold back dreams
> Decorate your soul
> Trust God.

SYLVIA'S STORY

Because of a ski accident at the age of twenty-eight, Sylvia lost the use of her limbs. And she lost more. She lost her husband and her children. She lost her faith and her vitality. She felt that she had lost her entire self. It took her thirteen years to reclaim her life. Approaching fifty, still paralyzed from her upper shoulders down, Sylvia travels around in a motorized wheelchair. She drives an equipped van. She works as an administrator at a large state university. She recovered and raised her children. She has become an accomplished painter. She has reclaimed her self and much more. She made it happen—through exercise of her will and spirit.

Although Sylvia's losses are significant, and many remain, her gains are enormous. How did she do it?

This chapter tells Sylvia's story, a juxtaposition of the ordinary and the horrible, the mundane and the unimaginable. How her life came together is the epitome of optimism and the desire to live.

Sylvia believed that her story would inspire physically, mentally, and spiritually challenged individuals. She believed she had a message to convey. A message about forging ahead. A message about not giving up or giving in. But she needed help to pull it together. That was where I came in.

A creative person, she struck a creative deal with me: she would instruct me in watercolor in return for my overseeing her book. Intrigued by the idea of perhaps also contributing to a chapter for this book as we prepared hers, we began our two-year association. Her book is well under way. I remain a frustrated painter.

My contact with Sylvia left me awed as well as curious. In preparing this manuscript, I sat with her informally for hours at a time and more formally interviewed her on a number of occasions to fathom her own perspective about her resiliency and what she believed contributed to it.

Surprisingly, with very little bitterness, she welcomed, rather than avoided, personal disclosure and discovery. She had a strong desire to contact the internal resources she knew lay inside her. She possessed drive and determination. Sylvia was a bundle of paradoxes: fiercely driven yet gentle, arrogant yet timid and retiring. Although the odds were stacked against her, she did not give up, never gave in. She thirsted for more and made it happen.

The Other Side of the Mountain

Sylvia begins by answering the question, "Why am I telling my story now?" with a simple reply, "I now have the courage." A friend, watching the movie *The Other Side of the Mountain* with her just two weeks before Sylvia's accident, suddenly shut it off, asking, "Do you know what happens to her?" Sylvia said no. Her friend said, "The worst things that can happen to anyone."

Because she had always wanted to be a nurse, Sylvia started nursing school when her two children were eight and six. During a recess from school, she went skiing. Her life was forever changed. Ascending the mountain fresh and vibrant, she came down motionless. Her neck was broken. She spent endless days in rehabilitation and underwent countless procedures. She was alive, but without the use of her lower arms and legs. One day an occupational therapist encouraged her to paint. With the brush strapped to her hand, she painted a tree. She threw away her first attempt. A friend retrieved it from the garbage, framed it, and put it in her hospital room, where it remained during her long stay. She did not know then that painting was to become her lifeline.

During this period of confinement, her husband, from whom she was already separated, talked of divorce, and then ended their marriage. He took Sylvia's daughter and son across the country. As if the accident were not enough, she then had to fight to get her children back. And fight she did. But Sylvia had always been a fighter.

With no motorized wheelchairs on unequipped planes, knowing no one, she took herself to court in Oregon. Unassisted, to prove that she could take care of her children, she wheeled herself into the courtroom. After several favorable point decisions, her children were returned. Her triumph made front-page news in a major newspaper.

The care of her children left her drained and depressed. One day, hating both the way she looked in her wheelchair and the way people looked at her in it, feeling sorry for herself, she nevertheless trekked out to make a rare foray to the local grocery store. There she met a stranger, from whom she expected yet another pitying glance. Instead she got a smile and a thumbs-up sign. It altered her perspective and rekindled her will to achieve.

Sylvia proceeded to enroll in a local community college and ultimately received a degree in psychology from the state university. Eventually, she got her first job. The commute, however, was exhausting. As she continued to grow, she found that she could strap a pencil to her hand and use a computer. She moved from one responsible job to another and attributed her ongoing success to determination. "I've always been stubborn and determined."

All during this time, painting was her salvation. At first she strapped a brush to her hand. Later she found that she could rest it against her fingers and paint. She took lessons from a prominent artist, traveling by van fifty miles to her sessions. She paints delicate watercolors of flowers and landscapes. Her paintings, especially her miniatures, are quite extraordinary, but not perhaps as extraordinary as the painter.

Over time her talent came to be recognized, and her paintings were exhibited at art galleries, universities, and private showings. She developed a style all her own that appeared as a special line of notecards, mugs, T-shirts, and pins. A unique feature of some of her paintings is the sayings she incorporates into them. One of her favorites explains her own tenacity—"And the day came when the risk to remain tight in a bud was more painful than the risk it took to blossom."

These aphorisms capture her own stamina and resiliency, but do they describe all of her strengths? Sylvia not only paints; but teaches painting as well. In her own studio, her students are both able-bodied and disabled. They find out there that having a disability does not mean one is not able.

But that is only part of her story. Surviving her background makes her triumph over the horrible accident even more remarkable. Alcoholics and difficult and abusive adults peopled Sylvia's early childhood. She has fought many battles. These are detailed later in the chapter.

RESILIENCY:
THEORY AND RESEARCH

Research (Harvey, 1996; Moran and Eckenrode, 1992; Rutter, 1990) suggests that sustained perception of one's own worth, coupled with confidence that one can "successfully cope with life's challenges" (Rutter, 1990, p. 206), result in resilience. Exposure to risk may have either a devastating or a steeling effect, argues Rutter. He goes on to note that vulnerability and protective factors are, in essence, two sides of the same coin. It is only through the interaction between risk and protective factors that resiliency occurs. The key in the development of resiliency is not in avoiding risk, but rather in accommodating to it successfully. Rutter identifies four primary processes that operate as mediators and/or moderators of risk: (1) the reduction of risk impact, (2) the reduction of negative chain events, (3) the establishment of self-esteem and self-efficacy, and (4) opportunity.

Another term for resilience, personality hardiness, represents the typical manner in which a person approaches and interprets experience. It seems to be an especially salient dimension in influencing how individuals process and cope with stressful life circumstances (Kobasa, Maddi, and Kahn, 1982). Hardiness, a term used to integrate various theoretical and empirical contributions, is described by Kobasa, Maddi, Pucetti, and Zola (1985) as being composed of a constellation of three closely related dispositional tendencies—commitment, control, and challenge. Commitment relates to a sense of meaning and purpose that the individual imputes to his or her existence, encompassing self, others, and work, that leads to a tendency to involve oneself in what one is doing or encounters. Control involves a sense of autonomy and ability to feel and act as if one can influence one's circumstances and contingencies and one's own destiny. Challenge involves a belief that change rather than stability is normal and a passion for life and living. One perceives changes as exciting and as opportunities for growth rather than as threats to survival or security (Kobasa and Puccelli, 1983; Kobasa, Maddi, Puccetti, and Zola, 1985).

In their recent study of resiliency in adults with histories of childhood sexual abuse, Liem and colleagues (1997) found that resilient individuals feel the capacity to bring about desired outcomes, tend less toward chronic self-destructiveness, possess an internal locus of control, and assume persons and situations to be controllable rather than resulting from inevitable and impersonal external forces (p. 601).

In their study of resilient children, Herrenkohl, Herrenkohl, and Egolf (1994) found that the will to create a better life is a driving force and reinforcement in the face of emotional pain. This will to create a better life is an important motive for finding new ways of living and coping. Although it may change over time (Herrenkohl, Herrenkohl, and Egolf, 1994), resiliency is generally conceived of as a fairly stable set of characteristics related to managing well in the face of risk factors. It is also defined as the capacity "to prevail, grow, be strong, and even thrive despite hardship" (Wolin, 1991, p. 3).

Perhaps the most inclusive definition of resiliency come from Garmezy (1994), who views resiliency as the skills, abilities, knowledge, and insight that accumulate over time as an individual struggles to surmount adversity and meet challenges. It is an ongoing and ever-developing fund of energy and skill that can be mobilized in current situations.

Saleebey (1997), while not directly addressing resiliency per se, echoes Rutter. He states that "trauma and abuse, illness and struggle may be injurious . . . they may also be sources of challenge and opportunity" (p. 23). Saleebey sees resiliency neither as a trait nor as a static dimension. Instead, it "is the continuing articulation of capacities and knowledge derived through the interplay of risks and protections in the world. The environment continually presents demands, stresses, challenges, and opportunities. These become fateful, given a complexity of other factors—genetic, neurobiological, familial, communal—for the development of strength, of resilience, or of diminution in capacity" (Saleebey, 1996, p. 299). Individuals are the experts in their own lives and there are continually open possibilities for choice, control, commitment, and personal development (Saleebey, 1996, p. 298).

McQuaide and Ehrenreich (1997) developed a "strengths questionnaire" (p. 209), based upon an intensive study of the extant literature, which identifies five overlapping and related conceptions of strengths that can be read as resiliency: cognitive and appraisal skills ("ability to perceive, analyze, and accurately comprehend a challenging situation"); defense and coping mechanisms ("characteristic mechanisms an individual uses to deal with problematic internal and external sources of stress"); temperamental and disposition factors ("characteristic ways of seeing and being in the world"); interpersonal skills and supports (the "ability to develop and maintain intimate and supportive social networks"); and external factors ("supportive social institutions, financial resources," etc.) (p. 205).

Although the literature and research cited above identify components of resiliency, none alone, nor even any or all considered in combination, explains resiliency in general or Sylvia in particular with a full degree of satisfaction. In all likelihood, all play some part. Clearly, resiliency is a complex and individualized blend of attributes that inextricably intertwine—individual attributes and personality, gender, familial, school, peer, and community factors. Most of these are descriptive, not explanatory. Questions arise: What explains resiliency when many of these factors, identified in theory and research, are absent? Are there yet unspecified factors? The next sections focus on two additional dimensions—*will* and *spirituality*. These are inferred in the resiliency literature cited previously. Oftentimes, they are considered anathema to one another, but it seems that in Sylvia's case they complement each other. Sylvia's resiliency involves more than her triumph over her body, more than the labor of her mind, but an exercise of will combined with spiritual and religious conviction and faith.

Existential Will

Existential thinkers posit will and self-awareness, coupled with the freedom to make choices and accept responsibility, as the greatest gifts humans possess. Choice is embedded in any situation, and many potential outcomes remain mysterious. Not knowing all the determinants of a situation provides freedom. Yet freedom implies courage; the courage to choose, to act, to choose being, and to accept responsibility for the choices.

Sartre (1960) avers, "man is nothing else but what he makes of himself" (p. 15). According to Sartre, life consists of choices, and the circumstances of life are the result of those choices. Briefly stated, we are what we act to be. We have the power to create ourselves. Camus, likewise, emphasizes choice in embracing life and being or nonbeing (1969). May (1969, p. 19) defines "being" as the individual's unique pattern of potentialities. Being is the process of self-aware existing.

May (1969, p. 37) speaks of responsibility as "the ability to confront reality directly and to respond to it in a positive manner. . . . To the extent that a person can accept responsibility for his life, he becomes a free moral agent." This view of responsibility permeates all life and translates to the concept of will—accepting responsibility and moving forward toward action, change, and life.

In addition to responsibility, humans possess the unique capacity for transcendence, "moving past the subject-object (self-world) split" (Bugental, 1965, p. 34). This explains the ability to overcome the past and the present in order to move toward the future. It implies growth and an ability to reach beyond the concrete; in other words, the capacity to transcend the immediate and present situation and strive for the future. Yalom suggests that the individual has freedom to create his or her own life, to desire, to choose, to act, and to change (Yalom, 1980, p. 217). He links responsibility to freedom—"one is responsible for one's life, for one's actions and for one's failures to act" (Yalom, 1980, p. 220).

According to Frankl (1992), meanings are found within individuals rather than given to them (p. 61), and we possess a spirit that is a source of healing and strength because it recognizes the human capacity to aspire to places beyond instinct, exposure, and environment. He asserts that meaning cannot be gotten hold of by mere rational means, but instead by existential means. This translates into *willing* it to be that way, *deciding* that there is meaning in the world rather than meaninglessness. It is possible to find meaning in all of life's events even when confronted with a fate that cannot be changed or manipulated in any manner.

Frankl's own life is testimony to the human ability to master even the most tragic and traumatic of events. He survived thirty-four months in Nazi death camps and the murder of his wife, unborn child, mother, father, and brother. It is living evidence that even in a situation in which an individual has no external freedom, when circumstance does not offer any choice of action, he or she retains the freedom to choose his or her attitude toward the tragic situation. You should not despair because this choice is always with you until your last moment of life. There is a will to meaning, and it is this that sets humans apart from animals. To be human is to strive for something outside oneself, for "self-transcendence," the grasping for something or someone outside of oneself.

Mastering the art of living is critical in finding meaning and purpose in one's life. Frankl (1992) noted that a person's attitude toward existence, the way one accepts one's fate and the suffering that accompanies it, can add a deeper meaning to a person's life, and that it is important for a person to see the limit to his or her "provisional existence. Thus, the individual must act on securing his or her future, to shape his fate or outcome. The striving for a goal or struggling to find meaning sparks tension, conflict . . . movement toward a goal. It helps the person transcend the suffering, and widen the picture of the world so the meaning is clear and visible."

The active operation of the will, a positive, active guiding force that mobilizes the personality, was also a central component in the work of Rank (1950). Rank speaks of the creative use of inner and outer experience. Although one cannot have everything without effort and without obstacles and restraints to contend with, positive willing makes it possible to move toward the attainment of particular things and to feel responsibility.

The synthesis of these concepts encompasses a concentration upon the healthy, aspiring, and positive aspects of humans and their capacity for choice and growth; the human dilemma of living and struggling to realize oneself; and an exploration into the fullest and farthest reaches of the self—mind, body, and spirit. In other words, will. Will, then, is the mental faculty, distinct from knowing and reasoning, responsible for choosing, deciding, and initiating, and directed toward the attainment of certain ends, even in the face of opposition. It is associated with "origination"—that is, escape from the past and the creation of a new beginning. The will, as with thought and feeling, is not seen directly, but is discovered from its external manifestations, acts, and behavior.

The Spiritual Dimension

Spirituality and religion are considered to be different, but in Sylvia's case both are involved. Spirituality involves the uniquely personal and subjective search for meaning, purpose, and values together with thoughts and feelings about the nature of life, the good or ethical life, and the nature of evil. Spirituality is seen as something within us that leads us to goodness and concern for others and the world. It is a belief system focusing on tangible elements that impart vitality and meaning to life's events. Faulkner, on accepting the Nobel Prize for Literature, commented, "I decline to accept the end of man. . . . I believe that man will not merely endure: He will prevail. He is immortal, not because he alone among creatures has an inexhaustible voice, but because he has a soul, a spirit capable of compassion and sacrifice and endurance."

Authentic spirituality is about the transcendence of captivity to the body, to ideals, to society. It involves the quintessential ability to address the larger questions of existence. Religion, on the other hand, is an organized, structured set of spiritual beliefs and practices shared by a community. It is one form of specific and concrete expression of spirituality.

Inherent in a spiritual focus is the resolution of issues of meaning and purpose. It posits that as humans we seek and hunger for deeper explanation, for answers, that are not provided by day-to-day existence. Being able "to draw upon spirituality gives meaning to life and, during crises, allows us to find solace and direction as we navigate change" (Angell, Dennis, and Domain, 1998, p. 616). It is of major importance in enabling individuals to deal with difficult and disruptive transformations and transitions in their lives. According to Flach (1997), spirituality is a form of resilience that provides individuals with the ability to understand and to overcome stressful, chaos-inducing events that in turn cause us to move from one state to the next by way of a normal cycle of disruption and reintegration. As such, it is a fundamental resource that can be drawn upon during times of adversity.

Canda (1988) defines spirituality as the "human quest for personal meaning and mutually fulfilling relationships among people, the nonhuman environment, and, for some, God" (p. 243). Involved is the fundamental yearning for meaning, purpose, and moral relatedness with others, the universe, and ourselves (Canda, 1989). Siporin (1992), in the same vein, depicts spirituality as the "inherent need for spiritual meaning, experience, and growth" (p. 79). Angell, Dennis, and Domain (1998) see spirituality as the "big picture" that establishes the value and choice parameters for daily decisions as an attempt is made to meet wants and needs (p. 617).

Religion and spirituality contribute another dimension to the understanding of essential resilience. They encourage activity over inactivity, imagination over concreteness, concentration over distraction, mastery over helplessness.

THE FIRST CHAPTERS OF SYLVIA'S STORY

What makes Sylvia's story compelling, and therefore instructive, is more than the fact that she overcame the dire effects of an accident that left her paralyzed, but also that she confronted earlier childhood and teenage turmoil.

Isolation was a fact of life for young Sylvia. She was an only child, a lonely child, it seems. By the time she graduated from high school, she had moved at least eight times. Although I know little about her parents, what came across in talking with Sylvia was pain—the pain of loneliness, of fright, of helplessness, the pain of constant adjustments to new people, new places.

Sylvia moved almost yearly between the ages of nine and eighteen. Imagine spending part of every one of those years adjusting to the painful knowledge that all the people one had just met, connected with, and possibly established relationships with were to be left. To survive each move, to make new friends, to find a niche, to fit in at all, Sylvia would have to work and work hard.

Home before the age of nine was filled with drinking and brutal fighting, which she referred to as "endlessly repeatable drunken scenes." Those were the stable years. They lived, the three of them, more or less, in one place, at least in the same state. Mother and father were probably completely incompatible, but when they were together, even if at each other's throats, Sylvia was the odd man out. She was the little girl all alone, no siblings to cling to, to comfort or be comforted by. Her parents had each other; Sylvia had only herself and her fright.

Children, like adults, do not know the future. Unlike adults, however, they still have exceedingly vivid imaginations. What did Sylvia picture as the next step while increasingly out-of-control parents fought within earshot? How terrifying were her prospects for the future?

By the time she was nine, Sylvia's parents divorced. The emotional instability was intensified at that point by geographical instability. For a while Sylvia lived with an aunt. After her mother remarried, she then moved from Texas to Illinois for the fourth grade and then to Arkansas for the fifth. By seventh grade, she had been put in a boarding school in Missouri where she said she was "alone, forgotten." By the eighth grade, she was back for a year in Illinois, but not in the same place she had lived before. By the ninth grade, she was packed off to boarding school again, but this time to one in Boulder, Colorado. She was always new. Never was there anything she could count on as being the same. Never was there anything she could count on except herself. And change.

She spent tenth grade in Idaho Springs, Colorado, but ran away. Sylvia's last two years of high school were spent back in Texas. But those are places. Then there are prisons. Not only are there the prisons of the places one did not want to be, but for Sylvia there were other prisons, ones that foreshadowed the life she would lead later on.

At age thirteen, diagnosed with scoliosis, Sylvia was placed in a Milwaukee brace, a source of shame and discomfort and an outward sign to everyone that she was different. To her father, it was an outward sign of ugliness. No adolescent would see the detestable brace as anything but ugly, but hopefully most children have a parent less adolescent than they are. Sylvia remembers, however, that her father did not want to be seen with her when she was wearing her brace. A beautiful girl in the making, but tall and gawky in the moment; all the insecurity of puberty was exacerbated by ugly metals and a father who made her feel even more disfigured than she already felt.

Again, eerily foreshadowing the future, not only did the brace cause enormous emotional pain, but it caused very real physical pain as well. It tore her skin in some places and caused horrible irritation in others. She wore it for years and felt imprisoned and persecuted by it.

Life went on as before. Mom was drunk a lot. There was loads of fighting as well. And "people stared at me."

Is it any surprise that Sylvia married young? So often when people feel that they never had a home, there is a great rush to create one.

Sylvia said, "I can look back at my childhood and many of the tragedies were building blocks to prepare me" for the even worse times that were to come. She learned early that "one moment your life is normal, the next it isn't."

THE END OF SYLVIA'S STORY

Sylvia died conducting her life as she always had—keeping herself active and independent. Having just fired her live-in aide for mistreating her, Sylvia, unassisted, entered the lift of her van in the garage. It was Saturday morning and she had errands to run. Although the lift-equipped van had malfunctioned the previous day, it had been repaired. Yet, that day a mechanical failure crushed her against the van's restraining bar. A few hours later, she was found by a friend who had planned to help her prepare for her next art exhibit. Unconscious, she was at first revived by an emergency medical team. However, she remained in a coma with severe chest trauma. Her children, the next day, agreed to the removal of her life support. Sylvia died.

Sylvia was to host her fiftieth birthday gala three weeks hence. Doctors had always predicted that she would not live that long. The party was to be yet another way she thumbed her nose at fate and celebrated life.

REFLECTIONS

Even with the odds stacked against her, as they had always been, and even though she knew it, Sylvia did not give up. She explains, "Being self-aware and taking responsibility go together hand in hand." How did she do it? Beyond our informal chats, I explicitly asked her questions such as: What sparked you? How did you and do you go on despite external and internal pressures and stresses? What did you learn about yourself? Following are her reflections in her own words.

What sparked you?

I always had a need to get away from how my parents lived. I hated their lives—I still do. Nobody had faith in me. But I did. I do. I wanted to escape.

My parents were self-deceptive. I was determined for as far back as I can remember to not be like them. The unfairness of the way I was treated and my own determination to not be a victim the way my parents were led me on. I wondered what better life there could be. I had to depend on myself; there was no one else to depend upon. I remember always feeling insecure and frightened. I pushed myself as a kid the same way I did after my accident by saying, "Keep going . . ." I had to prove, at least to myself, that I was OK. I was primed by my resolve.

There was always something in me, something that was healthy, something that said don't give up.

I think what makes me different from some others that may have a similar situation is my continual positive attitude. . . . A stranger stopped me in a parking lot just last night as I was getting in my van. Asking how I do what I do, etc. He then noted . . . I have a positive attitude. I suspect most folks think people who use wheelchairs are angry . . . or possibly they think that if they had to be in a wheelchair they would be angry.

I'm not a complainer. I feel I am blessed. I have a joy and enthusiasm for living. I'm truly glad to be alive. At one time, they said my chance for survival was pretty slim. When the priest gave me last rites, I thought he must have the wrong person.

Some say I have accepted my situation so well. I say I have accepted nothing: it is not okay to be in a wheelchair. It's not okay for anyone, man, woman, or child, to have to be in a wheelchair. And it will never be okay. For the most part I stay in the present moment. I cannot think about the fact that I might be in a wheelchair for the rest of my life. I believe that would be a depressing thought. Painting keeps me in the present. It is a process that I love being in. It is where my soul opens and reveals itself. It is truly where I am touched by God. God is in the present moment. He is not thinking about the past or worried about the future. I believe God holds the paintbrush.

Joseph Campbell says . . . we must be willing to get rid of the life we planned . . . to have the life that is waiting for us. I certainly didn't plan to spend my life in a wheelchair. This is certainly not a life I would have chosen. However, this life, though forever challenging, has many gifts. Every day I pray for courage. I can still remember my sewing table from the night before I fell. The little pillow, unfinished, waiting for my return. Many things I had to leave unfinished and incomplete. Just as I felt I was incomplete, broken and forgotten. I needed someone to return, to sew me up, put me back together again. No one could. Some tried. Most ran away. . . . This certainly was not my plan.

The chair certainly cuts through the bullshit. I have quality friends. People who choose to be my friends are a cut above the rest. . . . People are uncomfortable when they first see me or meet me. Folks immediately stop breathing or move away from me as if they want to evaporate into the four walls. I feel it is my responsibility to try at least to make them comfortable. I certainly can't change how they think and feel. But some are surprised that I am smiling, can speak and make sense, be somewhat intelligent. Some, if they allow themselves, begin to like me or feel inspired by me, although I hate that word—inspire. I once looked it up in the dictionary. I read, "filled with the divine." But aren't we all? I am no better than anyone else is. My woundedness is no more painful than others' are. Mine is just more visible. I hurt, feel angry, sadness the same as others. I recently went to Washington, DC, to learn how to teach diversity. Yugoslavia is at war; people are being killed and tortured because of one reason—they are different. If one takes the time to look a little deeper, they would find we are all the same.

How did you go on despite internal and external pressures and stresses?

. . . I take a deep breath, and tell myself to breathe. I talk to myself. I tell myself . . . this is only temporary. I ask, how important is it?

Usually these demons come at night. I try to remember I will feel differently in the morning: the sun will come up, and I do feel relieved just knowing it's a new day.

Twenty years ago, I don't know, I told myself one day at a time. I said the serenity prayer. It was the first sentence I typed in OT (occupational therapy) with the eraser of a pencil strapped to my hands. I focused on my children, I threw paint on paper, I banged on the paper with the paintbrush, I went to Al-Anon, I reached out to those who would listen. I hugged everyone because I needed it, I went into therapy . . . I screamed, I cried in the night.

What did you know or discover about yourself?

At first, the only thing or feeling I knew was how angry I was. I had only doubts about what I could not do. Recognizing along the way that life is precious, I learned to accept my limitations. I knew that if I put too many limits on myself I would feel very safe . . . and safety is a very expensive illusion. I learned to break fear down into small pieces, to define my own paralysis, to define my own defeat. I learned that I am where I am supposed to be right now, but I don't always like it and it's okay not to like it. It just is.

I learned a lot about myself. I learned that it is not acceptable to be quadriplegic. It's not okay and it will never be okay. I learned that I am not a burden; that writing is easier if I write as if I'm writing about someone else; there is no "how" in accomplishing a task. I must first believe in what I want to accomplish and then the "how" just comes; I am a strong and courageous woman; I can stand up for myself in a wheelchair. I discovered there is no such thing as trying, there is only doing. I discovered that in order to do something really well, I must first be willing to do it badly; even with paralysis one can move mountains; I am not alone; loneliness is a choice; I am my own worst enemy; I am lovable if I allow myself to be loved, and I discovered that my real disability is from the neck up.

I learned I am good enough just the way I am; to keep my mouth shut; to wait; to not have to be the center of attention, although I like to be; not to be afraid and to let go; not always to have to be in charge, and to say "no"; to take care of myself. And tulips can grow without my doing anything.

I learned a lot about people. I learned that they really do want to help and don't mind helping; people are just doing the best they can. I learned, if I listen to myself and I do what I am meant to do, doors open, money comes, people appear, everything falls into place. I learned that when hope is all gone, when I can't lift my head one more time, when hurt is all around, when I'm too tired to go on anymore, someone will show up or say something, a letter will come. Something happens that touches my soul and says to continue to hope even though there is no understanding.

I discovered God stands behind me, by my side, and in my pocket.

I learned that when the unplanned, unexpected, unwanted events occur in the process of life, there is wisdom in the moment. There is a new awareness, a discovery; "something" is being shown to me in that moment. I must be open to it. There is a gift in the moment. I must be open to see and receive the gift.

What Sylvia did not say, but central to explaining her resiliency, is her remaining true to her deepest convictions, her courage to stare defeat in the face, her mettle to convert tragedy into opportunity, and her humor to laugh at herself. How else could she have managed to bear it all?

TELLING THE WORLD

Sylvia prepared the following letter to Oprah Winfrey a month before she died. It was never sent. It poignantly and succinctly portrays her journey of triumph.

Dear Oprah,
  How do I remember my spirit? This is my story.
  In 1979 I had a skiing accident and broke my neck. As a result, I am quadriplegic. In that moment, my world was turned upside down. My children, six and nine years old, were taken from me while I was recovering in the hospital. Their loss was more devastating than the accident. I was lost and my spirit broken.
  My sadness grew with the losses. I felt like a burden. I couldn't understand the unfairness of the loss of my children. I was angry at everything. I worried about what I was going to be able to do. How would I support them? My focus was entirely negative. All I could see was what I couldn't do. While in the hospital, a recreation therapist (one of my angels) suggested I paint. I had never painted before. I thought to myself she must be crazy. Didn't she know I couldn't move my hands? But, then they told me crazy things like I was going to drive, work, and live independently. She strapped a brush to my hand and I painted a tree. In disgust I threw the painting in the garbage. My friend came to see me that evening. He saw the painting and asked, did you paint this? As he reached for the painting, I told him to leave my garbage alone. He asked if he could have it. After all I had thrown it away. He took the painting, brought it back the next day in a frame and hung it on the wall in my room. As I looked at it again, it didn't look so bad. I didn't know at the time that small gesture would change my life.
  I continued to paint. The process of painting turned my anger into joy, my negative thoughts I call "stinkin' thinkin' " into challenges and opportunities for success. While it did not take

any of my problems away, I was still on public assistance, I needed a job, I had a mortgage, bills to pay, and I was still in a wheelchair. Yet when painting I felt different. My fears were less.

The process of painting became God's healing grace. I believe painting is a lifesaver that allows one to step into their fear and live life to the fullest.

I learned to drive. I went back to school. I was one of the first quadriplegics to win custody of children. In Oregon, an accessible hotel was just built across the street from the courthouse. I believe God built that hotel for me. Working full-time, I raised my children as a single parent.

Twenty years later, the painting continues to renew my spirit. I believe my home studio is sacred space. It has become a meditation. Before I start to paint I close my eyes and listen to my breath. As I breathe . . . I breathe in God's love and feel it pour down my arms and legs with each breath. I breathe out all fear, anxiety, and negative thoughts. I may think of scripture or something that I've read. I open my eyes slowly and come back to the room. I paint and then write in my "painting journal."

It is a gift from God. I share with others as I teach the sheer joy of painting.

Sincerely,
Sylvia

PART III:
CRAFTING THE STRUCTURE
FOR STRENGTH AND SUPPORT

Chapter 9

Models of Helping:
Working with an Individual

remember one thing only: that it's you—nobody else—who determines your destiny and decides your fate. Nobody else can be alive for you nor can you be alive for anyone else.

e.e. cummings

. . . the purpose of life, after all, is to live it, to taste and experience it to the utmost, to reach out eagerly and without fear for newer and richer experience . . . The experience can have meaning only if you understand it. You can understand it only if you have arrived at some knowledge of yourself . . .

Eleanor Roosevelt

The helping process is greatly improved when assessment is precise and multidimensional. Clients' distress is caused by many things. Take note of as much of what constitutes their inner and outer lives as possible. Problems result from interacting intrapsychic and interpersonal processes that stimulate and reinforce each other. It is easy to forget that the functioning of a family as a whole is the product of individual processes and that, reciprocally, the functioning of individuals is influenced by their families. There is a tendency to emphasize one frame of reference or the other, individual or family, when doing an assessment or implementing a change effort. The truth is that they are compatible and complementary units of attention. When you are doing an assessment, ignore neither individuals' subjective experience nor their family system. Change in one foments change in the other. If you incorporate both into your work, synergy results.

The following story about Elaine precedes an overview of how three different major contemporary theories—psychodynamic, exis-

tential, and behavioral—conceptualize individual assessment and intervention. Brief sketches of each of these theoretical orientations is
followed by a vignette describing how one might approach work with
Elaine using each orientation. A mnemonic abridgment distilling the
principal concepts of each theory into a list of five C's concludes each
section. These theoretical summaries are in no way exhaustive or inclusive. Their intent is to highlight how these three theories conceptualize assessment and intervention. After discussing the three models,
I offer my own, including a list of ten S's, which comprise factors that
I consider when assessing and working with individuals. Integrating
the three theories highlighted above, together with ego- and self-
psychology concepts, into one inclusive guideline, provides a way to
incorporate the dynamic interaction among the myriad of biological,
cognitive, emotional, and cultural ingredients that influence individuals.

ELAINE'S STORY

Elaine, a thirty-year-old certified special education teacher from
an upper-middle-class background, was referred by a friend because
of her serious dejection and talk of suicide. She herself reported feeling depressed and anxious. Elaine had moved to New York City three
months previously from a Midwestern rural area where she had lived
for two years in a religious commune while finishing her graduate
study in education. Three months before first seeing me, Elaine had
left her home following the death of her lover, with whom she had
had a clandestine affair.

Although Elaine was not presently suicidal, she was despondent
and viewed herself as inept, of little worth, and "bad." She saw herself
and her situation as unalterable. The only relief she found from her
pervasive sense of sadness was reading and engaging in selected
handicrafts such as tatting and macramé. Also, she was able to find
support and a little solace from one or two trusted friends. She was
skeptical that any intervention could be helpful. Evaluation of risk
factors, resources, and lifestyle did not indicate a need for immediate
protective care, although the possibility was considered initially.

Although Elaine had suffered a series of recent losses, there was no
premeditation or specific plan for suicide. Likewise, she reported no
new symptoms, had a few friends available, and demonstrated little
tendency toward impulsive behavior. She indicated that she wanted to

give herself at least a "fair chance" and agreed to psychiatric evaluation.

· Developmental history revealed that Elaine had been in therapy four times and hospitalized twice during adolescence for serious depression and suicide threats. She suffered recurrent episodes of distress and discouragement. Recalling that all during her teens, through to the present, she felt intense self-hatred and unworthiness, she now often saw herself as despicable and continually apologized for herself.

Elaine would follow the mention of every difficulty with an expression of regret, either for "having" it or for talking about it. She was "sorry" that she would bolt up at five in the morning and was not able to get back to sleep. She felt terrible for "whining" about her loss of energy, lack of attention, and melancholy. She continually reproached herself for referring to these difficulties as if they were problems and felt "awful" and guilty for exposing to me defects in her discipline or "faith," not being able to resolve such "frivolous" problems on her own.

Her memory of the past was scant. Chapter 10 describes how it was expanded using a family systems orientation. Elaine did acknowledge her strict religious upbringing as having contributed to her difficulty. She was raised in a modern faith fellowship that emphasized humility, being "perfect," doing what the Bible says, and leading a life of self-sacrifice, service, and simplicity. Even though she was educated to be an enabler within the religious sect, seeking help for herself represented all that she was raised to abhor and reject. To her, it was self-indulgent and self-centered at the least. It violated all beliefs she held dear; it bordered on the "sinful."

Always educated in religious schools, Elaine had spent all of her high school, college, and graduate school years living in a faith community with her religiously fervent grandparents, who were more conservative than were her parents. Conformity was obligatory.

Suffering the loss of her lover and severing all ties to her family and religion, Elaine sheared her hair, which had never before been cut, and came to "Sin City," ostensibly for a good teaching job. Now "freed," she felt herself, ironically, "imprisoned."

Despite her despairing presentation of self, Elaine manifested strength and resilience in more than a few areas of her life. Her keen intelligence and sensitivity were drawn upon and expanded during the course of the helping endeavor. For example, she learned early in her life to fulfill her unmet social and emotional needs by contact with teachers and older children. Solitary fantasy play as well as precise handiwork gave her a sense of accomplishment and mastery. Her thoughts, impressions, and emotions were recorded in lengthy childhood diaries, which she still possessed and made available to me. These entries are described at length in Chapter 13. Concentrating and embellishing on some of these earlier gains provided renewed energy to break the inertia she felt about "getting hold" of herself.

Elaine's likely genetic susceptibility to depression, combined with early traumatic experience, such as the emotional unavailability of her mother (later confirmed while doing family-oriented treatment), and an inability to influence or control significant events in her life, undermined her sense of self. Her present losses—home, lover, and grandparents—placed cruel demands on her already vulnerable ego.

THE PSYCHODYNAMIC MODEL
OF INDIVIDUAL ASSESSMENT AND INTERVENTION

Implicit in the psychodynamic approach (Alexander, 1956; Brenner, 1973; Fenichel, 1945; Hall, 1973; Freud, 1966; Freud, 1915-1917; Hartmann, 1964; Shapiro, 1965) is a sense of determinism. Mental events are not viewed as random occurences; rather, thoughts, feelings, and impulses are considered to be causally related phenomena. Holding that crucial events of childhood generate conflicts that manifest and repeat themselves, unconsciously, in ongoing and present relationships, resolution of these intrapsychic conflicts comes only through a process of critical self-examination within a corrective emotional context. As insight is gained, light is shed on hidden conflicts, thus enabling clients to deal with stresses in their lives less defensively and more rationally.

The process of assessment and intervention begins by establishing a relationship. In the psychodynamic perspective, your role in developing and maintaining the relationship provides both the context and means through which change occurs. In other words, clients' understanding of the relationship with you is applied to understanding aspects of their trouble in relationships with others. Psychodynamic clinicians say little about themselves, so whatever the client feels is the product of feelings associated with other significant people in the past, which are projected onto the clinicians. They carefully monitor interactions with the client and seek to locate the sources of any confusion or anxieties in underlying fixed behavior patterns and early drives and wishes. The effectiveness of this approach relies a great deal on the phenomenon called transference—automatic attribution of attitudes, thoughts, and feelings toward someone in the present that originated in early relationships with significant others, e.g., mother and father. As clients become more comfortable with you in the relationship, over a long period of time, they begin to see you in a certain light, projecting onto you attributes that actually belong to a person in their past. These attributes trigger inappropriate reactions from clients, and by subtle questioning and interpreting you lead them to an emotional reeducation in which they learn more realistic perceptions and ways of behaving.

Because irrational forces are strong, and conflicts remain largely out of awareness, it is through a deliberative process of uncovering that clients come to understand their sexual and aggressive impulses, environmental counterforces, and the particular interactions among the various agencies of the mind. In making an assessment, the psychodynamic clinician sketches a broad outline of the nature of clients' conflicts and studies clients' characteristic resistances (internal impediments interfering with or interrupting progress), transferences, and defenses. Defenses are means, out of clients' realm of awareness, for controlling their anxiety by denying or distorting reality. Intervention is directed at enabling clients to reflect on possible original sources of underlying unconscious conflicts. The psychodynamic clinician, within the framework of the relationship, points out and explains the meaning and motivation behind these conflicts, interprets psychosexual developmental history, and seeks to correct clients' distortions, reconstruct and analyze their repetitive patterns of reaction, recognize their dysfunctional defensive maneuvers against anxiety, and understand their early developmental experiences and personality structure. Clients' insight, combined with the clinician's analysis and interpretation, consolidates change.

A Psychodynamic Perspective on Elaine

Assessing Elaine from a psychodynamic standpoint requires careful consideration of her presenting problems. It also involves attention to her countenance and demeanor within the helping situation itself, because this serves as a sample of her typical behavior. From her sketchy history, it seemed evident that attitudes toward herself were repetitions of internalized images from her past. Her depression was likely the result of having internalized her family's depreciating views of her, resulting in self-directed rage. Elaine's depression, in other words, could be viewed in part as a function of her aggressive instincts redirected against herself, possibly as punishment for harboring unacceptable wishes. Because her conflicts were buried deep in her unconscious, she could not recall precisely any outstanding events or "lessons" where they were evident.

Implicit, however, in her presentation of self was a sense of being inconsistently nurtured and of suffering emotional neglect and abuse. Her perception of herself as "bad," inadequate, and ugly, and her self-defeating behavior, which included self-denial, self-desertion, and turning against herself, reflected two significant dynamics. It mirrored treatment she likely received as a child. It also manifested her tendency to direct against herself the aggressive impulses she felt toward unavailable nurturing figures. A self-fulfilling prophecy resulted: out of fear, she did not strike out at others, but felt guilty and punished herself repeatedly for negative feelings toward her parents and later for abandoning her religious foundations. She closed off what she needed most—connection to others.

The traditional psychodynamic strategy for dealing with such depression relies on understanding defenses, transferences, and resistance through intrapsychic analysis and interpretation. To get at the root of the depression, its historical development must be fathomed and insight promoted, followed by giving expression to the rage. Rage, once expressed, externalized, and redirected to its appropriate source, brings relief.

THE EXISTENTIAL MODEL
OF INDIVIDUAL ASSESSMENT AND INTERVENTION

Existentialists (Bugental, 1976; Frankl, 1963, 1969; Fromm, 1941; May, 1981; Yalom, 1981) deal with ultimate concerns—isolation, meaning, death, and freedom. The struggle with these concerns is seen as being at the core of clients' anxiety. Existentialists renounce the psychodynamic conceptualization of humans as driven by regressive forces and as subservient to unconscious aspects of themselves.

Personal growth, will, choice in the face of despair, responsibility for the freedom of deciding one's fate, and the search for meaning, rather than intrapsychic conflicts or behavior, are central concerns to the existential clinician.

The existential view holds that the myriad of factors in an individual's life is too manifold to identify, much less to pinpoint, as causal. Past developmental history is not of primary concern: the here and now is. Indeed, the absence of prior information, the existentialist argues, allows more freedom to confront clients' present dilemmas. These dilemmas are assessed as arising from a sense of despair, loss of possibility, fragmentation and alienation of self, or lack of congruence with one's experience. While the psycho-dynamic clinician proposes that we are afraid of knowing our regressive tendencies, the existentialist proposes that we are afraid of knowing our progressive tendencies. Since humans are not static and are in a constant state of transition, and since they are inherently striving and self-affirming, no situation, however miserable, is a lost battle.

Postulating on the *will* (discussed at length in Chapter 8) with its power to act, to feel, and to organize experience, the existentialist directs efforts toward helping clients to open horizons and to release innate capacities by participating in the world of events. Intervention takes the form of an encounter in a dialectical process, which brings clients to fuller awareness of themselves and their potential and their will in the face of uncertainty. The key factor is the relationship—an experience in form—in which clients can experience a new and constructive way of seeing and being with themselves and others.

Self-conscious decision making and self-direction make it possible for clients to transcend the immediate situation, to design their own lives, and to find meaning. The authenticity and spontaneity of the helping relationship itself, combined with dramatization and deep experiencing of the here and now, actualizes clients' self-growth, self-determination, and self-responsibility. Existential clinicians use a variety of methods to identify and investigate maladaptive mechanisms. Techniques are borrowed from other approaches to relieve symptoms, but, more important, to enable clients to attain personal growth and mutually open relationships. A unique feature of the existentialist perspective is the belief that both the clients and the helper can be changed by the helping relationship.

An Existential Perspective on Elaine

The existential viewpoint would not see Elaine's despair and anxiety as originating from suppressed instinctual drives or conflicts. Rather, her angst would be viewed as alienation between herself and the "givens" of her existence. Assessment would involve an in-depth understanding of Elaine's subjective experience, which would free her capacity to rediscover meaning in her life and to stop numbing herself to her experience. Existentialists pay very little attention to external behavior. It is necessary to keep in mind that the feelings you perceive from clients, as they describe their lives, may not even remotely resemble their feelings as they perceive them.

This approach does not, as does the dynamic approach, aim at discovering signs of inferred states of intrapsychic conflicts or underlying disparities in affect, cognition, and behavior. There are no prescribed procedures or techniques. Rather, the cardinal intervention entails helping clients contact their own inner experience. Flexible and versatile in approach, a variety of methods are employed, resting mainly on the strength and authenticity of the dynamic encounter with you. Within this relationship, clients are encouraged to contact the present from their own internal frame of reference, making them aware of their potential and possibilities, recognize authorship of their own life stories, and take responsibility for editing and revising them.

THE BEHAVIORAL MODEL
OF INDIVIDUAL ASSESSMENT AND INTERVENTION

Behavioral theory (Bandura, 1986; Lazarus, 1981; O'Leary and Wilson, 1987; Wolpe, 1969) rests upon the basic assumption that behavior is a function of its consequences and of modeling. We are both the product and producer of our environment. Since processes of the mind, e.g., defenses and transference, are neither observable nor amenable to scientific analysis, they are disregarded. Abnormal behavior is not viewed as necessarily pathological and is assumed to be acquired and maintained in the same way as normal behavior. Behavioral assessment involves identifying the bond between anxiety and the stimuli evoking it.

In contrast to the psychodynamic and the existential orientation, the relationship is a deliberately structured learning alliance that develops in tandem with achieving identified goals. In other words, it is secondary, not essential, for desired change, and evolves from the integration of the contextual and interventive aspects of interactions.

Maladaptive learning is at the core of clients' problems. Behaviorists aver that clients learn a certain response and can unlearn it. Covert, unobservable needs, drives, motives, and wishes do not play a critical part, although cognitive behaviorists suggest that a complex set of expectations, goals, and values can be treated as behavior and have influence on performance. Maladaptive learning arises from involuntarily acquired, repeated, and reinforced response to stimuli in the environment. Successful change requires building an accurate and positive expectancy about results and structuring, rewarding, inhibiting, or reshaping specific responses to anxiety-producing stimuli. The behaviorist is active and directive and functions as an instructor or trainer, using guided imagery, role-playing, self-monitoring, and other techniques to teach more effective behavior. Clients repeat and practice these new alternative behaviors within and then outside the helping situation. Believing that insight is unnecessary, behaviorists employ other techniques including desensitization (reconditioning to associate pleasant rather than anxious feelings to certain feared objects or events), shaping (altering behavior by reinforcing progressively closer approximations of the desired behavior), positive reinforcement (offering praise and social support), rehearsal of new behaviors, and coaching. A careful process of assessment precedes treatment and follows a contractual protocol that involves identifying and specifying the troublesome symptomatic behavior; identifying its antecedents, consequences, and frequency; specifying objectives; formulating a modification plan; substituting alternatives; repeating and practicing newly learned responses; rewarding achievements; and evaluating change.

A Behavioral Perspective on Elaine

Elaine's depressive responses, to a behaviorist, would be seen as part of a complex, but circumscribed, stimulus-response chain. Indeed, the depressive responses themselves would be capable of stimulating the response chain. Behavioral assessment of Elaine would assume that her depressive behavior and symptoms were originally learned through operant conditioning and are presently maintained through the reinforcement of other people. To unlink the chain, identification and modification is required of the situations that reinforce responses. The behaviorist would also attempt to discriminate stimuli, i.e., events or behavior that precede feelings of depression or depressive behavior and utilize such techniques as desensitization, rehearsal, shaping, and coaching combined with prescribed tasks. Positive reinforcement for successful task completion comes from the environment and from you, who become an activator and validator of new or changed responses.

THE DSM-IV AND INDIVIDUAL ASSESSMENT

The *Diagnostic and Statistical Manual of Mental Disorders,* Fourth Edition, (DSM-IV) (American Psychiatric Association, 1994) is a comprehensive but controversial compendium for diagnosing individual problems in functioning. It is considered by many to be valid and reliable. Increasingly, it has become a standard tool for clinicians, educators, and researchers to arrive at commonly accepted descriptions and definitions of individual functioning.

Many years in development, the DSM-IV purports to take an atheoretical approach, incorporating several innovative features representing major advances in the field of mental health assessment. The authors believed that the inclusion of etiological theories would be an obstacle to the use of the manual by clinicians of varying theoretical orientations, since it would not be possible to present all reasonable etiological theories for each disorder described. Phobic disorders, for example, are believed by some to represent a displacement of anxiety resulting from the breakdown of defensive operations for regulating internal unconscious conflict. Others explain phobias on the basis of learned avoidance responses to conditioned anxiety. Still others believe that certain phobias result from a disregulation of basic biological systems mediating separation anxiety. In most cases, however, clinicians do agree on the clinical manifestations of phobia without agreement about its etiology. Classification, therefore, is made on the basis of symptoms demonstrated by clients rather than on differing theories. The DSM-IV also lists psychosocial and environmental problems that may bear on diagnosis and treatment.

Using the DSM-IV, clients are rated on five independent dimensions or axes, allowing you to evaluate different categories of information pertinent to your clients' situations. These are as follows:

Axis I.   *Clinical disorders*—current episode of the illness, more florid symptoms that are the focus of clinical attention

Axis II.   *Personality disorders and mental retardation*—frequently overlooked long-term disturbance, or underlying personality features or traits

Axis III.   *General medical conditions*

Axis IV.   *Psychosocial and environmental problems*—problems are grouped in an array of categories

Axis V.   *Global assessment of functioning*—a measure of psychological, social, and occupational functioning using the GAF scale

All these serve as guidelines in arriving at a differential diagnosis and are considered in detecting individual disorders and in planning appropriate intervention.

Because discrimination among diagnoses is challenging and difficult, for each disorder the description in the DSM-IV contains a list of essential features of that disorder. It also offers a clinical sketch, based upon a summary of characteristics, information about the typical onset and course of the disorder, and predisposing factors. Frequency of occurrence and information on similar disorders are also provided. A disorder is conceptualized as a clinically significant behavioral or psychological syndrome or pattern that occurs in an individual that is typically associated with a painful symptom in one or more important areas of functioning.

One can clearly see in this latest edition of the DSM, absent from some of the early editions, an attempt to broaden the diagnostic configuration to include physical, environmental, and functional measurements.

The DSM-IV takes a phenomenological, descriptive approach rather than an etiological and theoretical one. Its purpose is to determine the presence or absence of identified features in order to arrive at a coded assessment or diagnosis.

Supporters of this assessment system for psychosocial problems consider it to be pragmatic and empirical, classifying symptoms that develop a clinical picture that is understandable by other clinicians, leading to an effective treatment plan. A common misconception is that individuals are being classified. What actually is being classified or labeled are disorders that individuals have. For this reason, the DSM-IV avoids the use of such labels as "an alcoholic" or "a schizo-phrenic." Refinement in multiaxial classification is offered by deci-sion trees designed to discriminate among various symptoms. The aim of the DSM-IV is (1) promoting elegance in diagnosis for clini-cians, while simultaneously (2) improving communication between and among the different mental health disciplines, and (3) serving as a valuable tool for teaching about psychopathology and mental ill-ness.

Problems can arise from using the DSM-IV because it involves a labeling process in which clients become identified with stereotypic attitudes and beliefs associated with the label. This, in turn, as dis-cussed in Chapter 7, shapes the way others interact with clients and negatively influences clients' self-perception. A pattern of self-fulfilling expectation may hinder rather than enhance resolution of problems or relief from symptoms. Critics claim that few clients ex-actly fit DSM categories, criteria are vague, and discrete treatment is not indicated for specified conditions.

The DSM-IV is criticized as being a limited and crude but all too popular method of labeling disease that contributes little of practical value in terms of prognosis and treatment. It deals scantily with cli-ents' inner world and does not deal with deepened understanding of clients' strengths and aspirations. It does not add but, rather, removes information; it does not present a full picture and may deceive clini-cians into believing that they have uncovered some particular entity, a disorder, instead of focusing on the full range of client attributes.

Advocates of the DSM-IV claim that, although it has limitations, it is a clear and consistent system of classification which provides the first step of help to clients. They argue that it provides structure and organization which serves as a shorthand for communication among professional colleagues.

Do not be constrained by the DSM-IV. While it can be instructive and helpful, remain mindful of its limitations. Use it selectively and with discretion. Balance it with your clinical judgment, applying its criteria flexibly and carefully.

The DSM-IV Assessment of Elaine

According to the DSM-IV, Elaine would be assessed as having an affective disorder involving alterations in mood. More specifically, she would be labeled as having a dysthymic disorder (300.4). A secondary but not especially strong consideration might be a personality disorder, an enduring pattern or trait of perceiving and relating to the environment, others, and oneself, namely, obsessive-compulsive personality disorder (301.4).

Elaine presented the picture of being sad, dull, tired, and self-debasing, the intellectual picture of uncertainty and self-reproach, and the physical picture of loss of sleep and restlessness for at least a two-year period. She had never had either a manic episode or psychotic delusions. When examined medically, no organic or chemical imbalance was found that contributed to or maintained her disturbance. Earlier major depressive symptoms from her teen years were in complete remission. There was no suicidal ideation at the present moment. Axis III would indicate no physical disorder or condition. A number of psychosocial stressors were present, especially enduring circumstances in her life (e.g., family factors) in concert with acute events (occupational and living circumstances). Axis V, highest level of adaptive functioning with the past year, was rated at 60, indicating her functioning as fair or adequate.

OTHER DIMENSIONS IN ASSESSMENT

A number of other factors need to be taken into account when assessing individual clients. They apply as well to making an assessment of family functioning:

- Availability of friends and family
- Characteristics of clients' residence
- Illnesses and accidents
- Ethnic, religious, and cultural factors
- Clients' physical constitution and health
- Elements of clients' temperament

AN INTEGRATED APPROACH

To achieve a synthesis that brings together the available components of the person and the situation in an orderly and economic manner that permits comprehensive assessment and responsible decisions about intervention, you need to consider many variables. These variables include an evaluation of clients' past efforts at resolution of the identified problem, reasons for not resolving it, and current and past precipitants. The style in which clients address problem solving, their motivation, agreement or disparity between behavior and related feeling, degree of fear, and affective appropriateness are of vital importance.

Recognize the defenses clients employ and the extent to which they are used, their capacity to deal with feelings as well as reality issues, and the nature and quality of their response to you. Additional factors to consider in client appraisal are their intellectual functioning; judgment; self-concept; functional beliefs; misconceptions; dynamic interaction between cognition, emotions, and behavior; and range of emotions.

You learn all this by both direct and indirect means. Direct means include questioning, using existing reports, differential use of diaries, logs, histories, inventories, family trees, and spontaneous self-reports. Indirect means involve observation of behavior in the interview with you, body language, tone of voice, and correspondence between what clients say and the way they show affect.

To help you distinguish whether clients experience disturbances of feeling, thought, behavior, social relationships, work or school performance, and physical function, and to help you appraise the degree of severity or dysfunction in themselves or in the environment, pay close attention to their appearance, posture, facial expressions, and general body movements. Ask yourself these questions: What is the state of clients' general physical tension? Are they hyper- or hypoactive? Is anxiety expressed mostly through behavior or words? What is the quality of their relationships? Are clients domineering, submissive, suspicious, cooperative, withdrawn, or aggressive? To what extent do the clients' efforts at controlling or concealing emotions succeed? Do they try to evoke pity? Fear? Anger? Other questions include: How accurate are clients' perceptions? What is the content and abstractness of their thinking? What is the quality of their insight, judgment, and memory? How intact are their physical functions—sleep, eating, tics, spasms, seizures, etc.? How autonomous are they? What are their attitudes toward themselves? Is there environmental mastery? Adequacy in interpersonal relationships? How do they meet situational requirements and social pressures? Is there evidence of environmentally created problems or stress? Are resources available? What are their talents and skills? What is their education and work history?

An Integrated Perspective on Elaine

No one school or approach has a monopoly on assessment or interventive effectiveness. The following evaluation shows how a variety of theories and techniques were blended in individual work with Elaine. Chapter 10 details how individual work was complemented by a family systems approach.

Work with Elaine concentrated first on initial expression of feelings of sadness, low personal worth, incompetence, and failure. It also focused on catharsis, which is releasing energy by bringing repressed or forgotten material into awareness. Discussion and examination of recent relationships showed a pattern of arriving at unsatisfactory and premature solutions to problems by sacrificing her own feelings, as she had done as a child to win parental approval. As a consequence, she often felt resentful. The resentment was subsequently self-directed.

During our initial contacts, Elaine was unable to extract even a minute sense of achievement or progress in the work; indeed, for a while, the more she uncovered and felt, the more contemptible she felt. I encouraged Elaine to talk more with the friends she had and to develop some alliances with support systems—colleagues and fellow craftspeople.

Early individual work also drew upon a cognitive-behavioral perspective. Attention was directed at correcting Elaine's perception of being unable to survive and satisfy her own needs. We collaborated to examine how her style of thinking contributed to sustaining her depressive mood. She "sensed" that she had "somehow" acquired the negative concept of herself through harsh judgments by and identification with key family and religious figures in her life. She could be no more explicit about this "sense."

Elaine's own negative judgments reinforced a self-concept of being "bad." To compensate, she set extremely high expectations for

herself and then judged her inevitably poor performance by these un-
reasonable standards. She came to recognize how such a cycle crys-
tallized a pattern for ongoing negative attitudes, which eventually
became entrenched. Elaine was especially receptive to the process of
monitoring her automatic negative thinking, examining the interconnection between her thinking, feeling, and behavior, and continually
resorting to processes of overgeneralization and self-devaluation. I
assigned homework directed at her recalling and jotting down on index cards any present or childhood accomplishments that brought
misconceptions about her abilities into active awareness. Stimulated
by her intellectual recognition of achievements—academic awards in
school, excellent employment evaluations and promotions, prize-
winning crafts—and by getting a grip on her emotions, she began to
experiment with changing dysfunctional beliefs and perceiving herself more realistically. She substituted more reality-oriented thinking
about her accomplishments and her self. Her depressed mood and paralysis of will lifted.

Continuing successful experiences using cognitive and behavioral
methods, bolstered by acknowledgment of her educational, occupational, and personal achievements, despite apparent trauma in her
past, led Elaine to be able to express her feelings more completely
and to grant herself permission to make mistakes. She became increasingly self-assertive. Elaine began to come to terms with the distortion between her image of herself and objective facts.

Throughout our contact, gestalt experiments and dramatization
techniques were employed to slow her down and connect her more
fully with internal affects. They also kept her in touch with the details
of her experience. Such experiments brought into the foreground
Elaine's avoided feelings. They were successful in getting her to acknowledge, accept, and support herself and to contact and confront
concealed memories and emotions from her past. It was still very difficult, however, for her to overcome blocks to seeing the missing
pieces, details, or "holes" in her early experience.

As described extensively in Chapter 13, through the added use of
the log and the childhood diaries she supplied from her early teen
years, her memory gradually improved about early childhood events.
This phase of the work resurfaced reminiscences of episodes of early
childhood conflict. She became more amenable to intensive and active exploration of dim memories and associations leading to her un-

derstanding the impact that hurts, difficulties, and defeats in childhood had on her present functioning. Interpretation of her relationship with me, an authoritarian male who did not degrade, abuse, or manipulate her for his own purposes, as did other men in the past, enabled her not only to gain insight into her self-defeating cycle that resulted in inescapable feelings of shame, but also allowed her to draw upon her creative energy to confront these feelings and behave differently. Increased awareness of previously hidden aspects, when considered in historical context, enabled her to risk breaking a repetitive pattern of expecting to be treated badly and almost ritually behaving in a way to ensure its happening.

As Elaine's view of herself, the helping process, and her immediate present context became more realistic, she felt more positive, trusting, and hopeful, and her sense of guilt, shame, and failure diminished. Earning money from craft work, making friends and socializing with other volunteers at the Red Cross, and obtaining a promotion and salary increase at a new job all increased her sense of competence and supported the helping process. Over time, she embraced her gains. Her ambivalence was greatly reduced. As blocks to recollection of her family faded, she was encouraged to deal directly with them, which furthered her progress.

Integrated S's

The following summary, "10 S's," is one I use as a guide in assessing individuals. It attempts to integrate pertinent components from an array of models.

1. *Situational variables*—culture, socioeconomic conditions
2. *Symptoms*
3. *Structure of personality*—especially ego functions of perception, memory, reasoning, and problem solving
4. *Sense of self*—esteem, integration, spontaneity
5. *Strengths*—adaptation, achievements, resilience
6. *Solutions sought*
7. *Sources of conflict*
8. *Separateness*—differentiation, individuation
9. *Synthesis of behavior, affect, and thinking*
10. *Systems variables*—family context, social and environmental supports

The following chapter builds upon Elaine's story and describes how incorporating a family systems orientation enhanced Elaine's progress and development in a positive direction.

IS ANYONE HEALTHY?

As Elaine's story aptly demonstrates, making our way in this world is stressful business. While it is fascinating to understand what goes wrong with people and how their coping mechanisms fail and why they get burned out, very often our focus tends to be on what is wrong with them, rather than what is right. Try to figure out what the special something is that holds your clients together, that propels them forward despite some dreadful circumstances in their lives. If you concentrate exclusively on flaws and disabilities, you will find them. Look for strengths and resilient traits, appreciate talents, enhance what is positive and functional. Identify clearly what is healthy. Finding and relying on these is crucial if you are to proceed successfully in countering what is unhealthy and dysfunctional.

If you do not struggle with attempting to appreciate what health is, how will you recognize it in clients when they achieve it? How will you know it when your client has improved? What will you have to aim toward?

In many ways, we are mental disease, not mental health, professionals. Curriculum in professional schools, or even in advanced training, directed at our becoming effective therapists seldom deals with or defines health. Courses instead deal with sickness, disorder, and disease. Just look at catalogues for course titles—Psychopathology, Abnormal Psychology. Do you find any that deal with the explanation of mental health? Even though this is the state of affairs, is it not possible to take a more positive view, to move away from a too heavy emphasis on "sickness," even though you know it exists, to an emphasis on health, strength, resiliency, and growth? This need not be a naive Pollyanna-ish ignoring of the existing reality of serious disorders, symptoms, or problems but, rather, a departure. It is a matter of perspective. If your clients are simply a bundle of unresolved complexes or dysfunctional interactions, what then will you rely upon to effect change?

Following is my attempt to identify significant components of individual health and strength:

- *Identity*—clear sense of separateness, respect, esteem
- *Insight*—awareness of self
- *Intactness, reality based*—correspondence between one's own and others' view of oneself; congruence between thinking, feeling, and behavior
- *Intuition*—spontaneity and creativity
- *Intimacy*—freedom to relate to different people differently rather than in terms of one's compelling needs and wants; ability to love
- *Inspiration*—will, spirit, creativity
- *Independence*—autonomy, inner regulation
- *Interaction*—in social sphere; balance
- *Ingenuity*—imagination
- *Initiative*—goal directed; welcoming new experiences
- *Integration*—not isolation; deferred pleasure; self-mastery

Look for strengths and health in your clients. If you do, you most assuredly will locate them. Continually draw upon them. Point them out to clients. I believe that, in doing so, your clients and you yourself will find that therapy both deepens and accelerates.

Chapter 10

Models of Helping:
Working with a Family

Everything in this universe is linked to everything else.

John Muir

As you ought not to attempt to cure the eyes without the head, or the head without the body, so neither ought you to attempt to cure the body without the soul ... the whole ... ought to be studied also; for the part can never be well unless the whole is well.

Plato, Charmides

The traditional approaches to assessment and intervention, as outlined in the previous chapter, view symptoms as expressions of conflict within individuals (psychodynamic theory), between individuals and "givens" in life (existential theory), and between individuals and their environment (behavioral theory). This chapter presents another viewpoint, derived from family systems theory. It demonstrates how a combined systems and individual approach complement and enrich each other. When you take a comprehensive view of clients' functioning and integrate methods of assessment and intervention from individual and family schools, therapy is deepened and change is hastened.

Family systems theory views symptoms as evolving from within family contexts. The emphasis, therefore, in family systems assessment and intervention is on interactional and relational patterns rather than on intrapsychic or individual dilemmas. Problems are seen as emerging as a consequence of families' failure to accommodate to the developmental needs of individuals and to transitions in families' life cycles.

Often, as in Elaine's family (discussed below), when distressful symptoms manifest themselves in one individual, other family members are saved from facing severe anxieties. Ordinarily, if families come to understand the value of the symptoms, they can let go of them.

Elaine's story, introduced in the previous chapter, is developed further in this one from a family systems perspective. The usual process of engaging the entire family to participate in such a formal process of intervention was not possible. What was possible, however, was to utilize a family systems orientation to help Elaine come to terms with her depression. I introduced a broader scope of assessment strategies in relation to her family context. She was willing to reenter her family to undertake structured and rehearsed contacts, making it possible to evaluate comprehensively Elaine's depressive symptoms and to intervene more effectively to alter her maladaptive patterns.

ELAINE'S FAMILY

Elaine progressed well in her individual work, as described in Chapter 9. She became more comfortable with the helping process and recognized that it helped her to sort out problems. She felt relief from much of her distress. As she perused her logs with me, she became willing to take a closer look at her family. At first she resisted doing so, seeing it as disloyal. However, after experiencing some success from rehearsed scheduled visits home with prescribed tasks, she became increasingly absorbed in family exploration.

Elaine's logs, filled with a raging mixture of thoughts and feelings, gave both of us data clearly showing a disturbed family system and indicating how she responded to it. The logs also revealed how she maintained the very system that oppressed her.

For Elaine, everyone else's wants and needs had precedence over her own. Her family and her religion taught her to be all sacrificing, all giving, all loving. It also taught her to have no expectations for herself, to make no requests. She remembers her father often commenting, "You're a nobody, Elaine." She had a particularly vivid memory of him saying this after she had refused to enter a psychiatric hospital for her own acute depression because she felt obliged to take care of her sister, who had broken her leg. In effect, anything anyone wanted her to be or to do came first. Her compliance rebounded and further contributed to her self-contempt. She felt that she had abdicated her personhood. No boundaries existed between her, her parents, and her siblings.

Elaine reflected that even as a child she did not often think or act as a child. She certainly never felt like one. She recalled being criticized by her mother for "never being a child." She also heard the explicit message from her mother—no one would ever like her.

To make herself feel better, and to feel more accepted by the family, she dissolved herself. She accommodated to everyone's whims. Even when she lived with her maternal grandparents, away from home, she felt "pulled" back home. Once home, however, she was miserable and wanted to escape, feeling that her life "would be sucked out" of her. This made her feel guilty and shameful. Religious tenets and family lessons fed her already intense sense of guilt.

Elaine remembered her mother as always being in bed, crying or complaining. She was never available and always demanding. Elaine said that she felt like a shadow who stole into her mother's room to give her some unidentified liquid, for "medicinal purposes." She remembered her father as a church elder who violated every rule he preached and imposed upon her. He secretly drank and womanized. Abandoned by her mother, she was violated by her father. She dispassionately reported vague recollections of incest perpetrated by her father and by his brother.

Elaine learned early to anesthetize herself. The few memories she had of interaction between her parents involved her father berating her mother for being "lazy" and "sick," and her mother screaming at her father about his drinking and his affairs. Both of her parents tried to enlist her to side with them in their arguments. Feeling helpless about stopping them, she saw herself as inadequate and defective. Indeed, she came to see herself as causing the family's problem. She seemed to punish herself for not having "saved" her family.

Elaine's siblings conspired with her view of causing the family problems. They constantly let her know that they were distressed by her presence. They either joined in their parents' mocking her or ignored her completely. Her older brother, who disappeared when he was seventeen, resented her immensely and would not even talk to her. Her two younger siblings avoided her except when they needed her.

Elaine allowed herself to be manipulated and "used," only to end up feeling rejected, disliked, and abused. She could not say no. Feeling more comfortable in belittling situations, she almost automatically fashioned new relationships in ways to resemble the home she tried to cut off.

The second of four children, Elaine was born within a year of her brother's birth. It appeared to have been a time when her parents were having serious marital discord. She was the most vulnerable to increases in family anxiety and was the most poorly differentiated and most emotionally fused child. She became the "symptom bearer."

From discussion and reflection on her visits home, and with repeated interpretations based upon assignments dealing first with taking a back seat while at home and eventually taking an active proactive role in stepping out of familial patterns, she recognized that while she was a product of the family interaction, she had also contributed to shaping it. She was able to reshape it now.

Obedience, rigidity, and denial of feelings were highly valued in Elaine's family. Even though she sacrificed her feelings to win their approval, they disparaged her.

Elaine's parents' marriage was a vacuum. Her mother was mentally ill and unavailable. Her father was cruelly authoritative and physically and sexually abusive. A spiritually disciplined life was touted as the only one worth living. The trouble was, no one actually lived it. Instead, hypocrisy, verbal and physical abuse, and incest dominated the family picture. Elaine was exquisitely responsive to its emotional tumult and hypervigilant in all relationships. She felt torn and guilty for whatever she did, although she was eternally loyal and supremely responsible to her family.

THREE THEORETICAL CONTRIBUTIONS

Freud was the original family therapist. He postulated the central importance of the family in the formation of individual personality. His methods of intervention, however, were retrospective. Acknowledging the central input of family interaction, he and his followers focused on internalized figures or events from the past as recollected in the present. Contemporary family therapists (Napier and Whitaker, 1978; Framo, 1982; Haley, 1977; Minuchin and Fishman, 1981; Madanes, 1984; Satir, 1983) focus on current ongoing experiences of families and intervene directly to disrupt and alter dysfunctions.

Whatever your theoretical or methodological preference, it is important to recognize that individuals originate from and live in families and that families are composed of individuals, each with a separate history. Take account of families' past and present influence on clients. Work to have clients understand their subjective worlds and internalized images, as well as actively interconnect with available family members to break fragile and binding chains or to strengthen or create healthy links.

The following brief abstracts of three major family approaches—psychoanalytic, structural, and intergenerational—show how each conceptualizes family assessment and intervention. As in Chapter 9, Elaine's story is featured to exemplify how these theories are applied in practice. The theory of family assessment and intervention is not as codified as that of individual assessment and intervention. These abstracts, therefore, which offer a sample of an ever expanding assortment of family systems approaches, are merely suggestive representations of the broad range of possible ways to conceptualize family assessment and intervention. The newness and explosion of differing conceptualizations make it impossible to develop encapsulations similar to those offered above for assessing individuals. I present my own guide for assessing families, which is organized into a list of ten A's. It represents my attempt at integration.

THE PSYCHOANALYTIC PERSPECTIVE ON THE FAMILY

The psychoanalytic approach to family assessment and intervention (Ackerman, 1966; Framo, 1982; Zuk, 1981) stresses unconscious interactions among family members. Spouses bring impairments that are residues from unresolved conflicts with their own families of origin, which are unconsciously reenacted in the present with other members of the family. Often, partners unwittingly select each other out of self-destructive patterns learned in their own families. Their unrecognized and repressed needs lead them to coerce each other; their children repeatedly and compulsively reenact past scenarios.

Spouses get absorbed in projective identification, a process in which disowned aspects of parents' personalities are projected onto each other or onto their children and then are reacted to accordingly. In other words, clients' functioning in the family is seen largely as a consequence of remnants of parental relationships, which they spontaneously relive with spouses and children. Louis and Harriet's marriage is one example of this phenomenon.

> Born in Puerto Rico, Louis was raised single-handedly from infancy by his mother. His father had abandoned his mother before Louis was born. Shy and withdrawn as a child, he would hide in a closet whenever his mother entertained male friends because it was the only way he felt safe and comfortable. He would avoid his mother afterward; in fact, the more she tried to get close to him, the further away he moved.
>
> Harriet, from Indiana, was the youngest of three sisters. Her father was emotionally cold and physically distant. Her mother was repeatedly hospitalized for schizophrenia. To feel warmth and comfort, Harriet remembered literally crawling to the house next door where, encouraged by her neighbor, she would repeatedly lick her finger, dip it into the sugar bowl, and lick it.
>
> Louis and Harriet had trouble from the earliest years of their marriage. They were unable to get from each other the type of attention and affection they both longed for. When Harriet felt alone and insecure, she would flood Louis with demands for verbal and physical reassurances of his love. Louis' response would be to withdraw further from her. Harriet, panicked by his "rejection," increased her demands. Louis, overwhelmed by her needs, distanced himself even further. Blind to their underlying feelings and motives, they both felt trapped and unloved.

The task of a psychoanalytically oriented family therapist is to reactivate and decode the hidden meaning behind clients' repetitious cycles, such as those illustrated by Louis and Harriet, and free them to interact with one another on the basis of current realities rather than images from the past.

Problems are viewed as a function of individuals' personalities, which are manifested in the interaction among family members. They develop from compromises intended to meet suppressed needs and avoid threatening members. Having to face the stress of life transitions for which they are unprepared, families resort to earlier or more primitive and unproductive ways of interacting. Unconscious forces, then, propel the family into dysfunctional and maladaptive patterns. Since spontaneous interactions, occurring unavoidably even in the presence of the helper, manifest covert motives, assessment entails penetrating beneath the surface in a nondirective, neutral way. It emphasizes reducing families' defensiveness, thereby giving them access to hidden causes of problem interaction. This understanding fosters change.

The chief method of assessment and change in the psychoanalytic family perspective is to facilitate the emergence of forgotten and avoided feelings and relationship patterns. Objective recognition and interpretation of these leads to insight into how parents inadvertently but inevitably repeat their own idiosyncratic pasts between themselves and with their children. This insight, combined with analysis of how their defenses operate in dealing with needs and feelings where the present is misjudged in terms of the past, ultimately encourages and instructs families to continue on their own with the uncovering process. The goal of intervention is not merely the elimination of symptoms; it is also discovery of secret meanings and termination of troublesome cycles of interaction.

A Psychoanalytic Perspective on Elaine's Family

The scanty information provided by Elaine about her parents' backgrounds in her logs, in her reminiscences, and in her genogram suggested unconscious and conflictual residues from their own pasts, which they reenacted with each other and their children with dire consequences. Her family continually evoked dysfunctional defenses, including isolation, rationalization, projection, and denial, to avoid being overwhelmed by intrapsychic and interpersonal anxiety and to maintain equilibrium in the face of threatening events. Their unresolved inner lives and conflicts interlocked with each other and bound them together to form and perpetuate disturbances. In other words, they visited onto their children their own "stuckness." Deeper emotional currents of fear, suspicion, urge for vengeance, and power were rampant.

THE STRUCTURAL PERSPECTIVE
ON THE FAMILY

Structuralists, such as Aponte (1972), Haley (1977), and Minuchin and Fishman (1981), hold that problems in family functioning arise from a failure of families to adapt to changing circumstances. Individual symptoms are viewed as by products of this problem. Individuals' symptomatic behavior and distorted sense of reality result from families' governing, but maladaptive, superstructures. Superstructures are sets or sums of unstated rules of interaction that determine the behavior patterns and organize the view of reality, not only of the family system as a whole, but also of the individuals who compose it.

Assessment requires attending to families' boundaries and structure, which, because they tend to be rigid, lead to repetitive and predictable patterns of interaction. Referred to by Minuchin as "isomorphs," these patterns can be elicited, deliberately and selectively, in the helping process. When they are elicited in this way, they can be renegotiated and modified. Attention is particularly directed at the "executive system," the parental subsystem, and how it functions. Parents are encouraged to form an alliance with each other, rather than with their children, and to treat children age-appropriately—not made either too powerful or too subjugated. Assessment is called mapping, illustrated later in the case of Elaine, which identifies excessive flexibility or rigidity of roles, rules, and familial alignments. It measures a family's flexibility, richness, and coherence of functioning patterns; resonance or degree of enmeshment or disengagement; life context, sources of support and stress; developmental stage; and function of the individuals' presenting symptoms as protective, defensive, or conflictual.

Mapping is an experiential diagnosis of family functioning based upon observation of family interaction, either spontaneously or at your provocation. It conceptualizes the complex organizational system, ecological context, and developmental stage on paper by means of a symbolic diagram. The schematic in Figure 10.1 shows some of the symbols used in structural mapping.

The aim of structural intervention, unlike psychoanalytic intervention, is symptom resolution through recognizing and reorganizing the particular dysfunctional part of a family's interdependent structure. Focusing on the immediate in-session behavior, only secondary attention is paid to awareness and historical material. Dynamics are not interpreted.

A number of techniques are employed for assessment and intervention—"joining" or becoming part of the family system in order to experience its worldview and to redirect its interaction into more functional channels; and escalating stress by rearranging seats, giv-

FIGURE 10.1. Symbols for Mapping Family Structure

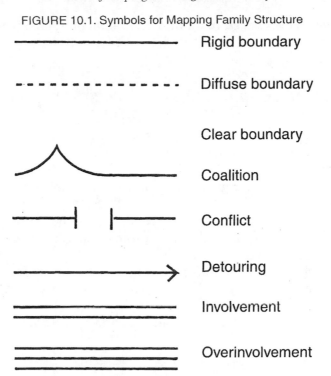

Rigid boundary

Diffuse boundary

Clear boundary

Coalition

Conflict

Detouring

Involvement

Overinvolvement

ing tasks, commands, and directions, and excluding certain members. Direct techniques include blocking communication, confronting individuals to speak for themselves, and challenging family myths. Offering metaphors, reframing, and challenging belief systems are some indirect techniques. These techniques are intended to modify the communication and relational system and reform a family's dysfunctional hierarchies, boundaries, alignments, and power structure.

A Structural Perspective on Elaine's Family

Elaine's family's rigid hierarchical structure and lack of clear boundaries maintained negative feedback cycles that trapped Elaine into an overly responsible role as caretaker not only of her siblings, but of her parents as well. The patterns of defeat, misplaced authority, and inflexible rules were supported and sustained by the family's strict religious and social context. The map in Figure 10.2 diagrams the family's entrenched framework, intruding on Elaine's space and resulting in a parental role for Elaine, even as a child.

THE INTERGENERATIONAL PERSPECTIVE ON THE FAMILY

According to intergeneration theory (Bowen, 1978; Guerin, 1976; Kerr and Bowen, 1988; McGoldrick and Gerson, 1985) individuals' self-image and chronic anxiety are formed in reaction to the anxieties and emotional neediness of parents who define their children through their own distorted perceptions. Pressure is applied to children to make them conform to established regimens in order to be rewarded with acceptance and approval.

This approach best interfaces with individual approaches. It encourages approaching family of origin members to facilitate a rapprochement with meaningful others in their lives. More important, it seeks actual contact with other family members themselves.

FIGURE 10.2. Elaine's Family Map

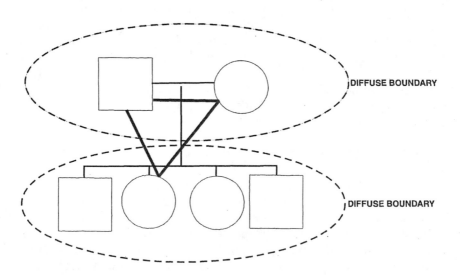

Bowen (1978), the most prominent theoretician of this school, identifies four ways in which families deal with anxiety and tension: (1) increased emotional distance between spouses; (2) physical or emotional dysfunction in a spouse; (3) overt, repeated, but unresolved marital conflict; and (4) impairment in a child. Bowen, in assessing families, takes a close look at sibling position and multigeneration transmission of anxiety. Since there is a basic emotional connectedness between the generations that results in each generation having a significant influence on the emotional process in the generation that follows, family projection, nuclear emotional systems, triangles, and individual differentiation are critical elements to address. Family projection occurs when immature parents create dysfunction in one or more of their children. The nuclear family emotional system refers to the way a family in a single generation controls fusion, "stuck-togetherness," or unresolved emotional parental attachment. The ways in which people manage the intensity of emotional attachments is through triangles. A two-person relationship has a low tolerance for anxiety and is easily disturbed by emotional forces within the couple or in the environment. As anxiety increases, the emotional flow in the couple correspondingly intensifies, and the relationship becomes uncomfortable. When it becomes oppressive, the couple involve a vulnerable third person, usually a child. The involvement of the third person, who forms the triangle, reduces the anxiety level. "Differentiation" describes clients' capacity to be aware of the difference between their intellectual and their emotionally determined functioning in relationships, and to have some choice about the degree to which each type governs their behavior.

The principle tool for conducting an assessment is the genogram. The genogram is used methodically throughout the helping endeavor, to assess all the patterns mentioned. Unlike structuralists, intergenerationalists do not "join" the family; rather, remaining calm, rational, and dispassionate, they stay outside the family's emotional and projection system in order to make rationally sound, objective appraisals of functioning.

Intervention, based on assessment, involves redefining individuals in relation to the balance of separateness and connectedness and reopening cutoff family relationships. In addition to developing a genogram, homework tasks, usually involving contact with a wide spectrum of family members, are proscribed to enhance assessment by providing opportunity for firsthand observation of functioning by the clinician and, ultimately, by the family members themselves. In this manner, a family's mythology and pressures placed on individuals to conform to dysfunctional patterns are exposed, reduced, and redirected. This approach relies strongly on planned systematic techniques of nonconfrontation and nondefensive reworking of relationships to change individuals' position in their families. The change in position forces families to adjust to these changes.

Intergenerationalists postulate that effective work is contingent upon your ability as a helper to look at, understand, and come to terms with the emotional functioning of your own family of origin. If you do not, you can unknowingly become triangulated into the conflict of the families with whom you work.

The Genogram

The genogram, an innovation of intergenerational theorists and practitioners in family treatment, captures information about family members in graphic form. Data include their location and significant dates—births, marriages, deaths. The genogram helps assess the legacy of families' unique milieu and patterns that played a significant part in the development of symptoms expressed by individual members. A graphic representation of families' structure and fabric, the genogram captures the details of at least three generations in a formal way. It provides a roadmap of relationships, patterns of closeness, boundaries, operating principles, and conflictual issues. It offers a glimpse at the characteristics of the extended family and red flags pivotal issues. Attending to incidental information, as the genogram is developed and discussed, gives clues that reveal central themes. These themes, in turn, become a rich source of hypotheses leading to solutions as well as to a better picture of problems.

The genogram opens up issues that have long been taboo, fostering an exploration of emotionally charged issues and suggesting alternative strategies. Family members' reactions during construction of the genogram reflect the private world of families' idiosyncratic characteristics. It can be utilized effectively in work with individuals, couples, or whole families. A schematic of the basic three-generation genogram is illustrated in Figure 10.3, and the symbols used to construct genograms are shown in Figure 10.4.

FIGURE 10.3. Basic Three-Generation Genogram

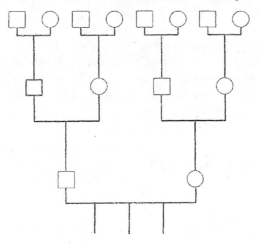

FIGURE 10.4. Genogram Symbols

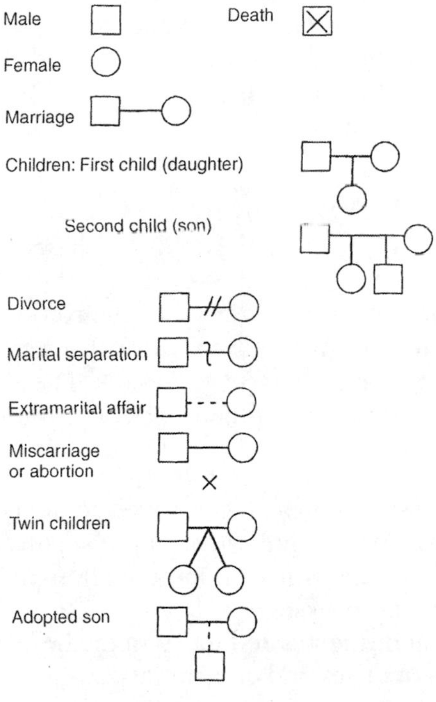

Male

Female

Marriage

Children: First child (daughter)

Second child (son)

Divorce

Marital separation

Extramarital affair

Miscarriage
or abortion

Twin children

Adopted son

Death

An Intergenerational Perspective on Elaine's Family

Elaine was caught in an overclose relationship with her parents in which each played on the other's fears and fantasies. She was programmed into the spousal pair to dilute their anxiety. The stability Elaine brought to the marital pair made it possible for them to tolerate each other, but at a price—Elaine's fusion. Projected onto her was the fallout of the parallel position each of her parents sustained as second, "replaced," undifferentiated children in their own respective families of origin. As the most emotionally bound child, she had the lowest level of differentiation and the highest level of difficulty in separating. The irony was that her identity was associated with this closeness. She had to "cut off" to escape and mask her attachment even from herself.

The genogram of Elaine's family depicts cross-generational emotional cutoffs, triangles, and patterns of interpersonal conflict between siblings and parents and similarly positioned children. Because the family would not cooperate in the helping process, it was impossible to precisely corroborate data. Nonetheless, even from Elaine's unidimensional and biased perspective, it seemed evident that the serious psychosocial stresses of the family were exacerbated by drugs, alcohol, and chronic infidelity.

COMMON ELEMENTS
IN FAMILY APPROACHES

Although different in many ways in their conceptualizations of family assessment and intervention, most theoretical approaches to families share some elements in common. These elements distinguish them from strictly individually oriented frameworks for practice:

- Belief that change emanates from the context of family interaction rather than from individual intrapsychic factors
- Emphasis on conscious communication rather than unconscious, covert processes
- Engagement of the whole family in the helping process
- Utilization of crises and confrontations

- Stress on recognizing present functioning, not recollecting past events
- De-emphasis of insight and understanding; concentration on behavioral change

When working from a family orientation, pay close attention to subtle and marginal clues produced by families in their interaction during sessions. Keep in mind such questions as: Who talks to whom? Under what circumstances? What makes the family tick? What are the alliances? What are the dilemmas? How do they function? How can they move to a higher level of functioning?

Assessment and intervention go hand in hand. Family assessment also devotes attention to families' developmental states, described differently by different theorists, as they progress from commitment through parenting to old age and retirement. It also includes an evaluation of how individual members negotiate the entire system on their own behalf, their ability to deal with their own internal emotions, and the manner in which they handle relationships within the family.

AN INTEGRATED PERSPECTIVE
ON ELAINE'S FAMILY

It is not possible for any one method or technique alone to provide complete and definite resolution of such complex problems as those presented by Elaine. Overexercising one specialized approach often leads to tunnel vision and restricted interaction; likewise, rigid adherence to one method often leads to being close but missing the mark. Integration of differing approaches offers the most solid base for family intervention. Work with Elaine, therefore, drew from both individual and family theories and relied upon a number of different, although interdependent, techniques. Adjustments were made in the intervention to accommodate to the changing assessment, which, in turn, was influenced by effective interventions. Every attempt was made not to fit Elaine to a modality but, instead, to fit the assessment and intervention to her individual and family dynamics and requirements.

Particularly because she felt even more rejected by her family's refusal to cooperate with her in the work, meeting her need for support while not interfering with her autonomous ego functions helped to thaw out her frozen views and patterns. It provided a cushion against her feeling totally misunderstood and isolated. This was accompanied by attempts to make sense out of the family's influence to complement the progress Elaine made in the initial individual work.

Elaine had geographically cut herself off from her family in an attempt to differentiate herself. She was not successful in this because she remained emotionally glued to it. She agreed to ask her family to join her periodically for a marathon meeting with an inducement to visit the "Big Apple." Although they took her up on her offer to come to New York, all flatly refused to participate in family sessions. This did not stop us from assuming a family orientation.

Elaine was encouraged to take an observer, "researcher" position regarding her own family. Work proceeded along two complementary lines. The first was the construction of the genogram, appearing earlier, over an extended period of time, which prompted new ways of thinking about and being with her parents, siblings, and friends. The second built upon the increased self-awareness and enhanced concept of her family to help her reestablish contact, at first by phone and then in person, with peripheral members of her family and ultimately with her parents themselves. Woven into the process was her willingness to take an "I" position in her contacts, much like the one she employed in individual sessions using gestalt techniques.

Taking an observer position made it possible for Elaine truly to separate herself from the family's emotionally consuming mass, and open up space for obtaining a different view of both her past and her present situation. Tracing the history of her nuclear family and its roots somewhat disentangled her from its emotional grasp. When she began to see her family as a series of interlocking emotional fields extending back through generations, the way and why of people's behavior toward each other and to her took on new meaning. She came to see that the long-standing, continuing transgenerational patterns of abuse and abandonment were not of her causing. Furthermore, when she remembered episodes of sexual abuse from childhood—and I agreed that they were real—she, for the first time, started to trust her own judgment and stopped succumbing to physical and psychological exploitation by friends and colleagues.

Elaine was asked to recognize times when she was able to do something positive for herself, not to conform to the dominant patterns in her family. This began a counterstory of being able to succeed despite having problems. Elaine came to appreciate instances when she performed in a way substantially different from the patterns she had previously learned. This generated a self-experience contradicting the original scenario she presented. It provided a new experience and a new map for her.

Before contacting her family, we talked about her expectations to minimize surprises. Elaine contacted her siblings and grandparents at first by letter, then by telephone. She followed these contacts by scheduled brief and coached visits home to her parents. Communicating directly with other family members provided a different and more balanced reality that further challenged the view offered by her parents and siblings. Reconnecting with her parents also released her from her triangled position because she recognized their scapegoating, hidden agenda, and lack of boundaries.

Repairing cutoffs in small doses on a one-to-one basis allowed her to come to terms with her parents' imperfection. She found ways to talk directly to each of them. With continual coaching, especially about predicting and preparing for the opposition she would face, Elaine was able to interrupt being automatically sucked back into an unhealthy place. This progress carried over into her relationship with me and with other friends.

The least successful and most dissatisfying aspect of the work involved her siblings. She had no way of reaching her older brother, and her contacts with her younger siblings were met with negativity and resistance.

Eventually, though, she not only identified dysfunctional family rules and codes, Elaine broke them. And for the first time; she felt clean.

TEN KEY FACTORS IN INTEGRATED FAMILY ASSESSMENT AND INTERVENTION

Following is my attempt to integrate relevant elements from various models into a framework for assessing families. It is formulated into A's.

1. *Attributes*—special features, distinguishing strengths, remarkable characteristics
2. *Abilities*—problem solving, coping abilities, competencies
3. *Affection*—intimacy, caring, need satisfaction

  4. *Affiliation*—belonging, boundaries, splits, alliances
  5. *Autonomy*—differentiation, dependency, stability, developmental stage
  6. *Arrangement of the infrastructure*—triangles, spousal and sibling subsystems, roles, scapegoating
  7. *Atmosphere*—warm, cool, trusting, conflictual, controlled
  8. *Adaptation* to the environment—cultural, religious, social
  9. *Artifacts*—rituals, rules, rites of passage
 10. *Anomalies*—myths, secrets, uniquenesses

This chapter has emphasized the contribution of family systems thinking to the assessment and intervention processes. Clinical practice is greatly enhanced when a comprehensive approach is employed. Here work with Elaine is traced using a family orientation, which adds breadth to individual work. The next chapter elucidates how additional creative techniques were incorporated into clinical work with Elaine and other clients. It presents some new ideas for understanding clients' life stories and ways to integrate these into your clinical practice.

FAMILY HEALTH

As was discussed in Chapter 9, there is a tendency to focus on what goes wrong with families. As with individual clients, give special attention to what is "right" in the families you work with. Search for strengths, for health, for what is positive and functional in your client families. Such examination will enhance your success in helping them to overcome their problems and difficulties.

The following are significant components of family health and strength:

- *Congeniality*—an atmosphere of nourishment (not suffocation), safety, security, compassion
- *Complementarity* and compatibility of roles; interaction where authority, pleasure, pain, and responsibility are shared
- *Closeness* without giving up separateness; appreciation of both dependence and independence
- *Celebration*—and receptiveness of different styles; rituals of commemoration

- *Collaboration,* not complicity, where problems are seen as issues influencing the entire family
- *Creativity* and flexibility—adaptability and responsiveness to changing needs; resourcefulness
- *Context*—structure, the framing of experience, stability
- *Construction* of reality; "family paradigm"; make use of capacities and support talents
- *Communication*—clear, direct, undistorted; conflict resolution
- *Clear boundaries*—both generational and interfamilial

Chapter 11

Clients Recommend Effective Ways
to Treat Trauma

. . . come home to yourself. Ask yourself. Where am I right
now? What am I doing? What am I thinking, sensing? . . . Just
seek awareness . . .

Anthony DeMello

The very cave you are afraid to enter turns out to be the source of
what you are looking for.

Joseph Campbell

The professional literature provides scant data about traumatized
individuals' views of their experience of treatment. It offers even less
guidance as to how to proceed clinically when working with trauma.
This chapter provides not only a detailed description of clients' subjective opinion about their treatment, but advances definitive recommendations for improving your clinical responsiveness.

Based mainly upon a qualitative case study of four male survivors
of childhood trauma and suicidal threat, this chapter presents, from
clients' perspectives, instructive explanations of how therapists can
best help clients confront difficult and painful material. Additionally,
reference is made to a different, although related, study of nine female survivors of rape who critique both their individual and group
therapy experiences. Clearly not generalizable in the traditional sense,
and certainly anecdotal, these two studies suggest ways that you can
best respond to serious client issues.

Although framed differently, similar questions undergird both
studies: What do clients tell us about therapeutic effectiveness?

About ineffectiveness? How do clients view their effect on therapists? What therapeutic interventions work? Which ones fail? As clients see it, what happens in therapy to help them resolve scathing
experiences? To foster and further their process of self-discovery?
Are there techniques or methods that prove to be better than others?
Worse than others? Are there interventions that clients object to?
What methods and techniques do clients recommend that therapists
adopt to be more effective? What encourages clients to stay in therapy?

UNDERSTANDING THE SEEDS
OF UNSUCCESSFUL THERAPY

The greater proportion of the professional literature related to
working with survivors of trauma deals with factors that negatively
affect the work rather than with those that contribute positively to it.
It largely focuses on understanding the inappropriate, ineffective, or
even nonresponsive qualities of therapists in dealing with clients who
have been traumatized. It highlights how working with traumatized
clients can generate powerful conscious and unconscious reactions in
therapists that can abort treatment goals without the awareness of either clients or therapists. For a fuller discussion of these factors, consult *The Effects of Suicide on the Private Practitioner: A Professional
and Personal Perspective* (Fox and Cooper, 1998). What makes the
reflections by these men, presented in a later section, so forceful and
convincing, therefore, is their emphasis on providing pointed and
pragmatic guidance for clinicians working with trauma and suicide.

Countertransference

It has been suggested that all psychotherapy involves an intuitive
sensitivity to clients' most profound emotional experience as well as
an ability of the therapist to absorb inner feelings and thoughts that
clients themselves cannot tolerate (Kernberg, 1975). It has also been
postulated that countertransference reactions cannot be avoided (Racker,
1957). When therapists are unaware of their own internal responses,
they may either overidentify with the client, seeing the world too
much from his or her perspective, or may underidentify, responding
unempathically or nonconstructively to the client. Even when they
are aware, they may abstain from intervention because of their own
fears of unleashing strong emotional reactions in the client or guiding

the client to reenter the traumatic memory and affect, which may be experienced as retraumatization.

Countertransference arises when therapists begin working with hurting clients. In this intensive intersubjective context, therapists' vulnerability may be triggered. They may defend against it by failing to respond to clients and instead produce interventions designed to allay their own anxiety rather than that of the clients.

Although there are varied and contrasting views of countertransference and its clinical implications, the formulation presented here clearly includes the range of countertransference reactions described by Orr (1954). Orr noted three central countertransferential responses: first, countertransference proper, the specific responses of therapists to the patient's transference; second, the responses to the patient generated out of therapists' experiences and dispositions as a whole— therapists' transferences to the client; and third, the specific responses of therapists, also generated out of their experiences and dispositions, to the therapeutic activity itself, that is, the variety of responses aroused in therapists by virtue of playing a crucial role in another person's life. Countertransference, in other words, is conceptualized as an "inevitable product of the interaction between the patient and analyst rather than a simple interference stemming from . . . infantile drive-related conflicts" (Greenberg and Mitchell, 1983). Therapists' conscious and unconscious reactions to their clients in any treatment situation are reactions to clients' reality and transferences as well as to therapists' own realities, needs, and transferences. Countertransference, therefore, can account for the inappropriate responses to the client based upon therapists' own inner issues and conflicts that create obstacles to effective intervention. When thoughtfully and sensitively considered, on the other hand, it can provide useful information in understanding the client, thus contributing constructively to the helping process.

Vicarious Traumatization

Vicarious traumatization refers to the effects that clients' graphic and painful material (e.g., abuse, violent ideation, sexual assault) produces in the therapist's own cognitive schemas or beliefs, expectations, and assumptions about self and others (McCann and Pearlman, 1990a). This secondary traumatization describes the failure of therapists to attend appropriately to a client's experience and issues and is a manifestation of counterresistance. Therapists are not immune to painful images, thoughts, and feelings presented to them by clients. The disturbing feelings of anxiety, vulnerability, hopelessness, and despair presented by clients can have profound psychological effects that may be disruptive and painful for therapists both in the short run and over time (McCann and Pearlman, 1990a).

McCann and Pearlman, after exhaustive research of the professional literature, suggest that when therapists are not able to assimilate or work through their own responses to harmed clients, they are themselves victims of "vicarious victimization." These authors identify seven fundamental psychological needs in therapists that are imperiled by working with trauma—safety, dependency/trust, power, esteem, intimacy, independence, and frame of reference (McCann and Pearlman, 1990b). They believe that the unique reactions of therapists are influenced by the centrality or salience of these schemas to themselves. Therapists may, for example, experience a heightened sense of vulnerability and an enhanced awareness of the fragility of life or feelings of helplessness, depression, or despair (McCann and Pearlman, 1990a) as a result of working intensively with victims of abuse and trauma. Such feelings may interfere with therapists' ability to attend to their clients' issues.

Compassion Fatigue

Compassion fatigue refers to how and why therapists, while not directly traumatized, nevertheless become traumatized and possibly secondary victims. Defined as the natural behavior and emotion resulting from knowing about a traumatizing event experienced by a significant other, compassion fatigue is the stress resulting from helping or wanting to help a traumatized or suffering person (Figley, 1995). It is viewed as a by-product of intensive caring, contact, and work with psychologically and physically traumatized people. Therapists are especially vulnerable to such secondary stress because of their empathic sensitivity, sense of personal integrity, and belief in humanity. These natural responses, values, and beliefs are shattered by overexposure to hurting clients and lack of relief from the stress of compassionate resonance.

Therapists, as supporters and helpers, may become indirectly traumatized through their intimate association with traumatized clients (Figley, 1995). As a consequence, they may experience a range of psychologically dysfunctional reactions, including emotionally distressful feelings (sadness or grief, anxiety, dread, fear, etc.); intrusive imagery of the client's traumatic material (nightmares, flooding, etc.); numbing or avoidance of efforts to work with traumatic material; somatic complaints (difficulty sleeping, headaches, heart palpitations); addictive or compulsive behaviors; physiological arousal; and impairment of day-to-day functioning (isolation, missed appointments, etc.) (Dutton and Rubinstein, 1995).

The concept of compassion fatigue contributes further to an understanding of why therapists may collude with clients to avoid psychotherapeutic work that needs to be done. Therapists receive little relief from the burden and responsibility ensuing from prolonged care for the traumatized and suffering client. Ironically, their empathic ability makes them particularly susceptible to emotional contagion, experiencing feelings of the sufferer. Taken together with traumatic recollections, which are provoked by continual contact with the traumatized client, therapists experience inordinate disruptions in their professional or personal lives, with inevitable and frequently negative consequences to their work with clients (Figley, 1995).

Burnout

Burnout results from chronic overexposure to traumatized clients, especially those presenting serious symptoms, threats, and issues, as in clients who have been brutally violated. In intensive work with seriously traumatized clients, the literature suggests that therapists are apt to experience the following:

1. Emotional exhaustion resulting from intense transactions
2. A profound sense of an inability to help acutely distressed clients
3. Cynicism arising from a lack of observable progress with difficult clients
4. Emotional numbness to the pain of clients
5. Isolation accompanying the absence of social support

A cycle results in which these factors interact with each other to precipitate distress and consequent isolation; these reactions, in turn, exacerbate the negative consequences that produce them in the first place. All, in turn, negatively affect therapists' responses to clients.

Clients who have been raped may arouse in therapists "unmediated stress" (Faber, 1983). This state of stress may develop when there is significant disparity between situational and environmental demands on the coping capacity of the therapist (Maslach, 1982). Working with clients who have been traumatized, and traumatized repeatedly, often produces in the therapist loss of drive and motivation (Pines and Maslach, 1978), and mental, physical, and emotional exhaustion (Freudenberger, 1980; Koeske and Koeske, 1989; Maslach and Jackson, 1981).

Therapists who feel overwhelmed by the strain of working with seriously traumatized and distraught clients tend to distance themselves from both clients and colleagues. Such withdrawal and isolation, coupled with the absence of social support, aggravates the burnout syndrome (Scully, 1983).

Thus, the experience of constantly dealing with pain, your own and your clients', can obviously interfere with your ability to address your clients' needs and issues. Maintaining a consciousness of these pitfalls, learning how to protect yourself from, while simultaneously giving yourself over to, the clients' trauma is an enormous task.

FOUR TRAUMATIZED MEN

Some years after concluding treatment with a number of traumatized men, who were suicidal as a result, I attempted to contact them to ascertain post-therapy reflections about treatment approaches they believed contributed, ultimately, to their continued well-being. I was successful in reaching four of them: Barry, a twenty-six-year-old dancer from America's heartland, victimized through incest as a child; Tyle, a twenty-seven-year-old black man, an alcohol and cocaine abuser raised in dire poverty in the inner city but many times over a millionaire; Brad, a twenty-six-year-old Ivy League-educated former Olympic swimmer, and Ramon, a thirty-year-old Latino infected with AIDS.

Each man, when interviewed by phone, spoke thoughtfully, poignantly, and deeply about his life and his therapy. All of them, gravely traumatized as children, overcame fierce obstacles in their lives, not the least of which were their own multiple suicide attempts, for which each had originally sought treatment.

The Stories of Four Men

Only a synopsis of each man's story is presented, since the whole narrative of each man alone would fill a book. The stories of Barry, Tyle, Brad, and Ramon, therefore, have been condensed to provide but a shadow of the whole, a background for their reflections on their therapy. More complete details about their lives, as well those of other traumatized men, can be found elsewhere (Fox, 2000). Each man came into therapy at a significant juncture in his life, more precisely, when facing a decision whether or not to live. What makes their stories compelling, and therefore informative, is not so much the choices they faced, but the choices they made in confronting the relative attraction of an outcome of suicide. These men chose life, and continue to choose it, through self-reinvention, overcoming anger, and pushing away the past to spring or, in some instances, crawl toward the future.

All desired strongly to contact the internal resources they knew lay inside of them. All completed at least three years of treatment, some of it regular and some intermittent.

All these men possessed an overall desire "to make things different." Upon completion of treatment, all showed an intensified desire to live, to get on with life, and a heightened degree of self-awareness, self-reliance, and goal directedness.

Barry's Story

A dancer, Barry came to see me when he was in his early to mid-twenties. Tall and lithe, he was frightened, terribly depressed, and highly suicidal.

Two years before, his sister, Yvonne, had taken her life. He was now approaching the age she had been when she had done so. He had been rather close to her, although she had tortured and sexually abused him when they were younger. In this family of four children, every one had been sexually abused and tortured by their father. Most had become abusers themselves. Yvonne, emotionally devastated and despairing, had actually shown Barry the razors a few months before she used them to kill herself.

All the feelings of shame and guilt that he felt in relation to Yvonne were unexplainably surfacing as he danced on stage. His dancing, which was his life, was being destroyed. Having his genitals semiexposed, as they were in tight-fitting leotards, was leaving him unable to perform. If he could not dance, he did not want to live. Yet here he was—in great pain, looking for a way to get beyond the pain, perhaps as Yvonne had, but also implicitly looking for an alternative.

Raised on a farm in America's heartland, with his wheat-colored hair, Barry looked like the proverbial Norman Rockwell kid. But he had led anything but a Norman Rockwell life.

Barry's mother was probably mentally ill, possibly bipolar. She was depressed, often unable to get out of bed, overwhelmed, unaware, alternatively unresponsive to the children or in a state of high drama, screaming and yelling and scaring them. Certainly no one felt that she could be trusted. A religious fanatic as well, she imbued in the children terror of the punishing God who would extract vengeance for their sins. Barry was often her preferred target.

His father, whom Barry likened to a raging bull, was a threatening, hateful, bestial sadist. He had abused Yvonne and Barry. He forced Barry to engage in sex with the farm animals, and if Barry dared refuse, his father would strangle Barry's favorite pets bare-handed. Just seeing him approach would cause Barry to defecate in his pants. His older brother, a clone of his father, would torture and kill small animals and abused Barry in the bed they shared growing up and suffocated him to keep him quiet.

No wonder, then, that Barry had trouble breathing when he became anxious.

Barry's natural bent for gymnastics and acrobatics led him to study dance by the time he was in junior high school, and dance was his ticket out of the household he had grown to loathe. His teacher invited him to live in the nearby town with her family, and by age seventeen, he had won a scholarship to study at a major New York ballet company.

He was extremely solitary, self-conscious, and paradoxically introverted for a performer. Though depressed, and with an obviously sad demeanor, Barry was highly disciplined, never missing a rehearsal or performance. Oftentimes he danced despite injuries, but he never ignored his injuries and always sought treatment for them. Interestingly though, by some unexpressed mutual agreement, no one in his family ever saw him dance, so that part of his life remained uncontaminated. When he returned home from his visits with them, he was always miserable, swamped by painful memories, acting out sexually and masochistically.

Therapy was able to break some of the pattern. It validated his experience and showed him that he was not the "bad seed," not evil as his mother often preached, that he did not deserve the abuse and punishment he heaped upon himself. Barry often wondered aloud if sharing and exploring his pain-racked background would ever bring relief; yet he was willing to grapple and confront his demons head-on. He eventually came to understand in treatment that he had a choice—to give up as his sister did or to believe in dance and himself.

Tyle's Story

Tyle came from dire poverty. He never went to college; actually, he barely graduated from high school. Yet he sought out and was willing to engage in the therapeutic process to help him deal with his anxiety and despondency as he faced the prospect of a long jail term for securities fraud. He thought that it would probably be better to kill himself than to rot in a prison cell. He essentially dared me to convince him otherwise.

One of five boys in a family of ten children, he was the second youngest. Each one, in his or her own way, was what might be called dysfunctional, alcoholic or drug addicted, and Tyle was no exception. Most could be called compulsive. Tyle certainly might have been classified as having attention-deficit disorder. But where the others might drift, Tyle would drive. The others might drown in their despair. Tyle was different. Tyle knew two things more than the others did. He knew what he did not want and he knew what he did want. He was fiercely determined to get what he did want.

At seven years old, he had a paper route. By eight he had three of them. Extremes were always part of his makeup, but extremes were necessary, it seemed, to go from being the poorest to the richest.

An African-American child, living on welfare in a neighborhood abutting a wealthy upper-class inner-city area, Tyle was continually beaten by his father as well as his peers because of his differentness. He learned early and believed strongly that anything he wanted he would have to get by himself. His parents could not help themselves, much less him. All the children overwhelmed his mother. His father was an artist who, despite his own creative talent, had nothing to show for it. He died unrecognized, poor, and downtrodden. Was it

disgust with his father's self-sabotaging unwillingness to be successful that drove Tyle?

Certainly, nothing came easily to Tyle. Everything he wanted he had
to struggle for—even if it meant going to the far edges of the law to get it.
He struggled for recognition; he struggled to be accepted and liked. Sexually abused by an older brother, he struggled to escape that fearsome
memory while holding on to the family. The struggles manifested themselves in extremes and excesses—sexually, addictively, and financially.

Though no great student, he was obviously bright, sharp, and quick.
Business and people who were successful in it fascinated him, almost
to the point of obsession. Working as a young teenager in a Wall Street
delicatessen at lunchtime, he discovered that the owner played the
stock market. Thus began his own career. Tyle picked his boss's brains
relentlessly until every penny he earned was being invested.

What he had, that his siblings and so many others did not, was a
very simple, one-dimensional goal—to get rich. He was confident
that he could always make money and believed that if he could make
money, he could escape the home that taunted him and the poverty he
hated. He discovered he could talk anyone into anything. And he did.

What he could not do, it appeared, was to rein in his own compul-
siveness. He was alcoholic, cocaine addicted, and sexually promiscu-
ous. Any gamble was worth taking, and financially it served him
well. He made his first million by twenty-three, but he led a double
life, one foot in the legal, the other in the illegal.

However, despite the appearance of being out of control, his deliberate decision to lick his addictions won out. He came into therapy,
perhaps negatively motivated to find an easy way out of trouble; nevertheless, he addressed his fears and convoluted thinking, and recognized the self-destructive ways patterned after his father's, whom he
maligned. Encouraged to join a twelve-step group, he did so and adhered to its dictates, gaining control over his vices, rather than serving them. His firm commitment to therapy spilled over into taking
responsibility for his life. Admitting wrongdoing, he went to jail,
faced the consequences, and revised his self-sabotaging choices and
actions of the past.

Brad's Story

When I try to describe Brad, I think of metaphors: he springs up, he
bounces back, he has nine lives. Like a child's punching bag, he is

self-righting. His ability to survive challenges the commonly held viewpoint that family influence is paramount, that early trauma is irrevocable, that adversity tends to promote damage, that children from dysfunctional families are doomed.

Brad was an Olympic athlete and an actor studying at a prestigious drama school. Nevertheless, in his late twenties, he had already survived three suicide attempts and years of alcohol and drug abuse.

When I first saw him, our goal was to keep him alive. That was not just my goal; it was his. His girlfriend had broken up with him while they were both in Asia. He had begun to decompensate, "dissemble" as he called it, and was obviously in a major depression and extremely suicidal. He had been neither sleeping nor eating and had been thousands of miles from anything familiar, but he had managed to make his way home. He wanted to die. He was determined to live.

Several years before, he had detoxed and since then had been religious in attending AA and NA meetings. They were now, however, offering no relief. His mental health was crashing around him, and yet he believed that "some internal, inexplicable force" had so far kept him alive. After another long-term relationship had failed, he had taken pills and then, when hospitalized, hung himself. This time he sought help and agreed to an antisuicide contract, medication, and a mutual attempt to understand the interaction between past and present.

Because he had grown up in a household where he was continually punished, dismissed, and forced to go to extremes to get recognition, Brad's ongoing emotional anguish and dysfunctional behavior was labeled "nothing but a lack of discipline." His father, a military man, believed in severe corporal punishment; Brad experienced this firsthand as his father beat him to "straighten him out."

Depression was rampant throughout the family. His maternal great-grandmother had received ECT; his mother had been on antidepressants since his birth; his paternal grandmother had been hospitalized for depression; her son, Brad's uncle, had suicided; and Brad's own brother was seriously depressed but untreated because of political aspirations. Choosing to live required sucking himself out of a strong genetic pool.

As if that were not enough, medication seemed to interfere with his ability to memorize lines as an actor. Brad felt as well that it bloated and distorted his face and would short-circuit getting the roles he wanted. He worried also that the medication would affect his sexual performance. Yet, while in excruciating psychic agony, attempting to maintain his sobriety, and fighting the medicine's side effects, he plowed on. He got up in the morning, went to work, and came to therapy. Treatment validated and appealed to his self-described "healthy insides," revealed destructive thoughts and damaging behaviors, and focused largely on exchanges within the therapeutic relationship itself.

Ramon's Story

By the time I saw Ramon, he was already in recovery and had been for four years. While only in his early thirties, he had already been diagnosed as HIV positive. An intravenous heroin addict, he had considered suicide as he battled his dependency. His life, he knew, had been ravaged by the drugs, and now it was to be further ravaged by the illness that had already taken so many of his friends. The antiviral medication ceased to work. Wasn't it better for everyone if he was dead?

Coming out of the fog of years of drug use and abuse, followed by years of getting and staying clean and sober, Ramon had adhered rigorously to twelve-step programs. During these years, even before his own diagnosis, he had ministered to both gay and straight friends, nursing several to the moment of their deaths.

As he himself was diagnosed, he again considered suicide, to take control into his own hands. He was ashamed, angry with himself, angry that he had wasted his life, angry at all the men in his life that had betrayed him, most especially the father who abandoned him when he was a child.

A Latino, Ramon had grown up surrounded mostly by women. It was his older sister, in fact, who had introduced him to heroin when he was nine. Childhood was a dark time. Having a serious speech impediment, he experienced life as great pain and was quick to seek the comfort heroin provided. As bright as he was, and despite a good mother who wanted good things for him, there was no male modeling that encouraged anything but the street life.

The street, however, led nowhere. For most, it had led only to jail or death. However, because of who he was, Ramon had somehow, until now, escaped both. Something had impelled him on; something had led him to choose life over death. Something had made him determined to make up for those lost years, to make something special of his life. He believed that if he could kick the drug, he could re-create himself anew. And he had.

When he came to see me, he was already a highly esteemed mental health professional—a writer, a teacher, a father. But becoming a success, overcoming all odds, does not protect anyone from new pain, present anguish, or past shame. He now had a daughter with an even more serious handicap than he himself had had, his divorce from her mother, and his own deteriorating health with which to cope. He questioned the value of going on.

His distorted and negative thinking was challenged. Provided with advice and practical information about AIDS and newer medications, about ways to handle himself, about his physical disease, and about relating to his family and friends, he took charge of himself and his situation. Appeals to his mental health and support for the strength that had already produced so many accomplishments were a further focus of treatment. He responded very well to probing, prodding, and coaching.

RECONNECTION

So, from the clients' point of view, what is helpful when you are treating traumatized individuals? The following retrospective comments by the four traumatized men provide some clues. Each of the men, when contacted, welcomed the opportunity to reflect back upon his treatment.

To frame their responses, I posed the following questions: What was effective in your therapy? Not effective? How did you or your situation affect your therapist(s)? What therapeutic interventions worked for you? Which ones failed? What happened in therapy to help you along? To foster increased self-discovery? What did you object to? What techniques or methods would you recommend that therapists adopt to be more effective? Why did you stick to therapy?

None answered the questions directly, but upon hearing them, "free associated." The following is a distillation of these associations.

Barry's Reflections

My parents were nonachieving and self-deceptive—losers. They had no power, no choice, no control. I vowed to be different. I always had a keen sense of not failing. Failure to me was unacceptable. I would be a famous dancer. I was determined for as far back as I can remember. The unfairness of the way I was treated and my own determination to not be a victim the way my parents were led me on. I had a couple of models—in my first ballet teacher and others along the way—who encouraged me to be different, to risk, especially as a man. Kind of the way you always did. I wondered what better life there could be. We all lived in the same two-bedroom farmhouse. I had to depend on myself; there was no one else to depend upon. I wanted out. I was always struggling to show that I was not silly, a sissy, stupid, flaky, "less than." I remember always feeling insecure and frightened. I wanted to achieve, to be OK. To excel.

I knew I could. I sort of took it as a challenge to show them. I pushed myself by saying, "Keep doing it, keep practicing, until you get it right." You promoted the idea that I had to take responsibility, even when it went against my grain. But that is what I was doing anyway. Punishment involved not doing what I wanted to do. I had to prove, at least to myself, that I was OK. I was primed by my resolve. Therapy pushed me along further. It was the turning point in my life. I learned to trust myself only because your belief in me got me to. You were always there, and you used my own progress "as evidence against me" when I doubted myself. It was amazing how much you remembered. You helped me recognize that even though my childhood still haunts me, it doesn't have to cripple me anymore. Mostly, you let me see that I was not fatally flawed, had a right to live.

Tyle's Reflections

I always had a need to get away from how my parents lived. I hated their lives—I still do. Nobody had faith in me. But I did. I do. And I knew that you did. I knew not because you said so, but because you made me feel safe and pushed me along. You even stuck by me when I went to jail, even when I didn't pay you. I had one very clear goal in mind. That was to make money. To be rich. I wanted more, much more. In ways, I always reached far, and, in ways, I believed that I would do it. God put me here—who am I to cheat him? I was always certain of what I didn't want. I wanted to escape. At thirteen and again at sixteen, I took a large piece of oak tag. On it I wrote what I wanted to achieve. I wanted money, friends, and family. I then crossed off things that wouldn't give me the sense of achievement.

Despite everything, I have come to like what I do because it gives me what I want. I gave up a lot, but then I have the only thing I always really wanted. Money. I never surrendered.

Next step for me is to have more time, to take time. You mentioned the importance of time to me a lot. You also told me to save some energy for my "self." I'm doing that. But I don't know if I'll ever stop putting myself out on a limb. I want to be bloody rich.

An anecdote. I remember my father had drawings. He laminated them. Nobody bought them. I brought them into school and sold them as book covers to 100 kids. I even took orders for them. His idea sucked—mine didn't. Then I rented space at a flea market and sold some more. I remember that my father didn't go anywhere. He stood by. I was always focused. Life is a contest. I will win. I never told you how much I appreciated your support when it looked like all else failed and everybody left me. You supported my drive, and it's my strength. I never met anyone more persistent than me. I think you are. You got me to look at and laugh at myself, recognize my overblown schemes, and see that if I couldn't reinvent history, I could reinvent myself. You cared, man.

Brad's Reflections

There was something in me, something that was healthy, something that said don't give up. However miserable I was, no matter what way I was hurting myself, I reached out. I got help. I decided to live. I found you, thank God. I guess I learned a lot from my swimming coach. He told me to dive in no matter how scared you are. Don't let anything stop you. Inside me was a voice that said stay alive; all will end up the way it should. It's like a matter of attitude. Maybe a mind thing. I was determined to stop the crap and get my dream. I think that you forced me to see how I sabotaged myself, always did. You said that you had confidence in me. I felt your confidence. When I asked you to prove why, you told me why and how. In chapter and verse. How do you remember all the details? I stopped drugging. I stopped drinking. I stopped cutting myself. Yeah, I stopped taking my meds too, but for almost a year now I've been working steadily, not at what I want, but close to it.

I think, now that I'm talking to you, that maybe I'll come back to see you. I want to get over the next hurdle. Put all my training to the test. You showed me how to really rely on myself. You kept showing me that I had choices. And most of the time, when I really thought about it, I came, with your help, to make pretty good ones. I'm a bit scared, but I will do it. You convinced me that I have the potential and raw materials. I will do it. I believe in myself. I will succeed, really, really succeed. I still believe that some internal, inexplicable force of health and place of safety will keep me alive and on course. Somehow you tapped into my stuff, brought the good stuff to the surface. I don't really understand how you did it, but I felt you were "for" me. Too, the "new" me didn't have to be a reincarnation of the "old" me, and even the old me wasn't "bad."

Ramon's Reflections

Ramon spoke in metaphors.

I was a sponge so saturated that I was sinking. I wanted to re-create myself. I cleaned out the closet. Each success, while not fully a surprise, drove me in spite of my physical limitations. I had hope and drive. Ever since I was young, I yearned for life. I've been a fisherman all my life. I check out every angle, trap the bait. I cast. I don't always catch a fish. I cast again. I sometimes do. I know that I'm in a rush to try to get so much in. Revenge played a large part. I was determined to get what I didn't get, what I didn't have in the first place. I wanted my daughter not to suffer the way I did. So, I was also determined to give what I didn't get. You helped me recognize that I actually had something to give. You even almost trained me how to do it. I always had a strong urge to prove myself. I will prove myself. I have the utmost confidence that I will beat the odds. I am not resigned; there is a light inside of me. I want to be viewed as substantial, reclaiming what my life is about. Over time I came to believe you that my life couldn't be thrown away. Even in the face of my physical deterioration, I can give up like so many and die, or live. Even talking with you now brings relief, support, and gives me motivation.

You asked what happened in therapy that helped me. I'll tell you. It's just this—you supported me and challenged me at the same time. You helped me realize that I could design my own life. That's powerful, man. I believe that our fate is ours and ours alone. We have only ourselves to blame or praise for both the good and the bad that happens in our lives. I thank you because you helped me figure out the way to live my life the way I want to live it. Therapy helped me realize that I was a turtle. I could, if I wanted to, close myself up in a shell. I could cut myself off. I could die without seeing what was on the other side. Or I could stick my neck out and go ahead. That's what I've always done, stuck my neck out and moved, maybe slowly, but ahead.

OTHER SURVIVORS' VIEWPOINTS

The gist of what these men report as effective therapy interfaces strongly with the responses of nine women interviewed in a separate study (Fox and Carey, 1999). These nine women had previously attended various rape survivors' support groups and had been in individual therapy. Each had been brutally raped. Natasha had been raped at gunpoint by a stranger during a robbery at her workplace; Rebecca was raped by an acquaintance when she was seven years old; Ellen was gang raped by her boyfriend and his male friends; Caroline was raped at knifepoint by a stranger who had broken into her home at night. Marie was gang raped by three acquaintances when she was a teenager and, as an adult, had been raped two and a half years ago by a stranger who had broken into her home. Tricia, Lyn, Alyse, and Joan had all been raped by acquaintances.

Key questions guiding the inquiry into what these women perceived as beneficial in their respective treatments were: What was effective/not effective in your therapy? How did you or your situation affect your therapist(s)? What role did your therapists play in avoiding your painful issues? What therapeutic interventions worked for you? Which ones failed? What happened in therapy to foster increased self-discovery? What did you object to? What techniques or methods would you recommend that therapists adopt to be more effective? And, perhaps most important, how can therapists remain centered, compassionate, and appropriately responsive when feeling overwhelmed, frustrated or inadequate, perhaps even emotionally assaulted and threatened as well?

All women expressed the belief that therapists should help them talk about their trauma, but should also to know when to back off. Joan, for example, commented, "I think somebody needs to bring something up that others really wouldn't want to talk about. I think somebody needs to bring it out in the open and then see if anybody comes and gets it, as far as deciding to talk. I think if you just had people who had the problem sitting in a room, especially in the beginning, I don't think anybody would start talking." You, the therapist, are that somebody.

Eight of the nine women reported needing to be pushed to do therapeutic work; however, there was agreement that they also wanted the therapist to back off if they could not stay with an issue. The therapist, then, needs to keep clients focused on issues, even when painful, but back off when clients request it. Tricia remarked, "It's good to be pushed, but on the other hand I'd rather just sit here and not deal with it." Joan reported, "I think the one thing you can't do is force someone to tell their story." In what may appear to be a contradictory wish, Joan continued, saying that a therapist can't force anyone, but should make every effort to encourage clients to talk. For victims of any kind of trauma, and in these cases of rape, the hope is that force will never again be used against them in *any way;* nevertheless, they seek compassionate urging to facilitate their speaking about the unspeakable.

A complicating viewpoint was that therapists should know that traumatized individuals are strong, not fragile. Six of the nine women cautioned therapists not to patronize clients, which diminishes them. Natasha stated that a therapist should be willing to take a risk, not be intimidated, not just "fluff me up and stroke my head."

Alyse, in expressing her view that therapists need to demand work from clients, stated, "I had said it in the beginning, that's what we needed. Somebody who was not afraid of us, not afraid of hurting us by making us talk about things. I mean our therapist never hurt our feelings but she didn't walk around us like on egg shells, like she was afraid of us, like we were these poor little victims, that was the difference."

When you interact with clients as if they are weak or fragile, clients intuit from you that they are incapable of the emotionally painful work necessary to become survivors. Using an analogy of a physically ill patient, Alyse described her therapist in this way: "I was annoyed and angered by the therapist, who was afraid of us because, I guess, it kind of made us feel like maybe there was something wrong with us. It's like a cancer patient or somebody who is in the hospital dying, and everybody is tiptoeing around them and whispering and doesn't want them to hear. I guess that's how she made us feel."

In struggling to explain how therapists can truly be helpful, Ellen emphasized that there were no hard and fast rules. She stated, "I think it's a fine line. I think it's trial and error every single time you do it. One day you may be able to push me really, really far and the other day you may think you can go back to doing what you did last week, but there's a wall there. I think it's trial and error."

Joan recalled when her therapist successfully pursued a painful story. "I remember one incident specifically where somebody was confronting something really, really painful for them and it was kind of a situation where it was a judgment call on the part of the leader. 'Should we pursue this or should we let it go?' The therapist chose to gently pursue it. It was one of those situations where you could hear a pin drop because the person was dealing with her emotions. I felt uncomfortable, but I think that, in the end, that person's disclosure helped. First of all, it helped the group to understand where the person was coming from. I think that if she hadn't been challenged perhaps that group member might not have so easily revealed what she ended up revealing."

Resistance, an expected part of the therapeutic process, especially with traumatized individuals, and more especially at the initial phases of your work, needs to be met with slower pacing, not avoidance. Sensitive to the timing of interventions, you need to be mindful of both the initial fragility and progressive ego strength of clients, so as to be informed when to push and when to back off. Such a stance informs and guides you in the pursuit of recall of painful memory and affect, which will successfully result in reentry into previously walled off emotional wounds and thus promote the process of healing.

All nine women identified emotional strength, empathy, understanding, caring, humor, and the ability to deal with rage, horror, and pain as requisite qualities for therapists. Tricia saw it this way: "You need to be strong and yet caring. It's not like you're going to rip people apart and try to tear down their defenses. But when you say something that is obviously true, I don't think you should back down and start apologizing." Additionally, you should help clients stay focused on the task at hand.

Natasha strongly recommended that therapists have a sense of humor. She said, "I think you need a sense of humor to do this work with people. It means a lot. It's an ice breaker sometimes, a relief of tension. I always think that laughing is as good as crying."

Four respondents, Alyse, Rebecca, Ellen, and Joan, avorred that a requisite for therapists is knowledge and training about trauma. Joan said further, "I am strongly in favor of specialized training for people dealing with rape survivors . . . because it's too easy to lack understanding of the shame, lack of trust, fear, the anger, pain, the rage."

THE KERNELS
OF SUCCESSFUL TREATMENT

What works? An overarching answer involves maintaining an integrated approach to your clinical practice with traumatized individuals of any kind. In other words, being self-aware, focused, flexible, and balanced in responding with appropriate techniques to clients' suffering and problems is what works. What should you keep in mind when working with traumatized and suicidal clients? What are some key elements that can be gleaned from the reflections by these four men and nine women? The guideposts below are interdependent, that is, they build upon and enhance one another.

Relating

Before intervening to explore painful memory and affect, it is imperative to build a relationship of trust and emotional safety. Initially, focus on the present and on the process of daily living. Daily routines and functioning, such as eating, sleeping, hygiene, health care, interpersonal relationships, safety, work, and play are comfortable, yet essential topics and issues. You may find yourself continually tested and evaluated by clients for your knowledge, trustworthiness, and skill. Empathically endure their scrutiny, accept their vacillation between dependence and contention, absorb and simultaneously promote their release of strong emotions.

More specifically, be consistent, available, on time. Return phone calls. Give credence to their free determination, right to decide, ability to make their own decisions, inherent strength, and capacity to succeed.

Hearing Their Story

Accompany your clients through the telling and retelling of their traumatic experiences. By so doing, you create a structure where catharsis of disturbing affects as well as a cleansing of disquieting and intrusive memories is made possible. The containment you provide models self-containment for them. Troublesome events conveyed symbolically in words to you, an attentive and caring person, allow them to relive and thereby relieve their trauma.

Naming Things for What They Are

Clients express their readiness to advance into troubled waters by beginning to allude to them. Avoid circumventing reality or using euphemisms when issues are exposed. Name the unnameable—abuse, rape, assault, victimization, trauma. In this way, you pierce the psychological trauma membrane that allows clients to distance themselves from the traumatic material (Fox and Carey, 1999). If you move too quickly at this juncture, you yourself may be experienced as yet another perpetrator of emotional violence. To successfully help clients reenter traumatic material, build on the safety of the therapeutic milieu in which trust is at the core, because honesty and naming the unnameable grounds the work and propels the process forward.

Striking a Balance

Along with problem solving, reframing experience, and teaching clients to self-soothe, you may find yourself taking a paradoxical stance. Endeavoring to effect a balance in your work so as to neither shy away from difficult material nor be too intrusive requires your accepting and validating clients' pain and suffering while maintaining a focus on change of perspective and cognition. Being spontaneous, perhaps even irreverent, sometimes moves such work along. Sensitively attune yourself to enhancing and encouraging communication while appropriately curtailing and discouraging premature or too detailed revelations. Your interventions are somewhat paradoxical—nurturing yet firm and demanding, compassionate yet confrontive, caring yet challenging.

Educating

Educate clients about the helping process itself and your methods, as well as about trauma and its aftermath. Provide practical information and advice appropriate to their special needs. Offer alternative viewpoints to consider in making decisions. Help them link past history to present dilemmas. Actively instruct your clients in self-sooth-ing techniques, normalize their symptoms, encourage them to practice more healthful behaviors, point out misinterpretations of their experi-ence, and counter distorted thinking patterns. Teach them to take a distanced position to view their feelings and actions while validating the fact that their original ones may have actually contributed to their survival.

Setting Goals

Prioritize targets of attention and agree on mutual goals, roles, tasks, and a timetable for your work. When you do, you honor your clients' internal capacity, demonstrate your respect for their intelli-gence and motivation, and promote their sense of mastery. Setting goals gives your clients impetus to carry on, direction for the future, and satisfaction in their own accomplishment as they move forward.

Believing

A strong belief in the process of therapy, coupled with a strong be-lief in the purposefulness of clients' unique responses to their trauma, undergirds the success of your work. It is crucial to encourage clients to be active rather than passive participants in the process. You en-hance their esteem for themselves when you show appreciation for their proceeding, and when you recognize and identify the ways in which they accept responsibility for their choices and actions. As I have continually mentioned, when you strive to create a meaningful and reliable relationship, one of mutual exploration and examination, clients come to recognize and appreciate their own uniqueness, come to believe in themselves as you believe in yourself and the process of therapy.

Creating Safety

For clients to master their lives, internal conflicts, and external frustration, you must meet their basic needs for security and affirma-tion. Building a safe house, the central dynamic of relationship, pro-vides them a context that is conducive to their facing the challenge of self-discovery. It also promotes taking ownership for themselves, their decisions, their mistakes, and most important, their triumphs. Clients are willing to exert great effort and endure considerable hardship when they sense your respect for and interest in them. You establish trust where it was shattered. Join them in celebrating their refusal to give up.

Taking an Active Stance

Move away from a neutral stance. That is, in addition to an attitude of positive regard, be actively caring and supportive, perhaps even vulnerable yourself. Challenge their belief systems, confront their self-destructive choices, and constantly provide options and alternative perspectives. This arouses and reinforces their inner strengths. It dignifies them. Breadth in viewpoint, genuine respect, and collaboration with clients effectively interrupts dysfunctional patterns.

Remind clients that their range of choices is greater in the present than it was in the past. It is essential to let them know that their range of choices in the future will be that much greater as they come to terms with themselves and rely on their inner resources. When you notice and explicitly point out clients' successes, their sense of mastery is activated. That sense empowers them and engenders a desire to grow, perhaps even to soar.

Confrontation

When there is a discrepancy between what your clients say and what they do, what they say in the present and what they have said in the past, between their visible pain and their silence, or any discrepancy for that matter, raise it directly. Even though it is risky, it keeps both of you honest. Often, it is through such confrontation that the beginning of true insight and change occurs both in your therapeutic relationship and in your clients' lives.

Overall, then, it seems that concentrating on the aspiring and positive aspects of clients and their capacity for choice, providing a climate conducive to deep exploration of self, building a relationship that is simultaneously safe and challenging, and continually exercising clients' capacity all converge to increase treatment effectiveness in working with trauma.

PART IV:
CUSTOMIZING AND CULMINATING
THE CONFIGURATION
FOR STABILITY AND GROWTH

Chapter 12

Creative Ways
of Capturing the Life Story

For this is the journey that men make: to find themselves. If they
fail in this, it doesn't matter much what else they find.

James Michener

. . . and if you are not certain who you are, you should realize that
finding this out is one of the most important jobs in your life.

Pete Seeger

THE LIFE STORY

Your clients' life stories give you and them access to regularities
and patterns of being and reacting and give both of you an appreciation of the interconnectedness of all events and responses. When clients tell you their life stories, they are confirming their reality, their
existence. Take them seriously. Explore "uneventful" as well as dramatic happenings. Be as fascinated with the ordinary as with the col-
orful. Seemingly marginal and minimal events reflect the person as
much as the outstanding ones do. Often mundane experience opens
the door to special drama.

Clients cannot be understood nor understand themselves without
knowing something of where they have been. Everything they do relates to everything they have done. It behooves you, therefore, to take
full measure of clients' constantly evolving life stories to give meaning and perspective to the helping process. Life stories provide path-

ways connecting the multiple factors, past and present, that influence clients and serve as a source for discovering something fundamental about their identity. Clients' personal life stories offer you incisive composites of their positive capacities and abilities, a chance to support them further.

The life story is certainly not a set of facts revealing historical truth. It is a narrative that sharply focuses attention on obscure patterns in clients' lives and their construction of reality, which helped them make sense out of their lives.

In telling you their life stories, clients reveal the fabric, structure, emotional substance, and themes of their lives, adding dimension to your understanding of their special way of processing, integrating, and differentiating experience. The aim is not to dig up the past for its own sake, not to reconstruct an exact replica of the past, nor to paint a picture of the past contained in the present. Such an approach would reduce your work to a treasure hunt for past traumatic incidents; indeed, it seems neither possible nor necessarily desirable to do this. If locating original traces is not the aim, what then is the purpose of so close a review of life stories?

Clients and you access the multifaceted, dynamic interplay among a vast array of factors—maturational, developmental, constitutional, and environmental. Examining them puts into perspective the effects of antecedent circumstances, determinants, and traumas on clients' current conflicts and behavioral difficulties. It promotes a far-reaching and profound portrait of clients' personality, makeup, fears, achievements, and disappointments. It helps to ascertain clients' sense of connections between the inner and outer life, the continuity of past, present, and future, as well as their transformation capacity— that is, their reaction to disruptions, vicissitudes, conflicts, restrictions, and constrictions. It gives a vision of their interpretation or misinterpretation of resistance patterns, symptom formation, and the ability to change. All of this is seen in light of their future goals, aspirations, and dreams. A rich repertoire of affects shaping and modifying clients emerges to distinguish them as unique persons.

Clients shed light on interfamilial dynamics, on the protagonists and antagonists in their lives, and on the effect and extent of these influences. In giving you such a closeup of interaction with caretakers, life stories offer a peek at the foundation for the transferential relationship. In brief, life stories supply the tissue that connects and guides your thinking and intervention. They anchor the helping process, giving it boundary and direction. They provide you and clients, at the same time, with a greater opportunity to draw upon that knowledge in the change effort.

Because the life story is such an inextricably interwoven composite of ongoing biopsychosocial elements, it is never possible to capture a complete picture of all there is to be known. How, then, can you see clients in the fullest possible way? What makes it possible for you to capture a relatively complete and cohesive picture through the active participation of clients as their own biographical historians? Encouraging them to narrate their life stories in their own way prompts reactivation, recall, and a sense of continuity of the life story over time. How clients tell about their intricacies, memories, triumphs, and defeats gives access to the actual life drama. How they process the subtleties of omission, discrepancy, distortion, and interruption contributes to a greater knowledge of transitions across the life cycle.

As they tell you their life stories, lines of communication open and insight is gained that reverberates within the helping process and in clients' interactions outside the process. Furthermore, the interest you display in the life story is a form of gratification for them that furthers your alliance. Clients' subjective accounts of the life story provide you with a schemata or template of the significant variables in their experience. It helps them to recover and reclaim perhaps long-forgotten bits and pieces of their pasts that were major milestones in their lives.

Your clients witness at first hand their distinguishing internal psychic apparatus—temperament, constitution, defenses, drives—juxtaposed against external forces—economic, cultural, religious—that mold and modify them. Life stories highlight the way in which stresses of daily life are handled, a sense of the self-concept, and thought processes.

Your clients come to understand that they are not at the mercy of random forces, but are able, to a significant extent, to alter their understanding of their histories. Spence (1982) pointed out that the objective allowing clients the opportunity to tell their stories is not "veridical historical knowledge, as such, but rather the construction of narrative truth in the service of coherence, continuity and understanding" (p. 137). He proposes further that such efforts to assign context and meaning to remembered experiences literally change the face of historical truth. The evolvement of the life story plumbs deeply and frees understanding; it is a reworking of the life script and, therefore, promotes healing and provides a new synthesis of clients' biography. Actions, emotions, and ideas are continually reevaluated and reintegrated. It revises the sense of identity and changes the plot that is vital for continued adaption and maintenance of a cohesive self (Fox, 1983). Another way of putting it is to analogize the telling of the life story to "replaying tapes from the past." Replaying tapes from the past makes it possible for clients to edit them, splice sections, add new segments, and, if not delete or erase portions, at least eliminate excessive static or noise and, overall, create a very different tape.

Clients' life stories, told in their natural language and style, give clues to their internal processes, both conscious and unconscious, of deletion and distortion. Understanding what portions or factors are deleted or distorted improves assessment and guides intervention.

Specifically inviting clients to tell stories is based on a positive expectation of change. It does not envision clients as fixed entities whose form can be analyzed once and for all. It envisions clients as capable of continual revision, refinement, and forward movement. Indeed, in the very telling of their life stories, clients alter them.

Significant Elements in the Life Story

We all create stories about the way we are or the way reality is. Drew's story is one illustration.

Drew, whose mother was distant in childhood, did not like to feel his need for emotional contact because it was too painful and frustrating. He explained his rejection of this need to himself by creating a story he lived by: "Women are not emotionally available. You can never trust them. I will never need a woman."

In relationships with women, Drew would oppose his own need. He would hold back from them emotionally because he never wanted to be in such a vulnerable position. As a result, women would always leave him because he would not let them connect with him. This confirmed his story, "You can never count on women to be there." His story became a self-fulfilling prophecy—the story created a reality guiding his actions, which, in turn, reinforced the story.

Even though Drew's story led to increased frustration, at least it was for him a picture of reality that was familiar and known. It made him feel comfortable and secure. Simply being present to the unraveling of his story helped him settle down and examine his experience.

He discovered that he did not have to hold on to the story to survive and that awareness did not destroy him. Drew gradually learned to trust me as a guide to the unknown and to fresh experiences of self and others. With this trust, he began to relinquish the old story, engage with women in new ways, and thereby construct a new life story. Figure 12.1 depicts the array of significant elements contained in Drew's and in all life stories as they are told in the "now."

Life stories are a composite of past, present, and future as well as conscious and unconscious phenomena that affect clients' lives. The "now," as told in life stories, is a product of the past, as revealed unconsciously in dreams and hidden conflicts and consciously in memories, family myths, and religious and cultural imprints; of the present, as experienced every day in relationships, actions, and feelings; and of the future, as conveyed in expectations, aspirations, and wishes.

GUIDELINES FOR DISCOVERING THE LIFE STORY

How can life stories become an integral part of the helping process? How can they be expanded upon? How can they be more than a

FIGURE 12.1. Dynamics of the Life Story

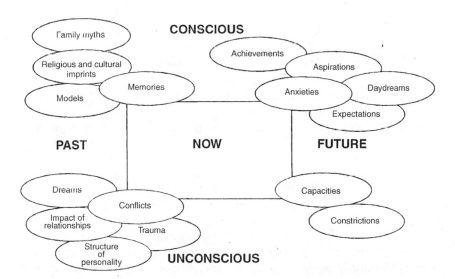

static or sterile exercise? How can they be stereoscopic rather than stereotypic?

Unfolding life stories is a joint endeavor. To obtain meaningful history, be actively involved in a joint exploration with clients. There is no ready-made formula. Uncovering life stories cannot be reduced to rules. Do not follow a rigid or preconceived pattern to which the clients' narratives must conform. Be flexible. Offer clients latitude in selecting natural ways of telling their stories. Give them general guidelines or suggestions. Explain what is relevant. Do not direct them, but rather invite them to tell you their stories in their own way. Such a commonsense approach is resourceful and humane. It also motivates clients to share their innermost selves.

Clients may respond quite easily and readily to your invitation. If they do not, do not be alarmed. There are other, less threatening ways to elicit them. Some of these are discussed in chapters 1, 4, 5, 7, 11, 12, 13, and 14.

These general guidelines may assist you in maximally encouraging clients to tell their stories:

1. Be simple and succinct in giving direction: overcomplicated instructions becloud the process.
2. Explain directly what information is desired.
3. Be alert to and enlist clients' unique style of storytelling and build upon it.
4. Proceed slowly and with care: neither rush nor force.
5. Strike a balance between when to lay back and when to prompt: it is only necessary to interrupt a spontaneous flow when clients are getting lost.
6. Give encouragement, being neither too gratifying nor too frustrating.
7. Help bring together the varied threads in an orderly manner (Fox, 1983).

TWO CREATIVE METHODS
FOR CAPTURING THE LIFE STORY

Two quite different but nevertheless effective methods of eliciting the life story are the family tree or genogram and a personal inventory. Depending upon the clients' and your own style, these can be employed in unison or independently of one another to supplement your face-to-face verbal work with clients. They do not have to serve as adjuncts but with uncommunicative clients can be the exclusive or principle vehicle for communicating. They are nonthreatening methods for eliciting clients' perspectives on events, feelings, people, internal responses, dreams, day-to-day events, and much more. They have the advantage of allowing clients to unload emotional baggage. They are not a substitute for therapeutic interaction but additional means to narrate the life story. Since human behavior is so complex, your efforts to change it require that you draw upon as many sources of information and as many strategies as possible.

The Family Tree:
Locating the Roots of the Life Story

Especially because of the interplay among family interaction, family role, and personality development, utilization of the genogram or family tree can maximize the effectiveness of individual and family intervention. Since clients' histories are constantly evolving and growing, they are frequently elusive. The family tree provides a diagram of a family over a few generations that grounds repeating family likenesses and patterns (McGoldrick and Gerson, 1985). It furnishes a clear picture of clients' nuclear families and the background of their formative experiences. The family tree continually grows; it is not so absorbed with past roots that it neglects to notice present modifications and branches. It creates an organic representation of relationships among family members—patterns of closeness, distance, conflict—and it delineates boundaries, structures, and operating principles (McGoldrick and Gerson, 1985). It also gives access to cultural, ethnic, socioeconomic, and religious influences. Constructing a family tree together with the client, you can gain an understanding of the origin and development of the process of internalization and identification that determine projections enacted by the client in current transactions.

Constructing the family tree together with clients is a felicitous way of beginning work together, because it neutralizes the tension of self-exposure and the onus of self-blame. It reduces the stigma of getting help. Emphasis is placed on the ecological context rather than on the troubled individual. It reduces the sense of vulnerability and permits deeper reflection on the problematic interpersonal framework so that it can be altered. The family tree can continue to grow throughout your work together. A more expanded discussion of its relevance to family and individual assessment and diagnosis appears in Chapter 10.

The very process of scaling a family tree with clients is as meaningful as the information it conveys. The aim of the family tree is to formulate an overview of the dynamics and subtleties of role performance, interfamilial attachments, and repetitive patterns. It is most illuminating, and perhaps even enjoyable, for both the client and yourself, especially when it follows clients' spontaneous musings, with you serving merely as a coach at times. You can be effective when simply following heuristic hunches—interjecting remarks, making comments, asking for clarification.

Although Chapter 10 elaborates on the use of the genogram in family assessment, the following brief example illustrates the usefulness of a family tree in helping to understand and intervene to "unstick" a troubled female client.

Paula, a twenty-seven-year-old banking executive, sought help for her "sexual unresponsiveness." In an unconsummated marriage of four years, Paula and her husband, both ostensibly wanting children, were referred by their family physician for marital counseling. Paula's husband refused to participate in the process. Paula was distraught and self-blaming about her husband's unhappiness, but was unable to state this clearly and directly. She spoke haltingly only of a dissatisfying and dismaying sexual relationship. While she presented a clinical picture of vaginismus, most frequently treated by behavioral techniques, the phobia had a deeper, more remote and hidden underlayer that required exploration; yet Paula persistently resisted talking about her history, very likely because she felt it would manifest information she felt a need to suppress. I suggested that we construct a family tree. This seemed sufficiently neutral, even intriguing to Paula. She agreed and was motivated to proceed.

Figure 12.2 shows an extended main branch of her family tree, yielding the repeated cycle of broken relationships. The genogram or family tree makes compelling what words only allude to—the unusual and uncharacteristic pattern of separations and divorces.

As we worked on and talked about her family tree together, it soon became apparent that Paula, the youngest of four siblings, was entwined in an intergenerational but disguised family ban on intimate relationships. Her two older brothers were each divorced twice; her

FIGURE 12.2. Paula's Family Tree

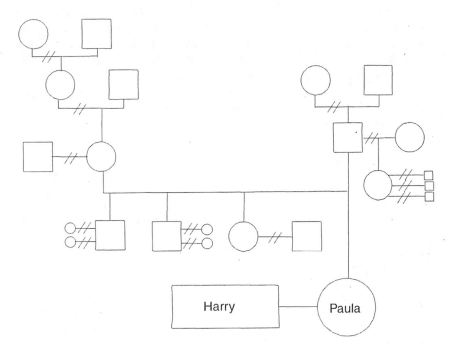

stepsister was divorced three times and her natural sister was in the process of a divorce. Her mother and father had been married prior to their own union, and, in turn, both of them came from split families. This was extremely unusual for that earlier generation. In each situation, as she tearfully described it, there was rancor and pervasive distrust in the relationships. The impermanence of relationships, a view of them as fragile and crumbling, led to recognition of her own conflict around attachments and abandonment; her ambivalence toward her father and, subsequently, her husband; and repressed fear, anger, hostility, and guilt about fantasized incestuous experiences. Recognizing that her sexual dysfunction was a means of symbolically expressing and sustaining a family pattern that she had internalized, she was able to make inroads on altering the self-defeating behavior that was manifesting sexually.

The family tree provided an important breakthrough for Paula and for me. It enabled both of us to get past the circumscribed presenting problem—vaginismus—which, if taken at face value, would have been treated quite differently. Looking at a broader, more enriched picture of her family made possible a more accurate, inclusive, and comprehensive assessment of the situation. At the same time, it provided a means for deepened understanding and examination of the lineage associated with the problem. The mutual endeavor, understanding the life story, opened up channels of communication in the initial stage, improved assessment, decreased resistance, and propelled us toward further work at resolution. Paula recognized that she saw her life through a filter of distortions.

The Life Inventory: Registering the Story

Another effective means of gathering data, especially in the initial phase of work, is to provide clients with a written inventory of questions and statements to guide them in recalling and then detailing their personal stories. I use this method as a stimulus for ongoing reflection; it is not merely a one-shot attempt to gather history. Instead, it offers clients some cues for approaching and flexibly relating their life stories. A series of comments or statements, some of which are amplified upon later, are intended to trigger clients' reflections about themselves and their situation and to guide them in writing an autobiographical narrative.

This inventory, unlike other standardized formats proposed by some authors or mandated in some agencies, does not straight-jacket a *post dictum* account in a rigid fashion. For example, Lazarus and Lazarus' (1991) Multimodal Life Inventory is a comprehensive, extensive, and inclusive questionnaire. It elicits in questionnaire fashion demographic information, a personal and social history, description of problems, clients' analysis of problems, feelings, thoughts, images, relationships, biological factors, and a structural profile. However, it poses a formidable and overwhelming task, particularly for confused and troubled clients and for those in crisis. My approach to the utilization of the inventory is more flexible. I suggest at the initial interview that the client take home the mimeographed inventory to peruse. The statements are instructions in themselves, insofar as they give clients an idea of the type of information I consider relevant to our ongoing work. It is, more significantly, a stimulant for them to recount reactions or responses in whatever way they wish. The writing helps to evoke memories, fantasies, and dreams, which remain unrecognized when not deliberately expressed. Putting thoughts and feelings into writing captures the ephemeral. It better promotes penetrating critical appraisal by the client and you.

No single set of statements is uniformly or universally helpful, either to clients or to clinicians. I developed the ones I use over time, and I continually revise them. You have your own theoretical orientation, method, style, and experience to guide your development of an inventory of statements or questions. It is important to remember that the inventory is intended to be suggestive, not absolute.

Just as there is no single set of statements that is uniformly helpful, there is no single way of responding to it. While some clients write out their responses discursively in notebooks, some clients choose other ways to express themselves. For example, one client wrote an epic about himself in rhymed couplets. Another client sang her responses. More than one client, wanting to answer more spontaneously than they felt writing allowed, spoke their responses directly into an audio recorder. This method makes it possible to hear their pauses, sighs, tears, laughter, etc., as they tell the story. It truly exposes much more of them.

Try not to let your own style interfere with the way clients naturally talk about themselves. When you are flexible, you not only facilitate the flow of vital information, but you give clients a rare opportunity to talk freely about themselves and give yourself the opportunity to see them in action doing so.

I ask clients to choose the order in which to answer the statements as it best suits their own situation and personality. Too, they are at liberty to find the method of responding that is most comfortable and effective for them. Clients are encouraged to pose and answer their own questions as well. If you are required by agency policy or governmental regulation to use a particular standardized format or questionnaire, employ it imaginatively. For example, hand clients one copy to examine while you fill out the second; allow clients to complete the form themselves at home; permit them to select the sequence and take responsibility for answering. There is nothing magical, mysterious, or secret about the need for historical data. In the long run, clients are the only ones who can provide accurate information anyway. When they are involved as fully as possible in sharing it, they are more apt to paint a full and clear picture.

Whether clients be individuals, couples, or families, they are asked to complete the inventory. A remarkable result of its use by couples and families goes beyond the stimulus it provides for reflecting on self-providing a clearer view of clients' dynamic counterpoint.

My own inventory, revised over time, is presently composed of twenty-seven statements. A selected few appear here. Later in this chapter, three statements and the responses from three separate clients, including one couple, illustrate how the answers reflect clients' differing and unique styles of being and reacting. Here are five sample statements:

7. Describe your feelings about your life during childhood, teens, and early adulthood.
21. Describe your present situation.
22. Describe the significant others in your life.
23. As you consider the whole experience of answering these statements, what insights, feelings, or questions have emerged?
26. Daydream! What are the most meaningful ways you see yourself living in the future? What are some of the things you would like to accomplish for the future? Don't consider whether they are possible. Just daydream and record them.

These representative statements stimulate clients to muse about their past, present, and future. They often come to appreciate the interconnection of all three time frames as they respond. Moreover, their account provides an avenue for your deeper exploration and examination. When you utilize a tool such as this inventory, have it reflect your clients' needs, patterns, and life situations as well as your own theoretical orientation and style. You might want to include other purposeful and open-ended questions, such as: What happened recently that led to your seeking therapy? What are various ways that you have attempted to solve this problem on your own? What factors may interfere with the problem occurring? What did you tell yourself about taking a new direction in your life? If a miracle happened, how would your problem be solved? How will you know when you don't need to come here anymore? What have you been doing to keep this situation from becoming worse? If I saw you in a video after you solved your problem, what would I see? What advice would you give me to help you out? What might be a warning signal that things are starting to slide backward?

Following are three statements with actual responses from three different clients. Their particular and different ways of responding demonstrate not only the rich and varied ways they perceive and define themselves and their experiences, but also illustrate the value of the inventory in providing information and in sustaining the work.

The following minimal background is provided only to orient you to the three clients. I believe that you will find that their own statements paint an amazingly intimate, rich, and accurate portrayal of them. Client A is a recreation counselor seeking assistance in coming to grips with two outstanding issues. He described the first as "staying too long" in his present job, where he kept "pouring himself out" without getting anything in return. He commented that "staying too long" was a familiar pattern to him. He enunciated the second issue as "getting the guts" to marry a woman fifteen years his junior, who had been a participant in a recreation group he led.

Clients B and C are unmarried partners. They came seeking couples counseling. They were gravely concerned about their increasing emotional estrangement following the birth of their son. They approached this transition in their lives very differently and found themselves unable even to converse with each other about it. They could not bridge the gap produced by their opposite styles of coping. Their responses to the inventory are particularly fascinating, since the manner of their responses, combined with the content, sharply pinpoints the very conflicts and differences that caused them distress and brought them for help in the first place.

Incidentally, client B's responses to the inventory occupied three typewritten pages; his partner C filled nine typewritten pages with her remarks.

Statement 1: Describe yourself.

Client A.

> I am a sensitive thirty-one-year-old man. From thirteen to eighteen I was in the seminary and since that time I have devoted my life to working with young people. I have overworked to limit my personal life and now have a few close friends in whom I confide completely and many acquaintances but few people I

socialize with regularly. I take criticisms to heart, I sometimes feel bad about myself even when criticism is wrong. I worry about things for which I am responsible so am therefore rarely remiss in my duties, but I have great trouble relaxing. I am not outgoing and therefore do not socialize quickly. I take friendships and commitments very seriously; I am ambitious to the extent that I like to do a good job and be the boss, or at least be independent. But I become anxious in competitive situations.

Client B.

Forty. Aging hippie. Precise. Mind for detail. Continually trying to understand the world, unify conflicting ideas. Thoughtful and considerate. Strong willed.

Client C.

The answer would vary considerably by the day. Today I'm tired but feel some accomplishment so there are mixed feelings about who I am. I am a woman of thirty-eight who appears younger. A new mother who works at home at two different jobs. I reach for different things with medium success. One friend described me as "caring so much and trying so damned hard." I would describe myself as worrying more than caring and as being too fearful to try enough.

Statement 13: Describe the atmosphere of the home where you grew up.

Client A.

We did not have much money so we lived thriftily. My father worked hard, often at two jobs, to improve our economic situation. My parents were strict Catholics and they were about twenty when I was born. They were loving with me and saw that I was well disciplined. My mother's side of the family was Irish and they were less affectionate than my father's Italian/French culture. We spent much time together and although I was an only child for seven years I was not spoiled because we lived simply. There was not any arguing or fighting or even friction between my parents.

Client B.

Many homes; many atmospheres. Until nineteen, lived with mother. Only child until eleven. Pseudo father for younger brother. Both parents married twice. Mother divorced twice, father once. Up and down the socioeconomic ladder; ranging from upper to lower middle class. Apartments, near mansions.

Client C.

From eight to thirteen our home was my mother and sister, both of which worked. Then ten of the twenty-three years at home, it was just my mother and I. The atmosphere was usually quiet as I was most often alone. But we always had animals and there was love and the three or two of us together. We spent a great deal of time sitting at the kitchen table but not usually eating. We all cooked for ourselves, which usually amounted to toast or TV dinners. My mother instilled the belief that one could always work to make things better and that one always should. My big Christmas present when I was twelve was a sewing machine so I could make my own clothes which I did.

Statement 24: What are the major priorities, goals, dreams, and frustrations of your life right now? How would you see them changing over the next few years?

Client A.

I am now concerned with changing from devoting my life to service to others at the expense of my own health to building a healthy personal life. My own happiness is a priority. I no longer want to be content with making others happy. I want to marry and have a family of my own. I want to stop taking on impossible tasks and do a good job with something manageable. Since I am in love with Peggy I want to marry her, help her get her career going if that is her wish, have a family if and when we see it being right for us, and devote my energies to us. Now I am spread too thin. I'm tired and burned out. I live too much through others. I am happiest when with Peggy.

Client B.

No response recorded.

Client C.

> To make more of my life with B. Occupying myself with work and caring for my child. I've shelved those personal needs and desires. But they are what determine the quality of life. I very much want a happy home which to me is an enjoyable, loving environment with good society from within and without. I would like financial security and to ensure I can provide the same for my children and family. The dream is tied with my frustration. It is a dream to produce a grand movie. I am afraid I will not be strong enough to meet and foresee the all-encompassing producer's duties. I have to learn to deal fearlessly with the powerful personalities I am tied to. Too often I act like the little girl, the sweet darling looking to please her potentially wrathful parents. When I am through with the first picture I will know whether I want to continue that arduous career or go on to something else entirely. My work at _____ is just what I call "bread and butter work." I would like to not need it anymore.

The life stories or autobiographies of clients based on this inventory have been invaluable in fathoming history and in forming differential diagnoses and a relationship that served as the foundation of further exploration and change. Life stories offer penetrating glimpses into clients' lives and often unexpected insights that advance the helping process. Furthermore, at termination, they provide the clients' own "before" picture against which to assess the "after" picture.

Client A, as was his choice from the outset, remained in the helping situation for only three months. Therefore, the inventory was instrumental, especially in light of this imposed time limit, in making it possible for him and me to quickly specify and address problem areas and long-standing dysfunctional patterns. His responses revealed other problems involving self-esteem and internal conflict; he did not choose to work on these even though they were in evidence. In the case of couple B and C, lines of communication were opened between them as they shared their responses to the inventory in interviews with me. They used their responses as starting points to launch in-depth discussion of themselves, their backgrounds, and their own relationship. Meeting over a period of approximately eighteen months, B and C's direct responses to the inventory told much about them but, more interestingly, led to our traveling along informative and intriguing side paths. For example, taking these detours together helped bridge their treacherous emotional gap. B, who did not "talk," was able to revise his terse and sardonic fashion of interaction with C. He came to realize that his very manner, coupled with his offering pithy and practical "little lessons," served no purpose other than to make C feel rejected. Although being rational was for him the loving thing to do, it was not seen that way by C. C learned to curtail her frustrated ramblings, which, in her attempt to make contact with B, ended up having the opposite effect. He would become more rational and distant from her. She, doing what she considered the loving thing, "reaching out," cut him off. He, reacting to her "unreasonableness," would become more impatient and closed. An impasse would typically occur, leading to total alienation, conflict, and unhappiness. This destructive pattern of interaction was interrupted as they exchanged and discussed their responses to the inventory statements.

A critical component of enhancing their bond was to obtain from the inventories an insider's view of each other's "life script." They came to recognize their own residual "stuff" from past experiences, triggered in the present situation. This led to dreadful reexperiencing of earlier pain, as if it truly existed in the present situation. Indeed, they saw how they fashioned this relationship to reproduce old scripts. Their roles changed after perceiving their parts in what they referred to as "this terrible circle." Reviewing the inventory facilitated interaction and the expression of affects, freeing them to hear and act on suggestions for experimenting with alternative modes of interrelating. Each also came to appreciate the special assets and unique worldview of the other.

For clients A, B, and C, as for many others, the family tree and inventory have made it possible to capture and encapsulate the uniqueness of their language, skills, and perspectives. The "structure" of the inventory, paradoxically, frees them and you for spontaneous interaction.

When Clients Do Not Respond

When a client declines to utilize the inventory, accept this noncompliance as yet another message about the client. Respect it. Meredith,

For example, a forty five year-old secretary, who had suffered multiple losses and trauma throughout her life, delayed responding to the inventory in writing. Although avid in maintaining a journal and fastidious in keeping her appointments, she was fearful of committing her thoughts and feelings to paper, fearing that doing so would reawaken past agonizing losses. She explained early on that just reviewing the inventory was excruciating. It dredged up painful memories of her mother's torturous death when Meredith was a young teen, her father's abandonment of her soon after, her many spontaneous abortions, and her husband's multiple and violent suicide attempts, as well as a host of other tormenting incidents. Over two years of regular contact, she continually alluded to the inventory and to the fact that she had not "done it," but would "someday." This having been said, Meredith would generally proceed to elaborate verbally upon an inventory statement as it pertained to a current dilemma or issue in her life. She not only responded de facto to the inventory, but as explained in Chapter 15, provided me with her handwritten version of the inventory at our last session, commenting, "this is now all past history."

Chapter 13

The Written Word:
Enriching Your Work

Our subjectivity is our true home, our natural state, and our necessary place of refuge and renewal. It is the font of creativity, the stage for imagination, the drafting table for planning, and the ultimate heart of our fears and hopes, our sorrows and satisfactions. For too long we have dismissed the subjective as ephemeral and of little consequence; as a result we have lost our center and been magnetically drawn to the shallow harbors and arid beaches of unrelieved objectivity.

James Bugental

While a poor therapist can conceivably do more harm than good, journal writing has the lowest risk factor imaginable, psychically as well as financially, providing you with the gentlest and safest therapies; at any given point, you reveal only as much of yourself as your comfort level permits.

Marlene Schiwy

Writing about oneself, others, and events is a powerful resource for gaining perspective. Noting personal history and identifying, understanding, and appreciating our patterns and needs helps us to realize our strengths and fulfill our dreams. Because of this, writing can be a valuable supplement to the helping process, stimulating self-observation and encouraging self-disclosure. I consider the journal as a container, a safe house, as it were, for all our wounds and triumphs. This chapter demonstrates the multifaceted and flexible use of writing for you and clients to add synergistically to verbal therapy, and offers illustrative examples to demonstrate its efficacy.

Up to this point we have intuited that writing eases pain, emotional as well as physical. But there is now mounting scientific evidence that writing can reduce psychological distress and can also literally reverse the effects of physical symptoms associated with rheumatism, asthma, and arthritis. It has been shown to be of considerable value in dealing with clients afflicted with Alzheimer's disease and those devastated by unemployment. The simplicity of a journal's blank pages allows both your clients and you to bring forth a creation that honors one's uniqueness.

CLIENT WRITING

Logging

Since time restrictions limit either the depth or breadth of exploration in each face-to-face encounter with clients, writing in a log provides continuity to the work and can be used in a variety of ways. Entries can be assigned or free expression encouraged. Open-ended, directed, or semistructured, the log facilitates your access to clients' memories, dreams, and everyday events. Clients' recorded reflections on content already discussed during sessions, or newly presented, amplify understanding for them and for you. Logging, therefore, continues the momentum of your work outside the formal structure of the interview, sustaining interest and focus in the helping process (Fox, 1982).

When a client brings you his or her log, draw from it in a non-constrained and creative way. For example, you might read it at the beginning of your session as background, concentrate on it exclusively, or not refer to it at all. You might select portions of it to discuss further or put it aside to peruse at another time. How you use it depends upon the circumstances of your immediate exchange with the client. I introduce the idea of logkeeping in the initial interview, explaining its purpose and asking that in his or her first entry the client record impressions, questions, omissions, concerns, or whatever else comes to mind about our initial contact. This early use of the log familiarizes the client with logkeeping and provides valuable data in itself; more important, the way the client approaches logkeeping guides you in its differential use. If clients choose not to use the log, it is never forced, always discussed. The log provides an added perspective on clients' situations because, progressive and cumulative, it furnishes instant history and instant participation and allows both of you to examine progress at different stages of the helping process.

Finding Oneself Through a Scrapbook

The log can take many forms—concise outline, lengthy letter, essay, scattered phrases or words. The way clients express themselves offers a transparency of their life projected onto the page. For Peter, a fourteen-year-old in foster care placement nearly all his life, the log, or "scrapbook" as he called it, became a declaration of his identity. Shifted among eight foster homes within twelve years, he was referred for help because of "poor memory," poor self-esteem, and presenting an elusive quality of being "lost." As we talked about his keeping a log, he proposed the idea of starting a scrapbook where he could organize the photographs and mementos that he secreted in many different places. In the course of our slowly, yet methodically, compiling a scrapbook together, Peter was able to piece together the fragments of his life as he gathered all the disparate pieces into a unified whole. He was able, thereby, to clarify his memory of events and himself. As time progressed, the scrapbook became a sourcebook of his milestones. It included snapshots, baseball cards, ticket stubs, library cards, official documents, and other keepsakes, all with significant memory traces that he was able to recollect as they were glued in. Because they all helped set him apart and define who he was, the scrapbook enabled him to find himself and to build a self-image. Peter was able to repair a fractured ego and establish an identity by working with me on creating his scrapbook and by expressing his thoughts and feelings.

An interesting variation on the scrapbook is the Fatherbook. As described by Holman (1998), the Fatherbook enhances therapeutic work with father-absent early adolescent boys. It is modeled on the life storybook used with children in foster care, providing information, thoughts, and feelings about absent fathers and ultimately a tangible object with which the child can begin to work through the experiences of being fatherless.

Diajournaling: A Play for Self-Discovery

Another way to express deep feelings is to write about them in the form of a dialogue. Imagine the voice of another person, or your own

Inner voice conversing with you. Capture the exchange on paper, Carol, an aspiring actress, sought help for severe anxiety attacks, a sense of incompetence, and sexual unresponsiveness. She chose to unleash her thoughts and images in the log in the form of dramatic dialogue. The dialogue, as she wrote it, resembled a play script, which facilitated expressing the conflict between her expansive needs and rigid conscience. She soon recognized that the dialogue represented polarities of her inner self. Fascinated by her own early discoveries, she played out these scripted roles. Eventually able to articulate and clarify her ambivalence and dichotomous modes of acting, Carol emerged with better understanding of her long-standing problems and sexual freezing. Finally she discovered that these polarities were her inner scared child's attempt to fathom her mother's desertion and father's sexual abuse, and at last she could relinquish her self-blame and deprecation.

Although it might be argued that some clients might misuse the log to avoid and rationalize, this has not been my experience. When it is employed with discretion, it leads to remarkably intensive self-analysis and honest disclosure (Fox, 1982).

Open-Ended Discovery:
Amplifying a Family Focus

An open-ended log often helps to loosen the constraints that have been built up for those whose fantasy life is minimal, who hesitate to let their imaginations run free, or who ignore inner irrational visions or intuition. Stream-of-consciousness entries enable these clients to gradually unfold and subsequently recognize and accept other than rational resources. Very often, paradoxically, for those with an excessive need for order and structure and little tolerance for ambiguity, as well as for those who have difficulty in relaxing and contacting and observing a spontaneous flow of thoughts, feelings, or images, the log provides impetus for less constrained expression during face-to-face interviews (Fox, 1982).

With one highly intellectual male, Jim, who denied and vigorously fought against the possible existence of any irrationality in his life, standard "talking" methods were employed during regular contacts to help him uncover suppressed and repressed feelings, but to no avail. It was only after Jim rambled in his log that he gained access to information and feelings of a more emotional nature. Logging reduced intellectualization and brought him closer to his experience.

Initial entries were suggested to Jim. One of his first entries was to trace his family's genealogy, to locate and discover his roots. Stimulated by this essay, he discovered some important clues to his relationship with his father, an abstemious, closed, and aloof immigrant. Writing freed Jim's associations and encouraged him to recall dreams and "log them in." (He first denied ever having dreams and then claimed to have forgotten them.) Over time, he was able to remember dreams, first in fragments, then in their entirety. He recorded them in the log, which helped him plumb an underlying and repressed concern about the nature of his relationship with his father. This was explored in depth over many sessions as he continued to turn away from logical, sequentially ordered thinking toward freer contact with experience and feeling.

Jim eventually recorded a dream of entering a tunnel where he met an older man halfway, a dream rather clearly connected with facing his father. In successively dealing with the unfolding dream, he surfaced inner conflicts laden with rage. Over time, the continual analysis of the appearance of his father in dreams, either literally or symbolically, allowed him to ventilate and explore his rage and its sources.

The log promoted examination of this powerful material, which might otherwise have remained repressed, and certainly would not have surfaced as intensively in so short a time.

Themed Journal Entries

The following three entries show how Hal, Jay, and Bill, three adult sons in search of their fathers, used writing in their journals to gain insights into their fathers and, thereby, into themselves. Hal, Jay, and Bill had very different backgrounds and viewpoints, but all shared in a struggle to make themselves whole by searching for explanations of their respective fathers' attitudes and behavior toward them. The following excerpts tell it all.

Hal's father died of Creutzfeldt-Jacob disease (CJD), otherwise known as mad cow disease. CJD is a mysterious brain deterioration, characterized by spongy holes in the brain, defying detection until it is too late and flouting any form of treatment. Hal, terrified, had eradicated any thought of it and, therefore, any memory of his father, whom he had adored. In therapy as a result of another possible loss in the form of a divorce after a ten-year marriage, he wanted to rediscover his bond with his father and attempt to fathom multiple deaths that accompanied his father's, including that of his brother-in-law, favorite uncle, and father's best friend. Abandoned by all the men in his life, he was bereft.

> I was talking to a friend at work today about my dad [who had recently died of mad cow disease]. After describing my dad's life to Harry I again realize what an extraordinary life he had. My dad was totally on his own from age thirteen on, fought for the partisans in WWII, lost his inherited property when the borders were moved, and came to the U.S. as a "displaced person." He worked in a factory for wages that were too low yet he raised a happy family and was a smiling happy man until he died. My life has been one of underachieving, discontent and endless pursuit of money. Since I was a child I made a lot of money. I could have everything I wanted and be happy. Obviously I was wrong. . . . I know I can do anything I want in this world yet I feel paralyzed. Why? Why am I so scared? I wish I had him back to talk to. I have discounted him for so long.

Jay, a forty-five-year-old squatter living in an edgy urban neighborhood, left home at sixteen to travel the world—more important, to escape his parents. Having no formal education, yet highly artistic and talented, he had secretly been an unpublished screen writer for many years. Counseling began when his young girlfriend, by ultimatum, forced him into it. Jay nonetheless engaged in therapy and struggled with the feeling of being a "total loser." Here he writes about what he considers to be his father's contribution to his being "stuck."

> . . . the fact that I was out there traveling and doing things eventually began to run me down . . . constructing my personal daymares (nightmares) over and over from a handful of the awful moments I endured in the past that I now magnify and there I am in a myriad of situations struggling to defend myself, winning battles but losing the war because of the fact that my father had no self-esteem and let me grow up in the same low ceilinged room he had where all you learned about the world was that it offered a very great view of the floor.

Bill, in his late thirties, began therapy following a bitter divorce that he rightfully attributed to his alcohol and drug abuse. He had a series of crushing panic attacks. Losing his breath, feeling like he was suffocating, resurrected sensations that awakened recollections of early life experiences, especially involving his father's brutality. His writing eventually led him to uncover massive amounts of cruelty directed by his father, unexplainably, at him. He wrote in the form of "short stories," quasi-fictional versions of the events that caused him so much anguish. It was only in "objectifying" it this way that he was able to tolerate the dreadful remembering.

Anyway, the purpose of this story is to help me find myself. You see my life began to unravel recently for lots of reasons. In my home as a boy violence abounded. My dad was a cop who ruled me and my siblings with his fist and his belt. I had an older brother and a younger one, an older sister and also a younger one. Me and my older brother took most of the beatings. I took the most by a long shot. Growing up was quite chaotic in my family. Friction, disharmony, yelling and screaming, anger and copious violations of everything holy and unholy.

My father never tried stabbing me to death like Uncle Pete once tried doing to his son. . . . My dad would beat the shit out of me and my brother. Usually with his leather belt and sometimes with his hands. He normally needed some provocation, which he got from my mother.

You see I never felt safe as a child in this belligerent environment. This feeling has followed me through my adult life. It has impeded my emotional growth and it's only through looking back and trying to unravel the truth that I may find peace.

Structured Writing

Although I prefer more open-ended, client-directed journal writing, structured journals are helpful means to deal with issues and to supplement face-to-face sessions. Pennebaker (1997) and Cameron and Bryan (1995) suggest quite different formats for undertaking a journal, but both are fairly structured. They have in common the sense that structured entries allow the therapist greater latitude in generalizing about clients. Workbooks, programmed writing lessons, exercises, or preset questions are completed automatically by clients outside the therapy session. Clients stay focused between sessions, assuming a measure of responsibility for themselves, which leads to self-mastery and self-knowledge.

BENEFITS OF LOGGING

The log is particularly helpful for clients whose myopia, rigidity, overcontrol, or impoverished fantasy life preclude deep exploration of their own worlds, because of possible pain, shame, or failure. It allows clients to "walk through" situations, in either retrospect or prospect, tens of times, and loosens the grip of self-constriction. Clients who feel silly or foolish when facing new or unusual experiences recognize the delimiting patterns that have made them reluctant to enter relationships in the past. The log is helpful also to clients who do not acknowledge their own strengths, trust their own capacities, or appreciate their own skills. Just maintaining the log is ego enhancing; it offers a fresh start.

I have found the log to be especially successful with clients who give up too easily or who do not start at all if they do not know the outcome in advance. Likewise, for clients who cling to obsolete coping methods, the log stirs the imagination in novel ways, and to new possibilities—ones clients discover themselves (Fox, 1982).

Poetry: Connecting Past and Present

The log enables both you and clients to probe inner experiences, identify irrational patterns, and find connecting threads between the present and the past. Whatever clients perceive is based in some measure on their background, which the log invariably taps. Although keeping a log is not strictly intended to locate historical sources, it does foster exploration. Entries provide valuable data about the multitude of ingenious strategies clients employ to camouflage troublesome feelings. The form of writing the client selects to express himself or herself speaks volumes, as with Joan, a personnel executive, who sought help for depression after a broken marriage. The breakup rekindled "tapes from the past," as she phrased it, about her self-image. She felt impotent, worthless, and empty and was particularly troubled by her interaction with men. She initially found it very difficult to verbalize her conflicts and pain to me, a man, but was sufficiently comfortable to unleash them in poetry. Verse allowed her to meter her feelings, but to do so in a disciplined way that reined in excessive or too rapid ventilation. At the same time, her poetry provided a poignant depiction of her internal life and hinted at sources of conflict. The following poem is excerpted from Joan's log:

I wish I could say
How hurt I am
In pain but
All I feel is the
Gray, cold walls of canyons
I have
Walked too many times
Before that even
The plains of your face
Are less familiar
And the shadows of your eyes
More strange
I wish I could say I
Miss you but today
It seems the only
Touch I
Really
Know
Is granite
Nightmare fingers
Holding me fast
And hard so often
I could not breathe
But these have stayed
The hours with me
Touched my body when I slept
And now they are become
The hands of my lover
Much more than yours
I wish I could say I
Would even die for you but
I have died so many times for

> So many things I did not know I
> Cannot even count it seems
> Even the ground would say
> What you again

Joan's poem offers a penetrating picture of despair that led, in our face-to-face sessions, to discussing how the experiences in her youth had deadened her emotions and led so frequently to suicidal thoughts. We gained a clearer understanding of a core problem with her husband associated with that of her father. Initial inquiry elicited only a dispassionate statement about early sexual abuse by her father, who permitted, and witnessed, her repeated molestation by his friend. The poem unleashed long-dormant and overwhelming feelings of rage, shame, guilt, and uncleanliness. It drew attention to negative attitudes toward herself and toward men and led us to trace the origins of these feelings back to repressed past experiences of abuse and rejection. I was able, furthermore, to encourage Joan to reach her own interpretations about the relationship with me, promoting a corrective experience that deepened our alliance. Had our contact been restricted to verbal dialogue, and our conversation strictly focused on the presenting issues, it seems unlikely that it would have unfolded as successfully as it did.

Glimpses Back: Documents of Verisimilitude

The following example shows not only how the log was used by Elaine (a thirty-year-old female client whose backgound is discussed in Chapters 9 and 10) as an impetus toward deepened understanding, but how it motivated her to make available journals from adolescence, which, when examined, catapulted the work forward. Elaine's teenage journals provided a slice of time to examine and thereby an increased understanding of her particular dynamics. They pinpointed central problems, ideas, and fantasies.

In and out of therapy for over fifteen years, Elaine welcomed the opportunity to keep a log, having been discouraged by counselors to do so. An exceptionally bright youngster, she had started writing extensively during her preteen years in an effort to clear her mind. When she first entered a psychiatric hospital in her early teens, her therapists discouraged her from writing because they considered it a form of resistance. In her work with me, Elaine welcomed the log.

She wrote about her history and background, and divulged, for the first time, her emotional reactions to past episodes in her life. She shared the entries with me but would talk no further about them. My responsiveness to her entries encouraged her to explore them verbally. More significantly, she entrusted me with a series of unedited childhood diaries she had kept hidden since her lengthy treatment began in adolescence.

Elaine's teenage diaries were filled with thoughts, wishes, and dreams. They provided a rare and vivid picture of everyday events in her life as they occurred. They furnished a glance at her complex history and family dynamics. After thoroughly reading these diaries, I returned them to Elaine, asking her to reread them herself and to make marginal notes of her present associations to them. Our mutual study and discussion of the entries during sessions led us to focus on her relationships with men—her father, ministers, teachers, and former therapists. The following entry concerns her father:

> 12/26/62—Daddy is downstairs throwing a tantrum because no one jumped to turn off the basement light the instant he told them to. Daphne woke up and started to cry. Did he care? No. If he would just be quiet, she would go back to sleep, but he has to keep yelling. If she does get up, he won't have to be the one to take care of her. Sometimes I can't stand him.

The following two more recent entries show Elaine's shift in attitude and feeling:

> 7/4/82—I wish to exclude men from the human race. At first it was only as if they didn't even exist. Then they existed but in some way undefined, nonhuman—more beastlike; then as "people"; now finally as men and often as individual men.

> 11/6/83—Spent last night with Harry. Interaction made me aware of how protective and defensive I am with men and I am, relatively speaking, far more open and relaxed with him. Particularly aware of this physically.

Of course, the value of having these earlier entries was inestimable. They offered a glimpse of how Elaine perceived what was happening in her life as it happened, rather than in retrospect, with its additional distortions of recollection, editing, and selection. This is not to say that there were not distortions in perception at the time of the earlier writings. Distortions are present even as an event occurs, but the secondary distortions of the past as remembered did not muddle reality further. Of course, the distortions themselves are a rich source to tap. Needless to say, the teen journals were a rich lode. Their exploration was a critical dimension of the entire helping process, because they revealed how Elaine's present relationships with men were repetitions of her relationship with her father, which led to still further analysis of her present interactions with men, including me. Focusing on understanding the development of maladaptive interpersonal relationships in the past, she untangled transferential reactions. As she discriminated between the past and the present, her present log, juxtaposed against earlier journals, enabled us to penetrate beneath the surface realities, documenting a shift from suspicion, fear, and bitterness toward men to a greater degree of openness and trust. Exposing her self without repercussions, she gradually exhibited new behavior outside sessions, in her transactions with men. This example illustrates how helpful logging can be in long-term work; it also has considerable merit in short-term treatment, as with José.

Logs in the Short-Term

José, a thirty-two-year-old father of five, twice divorced and living with his lover, was hospitalized for a back injury he sustained from being beaten with a baseball bat by his present lover's husband. After his release from the hospital, pain increased in his back, neck, shoulders, and head. His physician referred him because, after lengthy tests, there was no explanation for his experiencing so much pain so frequently. In collaboration with his physician, I encouraged José to keep a sequential and detailed log of the time when his pain began and intensified and the circumstances involved prior to these feelings. He also recorded his reactions and way of coping. Keeping the log and reflecting on it with me enabled him to become aware that the emotional stress of being pulled in so many directions without respite was directly related to the onset and maintenance of his pain and discomfort. Unwilling to explore this internal pressure, even though he noted its relevance to his physical distress, José agreed only to an eight-week contract, during which time he used the log, in conjunction with weekly visits, to master relaxation techniques and stress reduction exercises.

Angelic Intervention

Doodles, drawings, and sketches provide added sources of insight into the varied aspects of clients' personality and perceptions. Donna's log, for example, was a portfolio of angel drawings. At first, the angel's forbidding pose was like that found on cemetery pedestaled statues. Over the course of two years, the original pose softened; indeed, the angel descended from the pedestal and stood casually on the ground with a bemused smile on her face.

For Donna, raised with a rigidly religious background, the angel revealed her strict and punishing inner censor. She remembered having seen and continually dreamed of "fallen" angels and angels pursuing her for her misdeeds. Her drawings symbolically manifested her internal conflicts and tensions. These came more to light during interviews where she assumed these various angelic postures. She absorbed the experience and reflected minimally on it aloud in words, then slightly shifted her pose. Her drawings, which traced changes in the angel's posture from a forbidding to a forgiving stance, reflected her own psychological metamorphosis.

GUIDELINES FOR USING A LOG

The following guidelines will enable you to maximize the log's effectiveness as a highly unique and individualized means for self-disclosure and development. Remain flexible and adaptable, remembering that the log:

- Is voluntary, not forced. Any pressure exerted to maintain it would discourage clients from fully and honestly expressing what is really going on in them.
- Is not graded or judged. It is not intended to be an ordeal but, rather, an added opportunity to state ideas, beliefs, attitudes, and feelings in whatever manner best suits the client's needs.
- Works best when it is descriptive and explicit, expanding on themes in vivid detail, using concrete language, rather than generalities or abstractions.

- Has a distinctive form that is as important as its content. Its form is an integral component in the experience of expressing oneself.
- Is intended to be spontaneous and honest: requirements and restrictions usually associated with writing are put aside, allowing freedom in self-expression (Fox, 1982).

The absence of formal rules of structure, content, and style promotes ventilation, reflection, and description, accelerating the growth process.

AN EXPANDED DIMENSION
OF CLIENT WRITING

Noting Messages

Client writing can be of value in ways other than logging. For example, in some families and for some couples, verbal exchange inevitably deteriorates to name-calling and shouting matches. Indictments and rancor, rather than true dialogue, characterize the exchange. To prevent bouts of whining, arguing, or pleading, resulting from either a misuse or an overdose of talking, I suggest that such families and couples exchange notes to raise differences coolly and reasonably. Not strictly problem centered, note exchanging eases the awkwardness of expressing tender feelings or raw emotions, which often remain unsaid if not written. Notes offer family members a calmed and disciplined vehicle for giving each other encouragement, feedback, and advice as well as release of sentiments.

Letters of indignation, complaint, or outrage are another purposeful use of writing. The safety of the journal makes it possible to write feelings and thoughts that you might never be able to express in person. Doing so provides a catharsis through which hostile or painful feelings that are bottled up can be stated. I encourage clients to write letters, mostly left unmailed, to express aroused passions. Clients frequently suppress negative feelings and obsessively ruminate about what they "should have said." One client, for example, discharged his feelings of contempt in a letter to a public official who had supported legislation he found morally offensive. After reading and rereading it, he eventually sent it; more important than the relief he experienced from releasing his feelings was the satisfaction of a reply. An unexpected dividend was learning that uttering feelings rather than swallowing them can have impact and produce positive results. Even if letters are not sent, they can bring to the table unresolved conflicts, help resolve unfinished business, allow you to tell the truth, and ultimately trigger internal change.

Sent letters can also be enormously revealing. This letter, sent to me some years after a completed therapy, is one such example:

> i hope this letter (with the enclosed check—the most important part!) finds you well . . . this debt has troubled me for a number of years. i am only now in a position to repay it. that we had an arrangement, that you helped me immeasurably in our time spent working together, and that, hey, when you owe money to someone you owe money to someone . . . all of these have been a source of guilt for me over the years.
>
> it is my hope that you can forgive me for the time it has taken to repay this debt. as the new year turned, i committed, as i am sure did countless others across the nation in that old resolution fervor, to pay my debts. they are numerous (but manageable, i'm finding after years of paralysis [mine] in their face), and i've just sought the aid of a credit counselor to help me prioritize these debts and structure a payment plan. however, i didn't need to prioritize my debt to you. your work with me and my remembrance of your helpfulness and straightforwardness . . . well, there was no decision to be made on who to pay first . . . i owe you. here you go . . .
>
> i don't write much at all anymore, as this letter most probably indicates. it's unfortunate. i write code all day (which i hope explain why i write in all lower-case it's not an e.e. cummings thing—it's just how i type as a consequence of my job), but that doesn't count. i occasionally publish some technical articles, generally on web design and technology, which i enjoy. but it's not the kind of writing i'd really love to be doing. i'd like to get back to that craft at some point. but like anything else, it's a balancing act. hopefully i can do it again. nothing makes me feel better than writing. other than feeling better . . .
>
> i hope all is well with you . . . please do not hesitate to contact me for any reason.
> and thanks.
> best

Record Keeping and Agenda Making

I have found it useful in selected instances for clients to record interviews. This procedure may depart from one in which you exclusively document the work and keep notes. You may have heard clients say, "Gee, this session was good. I wish I had it to play back." I urge some clients to summarize their reflections in writing after sessions. Some clients literally take notes during the interview; still others actually audiotape it. Frank believed that he could not trust his memory to recall all the insights he gained during our interaction, so he sat with a pen and pad poised on his lap, taking notes. Some clinicians would criticize this as resistance and claim that it would dilute the relationship. I have not found this to be the case. Over time, writing has become a productive adjunct to my work with clients. It gives us a chance to correct distorted beliefs and to review movement.

Another client, Mike, prepared an agenda for sessions. In order to recall what had happened to him between visits, he formulated an agenda for each session, which in itself had a cathartic effect and enabled him to sift through concerns and generate ideas to face them. In handing me an agenda, he felt secure that "at least superficially, all bases are covered." When Mike could not address all the items on the agenda, he felt secure in knowing that he had given me a "bird's eye view" of his previous week in advance. We could focus on one item or put aside the whole agenda to attend to more immediate concerns that he, having "filled me in," was freer to examine.

Agenda setting is especially helpful for clients who ascribe equal importance to all events. It permits them to realign thinking, set priorities, and make decisions. This was the case with John, a seriously depressed twenty-two-year-old postal employee with a severe learning disorder that prevented him from completing high school. His weekly agenda, written on index cards, relieved his frustration of not being able to "share all," and freed him to feel his loss, pain, and grief more deeply during sessions. A sample of his agenda over a six-week period, exactly as written, follows:

> 11/8—1) want to know again if its O.K. for me to feel like your a step parent to me. 2) I dont like how my family develop thru the years, and wish it was better 3) party for Laurie 4) Monday: how I felt growing up, very hard to show how painful my life is every day 5) This week: Feeling not good enough, have nothing feel

so alone, what other have—I dont have having freinds, developing a relationship with a girl Being liked by other people; and
for me I need to feel it so bad, I really feel bad, I feel like crying

11/28—1) show concern for me, about being late and how it
made me feel. 2) feeling SAD about no friends 3) some days I
wake up feeling depressed, I stay like that for hours (SUNDAY)
4) I've been feeling, lonely, SAD, angry, dejected, a sense of
hopelessness, bitter about the way I develop, feeling very fragile
when I'm in certain situations or certain songs, wanting things
to be better 5) Feeling sorry for my parents awful marriage, but
at the same time, feeling VERY ANGRY at them for the mistakes they made. Also, wishing my parents could have been
more like some one else's parents 6) Having too many unhappy
feelings and not enough happy ones XXXXXXXXXX Having
XXXXXX so many feelings towards you, and for me to be allowed to express them verbally and in writing to you, means so
much to me.

12/2—1) When I left your office on Monday, I felt confused and
I feel I don't have the ability to understand every thing you try to
explain to me. 2) Monday and Tuesday were very trying and sad
days for me. Monday: it was hard to be at work Tuesday: late at
night, I put on that album and I became very sad. What I feel
about a song is probably very different than what the song might
mean, if it has one. Also, had another dream, where you were
the main person in it. 3) In general, just feeling very sad about
everything. It's so hard for me to go on with life, when I have no
friends and almost nothing else but work. I don't feel good
about myself. I just feel so lost and depressed about life in general and the way things are going, it hurts so bad.

John's agendas gave me penetrating revelations that he could not
talk about. The agenda made it possible for him to develop increased
clarity about himself, his family, me, his life, and the helping process.
The writing helped him locate underlying sources of his depression,
touch affects, and gradually open discussion and channel it toward
avenues of relief and redirection. Our contacts increased as a result of
the agenda. Slowly, he began to experience relief from his torment as
it was openly released, increased energy which he directed into struc-

tured social activities, and a more positive outlook on himself and his life.

The very act of preparing an agenda fosters orderly and discriminating thinking. It stimulates clients' acuity in focusing attention on specific issues.

Critical Incidents

One additional useful method of client writing is critical incident reporting. Here the client identifies a "charged" event with as much specificity as possible. The description includes relevant details and circumstances surrounding the event, people, and the role that the client plays. This is followed by brief summary and analysis. The helping interview, for example, may itself be one of these events. Musings in writing capture crucial episodes, patterns of response, and the interdependence between the helping process and real life. They are a core mechanism of communication, and their review helps direct focus. Reports of these critical incidents become reliable means for monitoring thoughts, actions, and feelings when they are fresh in clients' minds. They are a running account of the chronology of the changes that occur during the helping process. These narratives are not stuffy or static descriptions but dynamic unfoldings that reveal how clients draw upon their understanding to make meaningful connections and decisions as well as to solve problems.

YOUR OWN WRITING

Writing About Yourself

Writing need not be restricted to clients. It can be a valuable tool for you in various ways as well. Writing your own log, for example, has all the same benefits for you that it has for clients.

Writing about your own life experience is one of the best ways to give new meaning to your present personal and professional life. It also enables you to make an appropriate separation between the two. Certainly it is an excellent way to understand your own past more fully. Writing your autobiography puts your own contradictions, paradoxes, ambivalences, and unfinished business into perspective. Fathoming your own personal identity can be instrumental in freeing you from superimposing yourself, in unhelpful ways, on clients' lives. Consider composing a metaphoric life story. For example, imagine your life as a river and describe how it flowed from its source, how it branched off, where it was dammed up, and how it got to where it is. Think of yourself as a playwright preparing a script. Create and review scenes and the roles you played in them to convey the dramatic tension in your life. Your writing, like clients', clarifies your situation and better defines you. The very act of writing is a new venture and a new ground-breaking behavior. I have found "clustering" to be a particularly valuable method for self-discovery.

Clustering

Clustering is a method of open-ended writing, akin to free association, developed by Gabrielle Rico (1983). It gives shape to your experience. It is a writing approach that forms and structures the confusion that sometimes characterizes our inner and outer worlds, especially when we are faced with a dilemma, impasse, or vague ache. Beginning with a nucleus word and splitting off other words and phrases at random, complex images and emotional qualities associated with them become clear, leading to a pattern and organization of meaning not originally perceived.

To start, on a blank page, circle a chosen stimulus word or phrase that comes to mind. Let your mind flow and write down other words that you associate with it, each in its own circle, which radiates from the first. Connect the circles with lines. Start again when you have a new or different association. If it does not flow in any particular order, let each association find its own place. Be receptive to what comes. Do not censor. When you have exhausted this "playful" association, suspend your circling. Begin to write. You will be amazed at what comes together, at how the most troublesome thoughts can turn out to have unexpected depth and resonance. Figure 13.1 shows how a typical cluster might look.

Starting from the word "transference," the cluster expanded into five directions, each with very different types of associations, until the sixth direction led to "blank," ending the process. The translation of the cluster into a definition of transference led to this statement: "Transference is psychoanalytic jargon for a Freudian concept, developed in the remote past, explaining a client's uncanny, 'under the skin,' response to a person in the present, duplicating one from

FIGURE 13.1. Clustering

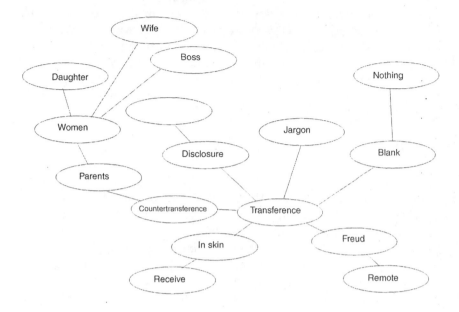

the past that rightfully belongs to his or her parents: for example, Larry inappropriately feeling rejected by his wife, boss or daughter whenever they are involved with other people because as a child he felt 'left out' by his mother whenever she was engaged in activity that did not include him, for example, playing bridge with friends. This phenomenon, once disclosed, leads to insight and changed behavior. Countertransference is the helper's transference."

Clustering is a kind of brainstorming process, beautifully explained by Rico (1983). It is a process of creative writing that can be freeing for you as well as for clients. It helps you to contact inner processes and gain self-awareness by accessing memories, freeing emotions, and capturing forgotten experiences. I highly recommend it to you as I do to clients.

Process Recording

Yet another form of writing for yourself, which also benefits clients, is process recording, described fully in Chapter 6.

Writing to Clients

Writing to clients can sustain and improve communication. Verbal interpretations to clients, for example, can be easily distorted, ignored, or repressed. Written messages that reinforce oral interpretations are tangible, visible, and hard to repress. The same is true of advice and prescriptions.

Writing is notably helpful in couple and family work where there is considerable potential for distortion. Writing to families and couples has advantages, as it does for individuals, including the following:

1. Clarifying your perceptions and observations
2. Breaking impasses or repetitive destructive patterns
3. Expanding and accelerating the work
4. Confronting issues that are denied and avoided
5. Specifying vague issues
6. Desensitizing emotionally charged issues

I ask families and couples to post a copy of my correspondence on their refrigerator so that it is visually present as a reminder to them whenever they go for a bite to eat. This may identify certain tasks they are to perform, remind them of homework they agreed to do, or post schedules for specified interactions. Messages to clients should be short, no more than a page long. They should consist of no more than two or three main points. When they are longer, they become burdensome for clients and harder to digest. The ultimate effect can be to overwhelm rather than clarify. Even postcard reminders of appointments, vacations, etc., become helpful reminders and transitional objects for clients.

I have found it helpful to share some of my professional writing with clients. For example, Sam, a rather restrained and rigid computer programmer, did not understand the idea of identifying his goals for therapy during our first few visits. After giving him a copy of a professional article about goals that I had published, he got the idea and at the subsequent session launched immediately into naming and prioritizing his goals for our work together.

ABOUT WRITING

In all its forms, writing is an efficient and effective tool for observation and disclosure. It is not a substitute for, but an enhancement to, interactive person to-person transactions. Writing helps clients and you to capture ideas, feelings, and behavior in unique ways. It is a powerful tool for developing a high level of awareness. It facilitates communication. It can provide a bridge in relationships and can supply information that might otherwise be too overwhelming or too painful to face in verbal discussion.

Clients' writing, as well as your own, does not have to be about negative events, problems, trauma, or crises. Journals are usually prescribed to keep fear under control, to access painful memories, and to release emotions. Although this is valuable, it can obfuscate what is healthy in us. It is important to write about positive experiences, as well as negative ones. Doing so pinpoints achievements and highlights good feelings. A springboard for focusing attention on goals and dreams, writing can freeze-frame happy moments. The journal, used in this way, promotes healing.

Writing puts clients and you in touch with patterns of behavior, feelings, and thinking and adds coherence to memories, fantasies, thoughts, and intuitions. Its impact on both of you is great, and it invariably leads to deeper understanding. Writing enriches the helping process.

Advantages of Writing

You may wonder, with all the paperwork you already have, how you will find the time or inclination to deal with the various forms of writing I have suggested, since they can seem so time consuming and burdensome. Very likely the long records you keep are neither relevant nor helpful in your ongoing interactions with clients; however, the advantages of writing are more than fringe benefits. It enables both of you to gain clearer access to rich, interdependent complexities and multifarious dimensions that make for success in the helping process. Some advantages of writing bear repetition, and others should be more clearly explicated:

1. Writing encourages a stance of inward attention.
2. It develops a degree of comfort in self-observation and self-reporting.
3. It heightens self-awareness and fosters alternative ways of viewing oneself.
4. It establishes a sense of competence in being able to discipline and reveal oneself, which is ego enhancing.

5. It lends itself to incisive self-reflection, especially when entries are reviewed over time.
6. Writing supports an appreciation of strengths, rather than debilities, in patterns of thinking, feeling, and behavior.
7. It helps trace the antecedents and consequences of patterns of thinking, feeling, and behaving.
8. It unfreezes thinking and feeling, making possible reinforcement of movement and change.
9. It heightens sensitivity to others and their conduct in relationships.
10. It documents clients' progress while going through the helping process.
11. Writing helps clients and you to be more receptive to spontaneous perceptions.
12. It helps you better attune to what is happening within clients.
13. It provides you with comprehensive data about clients.
14. It provides, for both clients and you, continuity during breaks and other separations.
15. It offers a way to explore and clarify the dynamic contexts in which clients live.
16. It promotes clients' self-monitoring of behaviors.
17. Journals can serve as vehicles to teach clients to focus on their unique situations in an organized and conscious way to promote better functioning in the future.

An important dimension of writing is that it can provide a "before and after" picture of the helping process. Particularly at the time of termination, as well as at any interval along the way, it provides tangible documentation of change.

A FINAL TRIBUTE TO THE JOURNAL

The following two entries, by clients referring to their journals, speak to the heartfelt, central, and crucial place the journal can play.
Mary's salute to the journal reads,

> . . . Boxes filled with the scribblings of my life contain the answers to all my questions. I have written for the greater part of

my life, perhaps to maintain my sanity, perhaps to mask my insanity, either way I am the better for it, this I know beyond all certainty. . . .

I have been journaling on and off for twenty years about all things that have given me pause in this world. There are the moments in nature when I am truly struck with awe by the beauty, as well as the moments of natural disaster that reveal the incredible power. . . . So too I have recorded travel and the moments of joy when each unfamiliar corner is turned, in addition to the comforts of home and the familiar. Present in most writings is my preoccupation with philosophy and theology, as my constant quest for answers is strewn throughout the pages of my life. I have written of love and the incredibleness of having one's cup overflow. . . . I fill pages about all those dead yet living eternally, as I stand in a museum or read a book, as sparks from the viewer renew life to authors and artist always. . . .

More pages than not are dedicated to the wacky crew of friends and family I love so dearly, but not without the ties of stress and annoyances, as I am to be part of their journeys as well. There are my many struggles to success, that I revel in noting, as it ensures I stop to notice and own them. So many entries are of strangers, people watching, and overheard words, and what I gathered. . . . And of course there is a whole journal dedicated to Jade my rabbit. . . .

All of my pain and sorrow has poured out of my heart and on to the pages throughout my life, and for this I am grateful. It has been said our greatest lessons are found within our greatest tragedies, and so through noting and later observation is the only way I could ever view such, and in turn I did not miss many lessons, nor was such anguish in vain. . . .

What do all my prior ramblings amount to? I would imagine there is nothing much here of interest for another to read. As for myself I have watched the anger of the pen ignite the pages, later to discover peace within the ashes. I have seen the spiraling confusion of words being strewn till the pen was able to gain flat ground of understanding. I have watched the pain stutter ink everywhere till the even flow of healing could be restored. The deepest darkest sorrows of the pen have trudged on till there is light both of God and the lessening of the burden. While never has it been invited, forgiveness has always managed to show. What prevails are the pages filled with the pen's struggle for the essence of love. And so in the end the pen fades, pages disappear, and it is only I in the midst of self.

Phyllis praises the journal as follows:

> . . . A simple request. . . . I'm doing an article on journaling . . . "I would like a copy of a journal entry with your permission"— Almost two months later here I sit. . . . I'm sure that says something in itself. . . . My first reaction was how can I do this. . . . *My Journal.* . . . It's never far from where I am. . . . It is as much me as I am. . . . Each page has my name written all over it. . . . It still surprises me that I am willing to let another in . . . to hold it . . . to read it and turn its pages . . . a sacred trust. . . . I said to myself certainly he knows others who are more intelligent . . . better writers . . . more insightful. . . . Is there a method in the madness . . . what did "it" say if I said "Yes, I will" . . . what did "it" say if I said "No, I can't" . . . I have sat in the quiet of my world and read and reread . . . I give to you this part of me . . .

Chapter 14

Metaphors in Our Lives

... there are essential differences between the uncovering made by the creative person and that made by the psychoanalyst. Whereas the psychoanalyst analyzes or separates the various elements, the creative person puts those disparate elements together.

Silvano Arieti

... metaphor is medium for fuller, riper knowing.

Phillip Wheelwright

Mark, a forty-three-year-old computer programmer, thinking about a change of career, repeatedly referred to "nature." Having been raised on a farm, he alluded frequently to images of hay and cornfields and to the senses evoked by their smell and texture. These nostalgic musings exacerbated his dissatisfaction with his day-to-day work. All day long he sat in a sterile city office staring at a machine. He painted this picture of his life—sitting on a riverbank intently watching rapids tumble downward over immovable rocks toward a valley below. This vision slowly, yet certainly, affected him as a sad but true vision of his life. Yearning again for nature's surface beauty, but more so for its profound, inexplicable effect on his sense of well-being, he became determined to "ride the current."

Mrs. G, described at length later in this chapter, juggled a career and motherhood. She was overwhelmed by having to maintain so many "balls in the air at once." She occasionally shifted their pattern but never was able to let any one of them down for even a second, fearing all of them and herself would plunge into chaos. Her "juggling act" became a blur as she incessantly kept the balls circling in motion. Her life was frantic and precarious. She was off balance and exhausted. She remarked one day that different balls represented different aspects of her life, except that an accurate representation required too many balls. A new act was needed.

Metaphors speak volumes.

My interest in metaphors arises from brain hemisphere research, from narrative approaches to therapy, and from my own exploration. Brain research has produced evidence that our ways of knowing with our "left brain" and our "right brain" are quite different. Studies indicate that the right brain is activated by metaphorical communication. It follows then, that metaphoric intervention, aimed at the right brain, may contribute to therapeutic change, which has relied almost exclusively on left-brain logic and reason.

Narrative approaches to therapy, discussed more at length in Chapter 12, stress clients' stories or maps of their experiences, views, or beliefs. They construct these to make meaning out of events in their lives. These personal stories have main characters, plots, and settings that are frequently cast in metaphoric terms. Healing occurs because you are attuned to them.

This chapter explores my own utilization of metaphor in therapy. It builds on some of my earlier writing about metaphor (Fox, 1989). It offers you guidelines for discovering and developing metaphors—your own as well as your clients'—to extend, enlarge, and shape your diagnosis, redefine problems, look for the unexpected, and creatively touch the rich fiber and texture of your clients' lives. It is important to note that metaphors do not cure problems; rather, they open clients' and your own senses, mind, and heart to new possibilities, new visions of past, present, and future.

THE POWER OF METAPHOR

Metaphors are ubiquitous in everyday life and have special relevance for your therapeutic work. When you creatively build upon them, metaphors can at the same time develop rapport, enlighten understanding, reduce resistance, stimulate unconscious processes, retrieve memories, and contact dynamic themes. Metaphors enable you to convey to clients, at their own level of communication, an understanding of connections between their past and present and their inner and outer reality. Metaphors promote the discovery of connecting patterns and unite these into a holistic picture.

Introducing and developing metaphors with your clients may require you to use yourself in a new way. That is, you yourself must become open to exercising your own right brain more fully.

Because metaphors speak more softly but directly to the right brain, they avoid stirring up the rational left brain's analytic resistance. They paint different perspectives and establish a sense of alignment as they make a correlation between a client's real-life situation and the metaphor.

Metaphor's Magical Attributes

Technically speaking, metaphors are comparisons between two dissimilar things in which qualities of one are transferred to the other in ways that imaginatively construct "some underlying principle that unites them" (Siegelman, 1990, p. ix). Metaphors, more significantly, are full of "mana," magical power.

Metaphors' power lies in their ability to evoke responses, recollections, feelings, and imaginings in discrete and often subtle ways. As in the metaphors of the river and the juggler above, they telescope meanings into simple, succinct images. The fact that a metaphor can evoke a mass of experiences, events, fantasies, wishes, recollections, and basic emotions—all by association—is their remarkable psychological property. Onto a single, usually visual representation, clients condense an enormous body of dissociated elements, all or part apprehended with immediacy. This telescopic endowment makes it possible for you to more readily identify clients' adaptive patterns and recurrent themes.

Metaphor has a powerful ability to pique interest and to foster the development of new perspectives. Since therapy involves helping people to see things differently, in a new light, so to speak, metaphors move well beyond the literal exposition of problems or issues. They offer new ideas and angles toward understanding and solution. Metaphors shuttle between the conscious and the unconscious simultaneously, activating a revised consideration of implications and connotations.

Words are limited. Symbols are expansive. It has often been said that a picture is worth a thousand words. A picture provides a visual shortcut to the larger entity it represents. Likewise, a metaphor condenses complex and even opposite feelings, needs, wishes, fears, and experiences. It does so with great economy and apparent simplicity.

Metaphor's Connotative and Comparative Power

Metaphors are comparisons that express sensations and states of mind in specific and meaningful ways and make concrete and tangible what is vague or abstract. A metaphor is connotative rather than denotative. On one hand, it symbolically expresses hidden emotion-laden content (a memory, a meaning, a dynamic conflict), and on the other, it fits an outer configuration of facts. Because it bridges the gap between inner and outer factors, it delivers a strong emotional impact (Lankton, 1983).

Metaphoric language is rich in association, making it more or less inexhaustible. Built on observable realities to represent less visible experience, it teases perception and stretches imagination. To be more precise, a metaphor enables you and your clients to find a vital connection between visible objects and the invisible realities they may represent. It sparks deep and complex responses while stimulating and activating associations.

Truly, metaphor is change (Greek: *meta*) bearing (Greek: *pherein*). It alters perspective. It provides harmonious and clear vision of what initially seems ambiguous and disassociated. It breaks ground for clients and for you as well.

Metaphor's Therapeutic Function

Metaphors provide a route to profound understanding of experiences that defy description in literal or direct terms and provide a shortcut to hidden material with great economy and apparent simplicity. Essentially they consist of four components: medium, form, content, and context. The medium refers to the language, idiom, or vehicle of expression. The form is the specific ordering, syntax, or use of this specific medium. The content is precisely what is expressed in and through the specific form, and the context suggests the underlying theme or meaning of the whole. Metaphors allow clients to perceive a different reality around their problems while still remaining in touch with them, and they enable clients to see different solutions and/or different ways of viewing their problems (Atwood and Levine, 1991, p. 202).

In your clinical work, metaphors have a threefold function. They present you with the client's current state of affairs, they appeal to you to share in understanding their meaning, and they reveal the internal condition of the client's mind. Metaphors suggest more than they actually say. They conceal what they carry and resist total explanation because they find their source in the primitive and irrational.

Perhaps the least explored but possibly the most important aspect of such metaphoric communication concerns the vitality and protean possibilities evoked from a shared symbolic interchange. The achievement of this intimacy provides not only empathy and rapport but a renewal of energy and hope springing directly from the symbolic activities' close relationship to unconscious processes. Something of the playfulness and magic of primary process thinking surrounds the successful metaphoric exchange.

WHAT ABOUT COMMON PLATITUDES?

All human behavior can be thought of as analogical and metaphorical in different ways and at various levels of abstraction. Common remarks about existence become clichés because they convey an element of truth; nonetheless, few of us, even therapists, listen. "Those who cannot remember the past are condemned to repeat it." "As you sow, so shall you reap." For example, men rely on sports platitudes in referring to sexual behavior. One young female graphic artist spoke of therapy as "interior designing," and continually relied on variations of that revealing but comfortable analogy throughout her treatment. Interestingly, when I alluded to my own interest in "interior designing," she commented, "but that is exactly what you are doing."

By telling about a memory, idea, experience, or feeling in terms of another, clients create a framework or image that reveals what is significant for them. These metaphors need not be elaborate. They may, in fact, be deceptively simple in conveying complex messages. Thus, metaphors stand closer to the spirit of what is felt than do elegant lingistic abstractions. Indeed, the very language of therapy itself often draws upon imagery from a variety of unexpected sources. From the business lexicon comes such metaphoric allusions as "contract," "role negotiation," and "investment." From the military lexicon comes "maneuver," "strategy," and "intervention." And from traffic control comes such terminology as "dead end," "bottleneck," "detour," and "hitting the brakes."

In everyday discourse metaphors prompt less visible connections; in therapeutic work they access invaluable associations. Especially when there is an atmosphere of expectancy and discovery, whatever clients spontaneously say and however they behave during a therapeutic session give a clue to what is going on within them. Whatever topics are raised, no matter how "superficial" (travel, hobbies, weather), or "serious" (careers, studies, arguments), can be metaphoric statements about their inner life, self, and view of the world.

John T., for example, a prominent researcher, hated his job. He had spent twenty years studying heart disease without really understanding why. He came to therapy complaining about his dissatisfaction with his job and concern about his compulsive jogging. His career as a medical scientist, as well as his obsession with physical fitness, were metaphoric statements about his unconscious preoccupation with undoing the traumatic death of his father from a heart attack when John was thirteen. It was also a means to assuage his fear and to prevent his own untimely death from a similar disorder.

Wordless Metaphors

Metaphors can be nonverbal. A client's breath, laughter, sighs, and movements are metaphors. Raised eyebrows, frowns, and grimaces are all forms of metaphorical expressing. Even when metaphor disguises, as with children expressing difficult circumstances through play therapy, the choice of the toy—animal, weapon, etc.— has special significance. To further develop an illustration, Mary, a seventeen-year-old student in fashion design, always walked on her tiptoes. This apparently began when her parents discouraged her from continuing ballet lessons at the age of eight. She was "not good enough." Tiptoeing was a sign of ongoing defiance. It explained behavior at different levels as well. She was wary, vigilant, "on her toes" whenever she was at home. Outside of home she positioned herself "above" everyone else. She simultaneously followed and rebelled against her parents' message metaphorically by walking on tiptoes.

Clients' metaphors usually contain information you need to know to be helpful. Your ability to absorb clients' metaphors, to hear what they are saying, enlivens communication enormously. That empathic ability to let clients know in subtle ways that they are being heard cements relationships as little else does.

The metaphors of daily speech transfer qualities from one sensual experience to another. These synthetic metaphors allow us to speak of a "velvet tone," a "loud color," or say, "green with envy." Warmth and light provide us with early and intense experience of gratification, and so we speak of a warm friendship, a dark mood.

Metaphors can put the client's situation in a new perspective. A story about a plant that gets accidentally chopped down, but then grows back fuller and more beautiful, can metaphorically reframe a client's crisis as a potential for growth.

Art offers another form of metaphor. Individuals or whole families can draw what their problems look like, what is necessary to create needed change, and what a solution looks like. An example of how one client tracked improvement in her mental health by drawing a succession of angels in her journal is discussed fully in Chapter 13.

Working with Resistance

Metaphors provide analogic ways of dealing with resistance without the risk of provoking even more resistance. Processing what clients present indirectly and helping them draw upon it arouses their ambivalence, of course. This ambivalence is related to discovering new things about themselves while protecting against the possibility of adverse results of discovery. No one wants to see themselves all that clearly if it's going to hurt. Tony, an accomplished musician, was no exception. He presented a musical metaphor, but variations on this theme had to be played tenderly, gently, for him to hear without being overly threatened. He sought therapy because he felt out of sync, not in harmony, with his career, his family, his friends.

Tony had broken up with his partner of six months, the third such split in four years. He complained of being out of sync in relationships. Just when he was getting involved, the relationship would fade.

Establishing relationships was easy for him; maintaining them was not. As you might expect, he found the introductory phase of therapy pleasant and exciting. Before long, however, he became bored and impatient, wanting to move on beyond the tedious and sometimes tense exploration phase.

No direct interpretations were made about his repeated pattern of behavior or his resistance, both inside and outside of treatment. Musical terminology began to punctuate the therapeutic dialogue at this point. "Sonata form" and "relationship" became indistinguishable for a time. His ease with overtures, with introduction, with exposition, was examined. By contrast, his inability to sustain interest or excitement during repetition and his impatience to quickly advance to the next movement were also examined.

The quest for novelty, the obsession with the next step, avoided the riches produced by the dynamic tension, the central working through of the theme that made one feel satisfied. To find joy in music was to play with these variations, to fondly shape and reshape, to examine from every angle. Without development, there is never more than outline.

As he became engrossed in the metaphorical interplay, he was able to use the therapeutic interaction as the counterpoint to his life. The recapitulation of past themes and behaviors was found to be stimulating rather than deadening.

Changes began to unfold outside of therapy as they occurred inside it, and Tony was able to modulate the tension. About seven months into therapy, he handed me an authoritative musical dictionary that explained sonata form in detail. He had underlined significant portions that resembled his own process of interpersonal relationship, both inside and outside of therapy. He smiled as he gave it to me, saying, "I got it."

When clients enter into and experience metaphors, they "see" more at a preconscious and unconscious level. As preconscious material enters consciousness, it not only makes room for unconscious material to move into preconsciousness, it also stimulates it to do so. The fortress of resistance can be penetrated without being destroyed.

The indirect nature of metaphoric interventions makes clients less threatened and less likely to mobilize resistance. For these reasons, anecdotes and parables are effective ways of communicating ideas that might be resisted if they were presented directly. Again, such methods are not the only ways of communicating indirectly. Many techniques involve indirection, which produce change spontaneously, though possibly without accompanying insight or interpretation.

Spontaneous metaphors serve many of the same purposes as those generated by the therapist. A more indirect expression is often the only way a client can approach unacceptable, intolerable impulses. The metaphor allows for discussion in a middle ground, which is neither too primitive nor too intellectualized. In addition, if you are willing to leave some metaphors uninterpreted, you save the client from having to engage in unproductive defensive operations. This was the case with Adam.

Adam was a cellist who had trouble verbally expressing his emotions. Writing music in his journal, for the first few months of therapy he barely spoke but, during sessions, played the music of reverie he had written during the week. He believed, as did I, that the soft, rich, melodious resonance of the cello, conveying the melancholic tones of the notes, aptly bared his emotions.

INDIVIDUAL METAPHORS

Metaphors are invested with emotions, which in turn are associatively linked to some of the circumstances condensed in the metaphor. In other words, affectively charged values are displaced from the circumstances in which the metaphor originated. Thus, metaphors exhibit two basic properties—condensation and displacement of significant experiences and emotions. Metaphors are the passkeys to doors that remain locked to many significant events in clients' lives.

Metaphors can also deepen an examination of the intricacies of relationships. Mr. R had a special bond with his father. Through metaphor, he was able to arrive at dynamic understanding of that bond.

The third oldest male of ten children, Mr. R was recalcitrant when it came to talking about his relationship with his parents, especially his father. His father, an attorney who had never practiced law and a lifelong alcoholic, had amassed a sizable fortune in a family-owned business. Three of Mr. R's siblings were alcoholics; two were drug addicted. Mr. R himself, a heavy drinker and periodic cocaine user, had been recommended to therapy by his younger brother, who was greatly concerned about Mr. R's bouts with serious depression, drinking binges, and blackouts. Chief operations officer of his father's company, Mr. R, because of lapses in memory and problems in attentiveness, was losing considerable amounts of money.

Unable all his life to deal directly with his father, Mr. R spent the first six weeks of treatment educating me about galvanizing, which was the family business. He talked of the special properties of the two metals involved in galvanizing: the iron or steel core—strong, rigid, unyielding, appearing invulnerable, yet highly susceptible to corrosion; and the zinc—active and soft, yet protecting the iron from corrosion. He explained that molten zinc reacts with iron to form a brittle alloy that effectively cuts off the iron from interaction with the elements around it. He instructed me further in the process of joining the two and how it is accomplished by hot dipping the iron into a temperature-controlled zinc. He explained that both advantages and disadvantages resulted from joining the metals together. The zinc, for example, lost its own physical properties because of the heat involved. It ultimately sacrificed its natural features to the base metal. Thus, in being part of an alloy, zinc loses its own individual qualities and purity.

We discussed the benefits, liabilities, and very real hazards of being part of an alloy and eventually came to discuss if and how it would be possible to separate the two metals if that were necessary. All this occurred without Mr. R's conscious awareness that he was, in speaking about the symbiotic relationship between iron and zinc, speaking about his father and himself.

We continued in this vein, speaking in indirect allusive terms throughout our work together. Reference was never explicitly made to Mr. R's fused relationship with his father. Proceeding in this fashion, Mr. R was not overwhelmed by reality, but approached it slowly. Understanding dawned in a most profound manner.

In a way, the client-as-poet and therapist-as-appreciator enter a creative dialogue that enlarges scope and depth of their contact.

FAMILY METAPHORS

It has been my experience that families build metaphors that act as central organizers for their shared constructs, expectations, and fantasies. These metaphors serve as repositories of family experience and as guides for behavior. Metaphors spring from the need to stop the continuous flow of reality in order to possess it, to recapture what is lost in everyday experience by means of something that resembles it.

I have discovered that families have visions of themselves that are frequently expressed in a shared metaphor. When individuals are asked about their image of their family, all members tend to concur. The T family, for example, likened itself to a crumbling house. The family consisted of four members: Mr. T, a forty-year-old architect;

Mrs. T, a forty-one-year-old part-time rehabilitation counselor; Tom, their fourteen-year-old intellectually gifted son; and Tara, their ten-year-old daughter. They had come into family therapy as a last resort after a series of unsuccessful attempts at individual therapy for Tom. Tom was not achieving his potential in school. Indeed, he was not even attending school much of the time. An improvement in Tom's school performance, therefore, was Mr. and Mrs. T's stated goal. A more important goal, however, came to light during the family session—the improvement in the relationship between Mr. T and Tom.

In the first session, Mr. T's desperate statement that the family was collapsing around him and his allusion to their crumbling house brought immediate and spontaneous response. All agreed that the house was in disrepair and that the foundation was weak. However, they were committed to rebuilding it. Together, with my inclusion in the metaphor as a "structural engineer," we set out to design the kind of house they wanted and could call home. We excavated what they saw as faulty foundations and cast these into concrete goals for erecting a new structural framework for relating. The Ts chose to get beyond the ornamental, to pare down to the basics in order to brace the family.

Speaking metaphorically enabled all of us to receive and respond to multiple messages at varying levels of abstraction. On a literal level, we were communicating facts. On an analogical level, I was gathering information from a rigid and defensive family that would be difficult to elicit in other ways. During the task of restructuring the new house, a family was being built from the ground up.

Metaphors offer incisive clues to how families operate and helpful cues to how to work with them. During the first interview, I ask family members to comment upon how they see themselves. I may ask them to complete the statment "To live in this family is like being . . ." Responses to this statement are telling. It has been rare that any one member deviates very much from the one overarching and central image. Some typical responses to this inquiry have been, "this family is a zoo," "a desert," "a circus," "a closet," "a railroad station," and "a jungle." These metaphors are vibrant and offer insight into the emotional climate, structure, interaction patterns, themes, roles, and missing parts of a family. They also focus your attention as a therapist and frequently prompt dramatic activity that more resembles play than therapeutic work.

Figure 14.1 suggests some possibilities for viewing the metaphor as a source of diagnostic information and intervention planning. Three illustrative and common scenarios are depicted—the family as circus, desert, and railroad station. It highlights the possible meanings of various dimensions of what the metaphor reveals about the family's emotional climate, structure, pattern of interaction, roles, and missing part. Understanding these leads to a better ability to figure out your role with the family.

This matrix of metaphoric family types is intended to assist you in navigating the underlying meanings of family metaphors. Viewing these possibilities may spark you in figuring out your clients' unique features and your role in working with them metaphorically.

FIGURE 14.1. Dimensions of Metaphors

METAPHOR

FEATURE		CIRCUS	DESERT	GRAND CENTRAL STATION
	EMOTIONAL CLIMATE	Hyped Chaotic Tawdry	Extreme Barren Desolate	Frantic Flustered Transient
	STRUCTURE	Entangled Tight Artificial	Disengaged Vertical Isolating	Disordered Loose Irregular
	PATTERNS OF INTERACTION	Distracting Deceptive Regulated	Armored Disengaged Hollow	Disorganized Desultory Superficial
	SIGNIFICANT ROLES	Ringleader Scooper Juggler Tightrope Walker	Cactus Reptile Tumbleweed Sand	Passenger Announcer Porter Engineer
	MISSING PART	Spontaneity Naturalness Autonomy	Lubrication Relief Moderation	Simplification Synchronization Personalization
	WORKER ROLE	Clown	Oasis	Conductor

Dramatization

Building upon the metaphor of the family has led me and gradually the family with whom I work to recognize that the family's metaphor for itself offers considerable information about varying elements of its structure and style of being. I encourage the family to construct an interpersonal scenario directly within the session depicting the various elements of the metaphor. Family members dramatize their particular roles. While "directing" this transaction, I observe the family members' verbal and nonverbal ways of signaling each other and monitor the range of transactions. Altering dysfunctional patterns, as they happen directly during the session, revitalizes what had become stale and unhealthy interactional patterns.

I intervene in the process by increasing the intensity, prolonging the time of transactions, involving other members, alternating or reversing positions, indicating alternative transactions, and introducing experimental probes. By so doing, both the family and I receive information about the nature of the problem, the flexibility of the family's transactions, in the search for solutions, and the possibility of alternative modalities for coping within the therapeutic framework. Moreover, these dramatizations provide an immediate alteration in the very patterns that need revision.

Since members of the family "play" with each other instead of merely talking to each other, a context is created for experimentation and change. The utilization of metaphors facilitates communication across cultural and age boundaries.

Amplification of Metaphors

Amplification of the metaphor, including dramatization rather than analysis, is the hallmark for working affirmatively with the family metaphor. Enactment is not a rare event that occasionally punctuates the therapy. It is a spontaneous and ongoing way of responding in the moment to foster change. With the clinician's coaching, the family reaches for deeper levels of communication. In one instance, for example, the G family pictured itself as a circus.

Creating the circus in the safety of my office allowed the G family to take its first honest look at itself. The circus metaphor until that point had always been a humorous one used by the family to describe the chaos in which they lived. The analogy to the circus had a benign quulity, and it allowed the family the hope that others interpreted the chaos as "fun." Like a circus, the family drew attention to itself in the hopes that it would be laughed at, but only with affection.

As the metaphor was enacted in therapy, however, its shabby side began to be uncovered. As in a three-ring circus, many events could be going on simultaneously but with no apparent connection. The isolation of family members was profound. Mr. G, the father, a salesman and the circus ringmaster, represented the family to the world with good looks and great pizzazz. He did not, however, relate with any intimacy within the family. His delinquent adolescent son, Sam, the lion tamer, as seen by parents and siblings, took terribly impulsive risks, endangering his future, his life, and, of course, ultimately his family. He related solely to his pride, his fellow gang members, and not at all to the circus family.

The younger brother, Charlie, was the clown. Not close enough in age to compete with his older brother, he used his clown status to divert the audience's attention from his parents or brother when things got too frenzied. He gained their affection as he kept diffusing the tension with laughter. The circus showgirl, Lisa, the younger sister, knew her job—smile and look glitzy. Stand on that elephant and maintain your and our balance at any cost. Like her mother, the juggler, she knew that the balancing act was paramount. The smile must hide the alienation, the garbage under the glitter. As the metaphor is an exaggerated reenactment of life, an experiential reassessment occurs in tune with it. This attunement is vital if change and the recasting of roles can occur.

Discovering Metaphors

Knowing the family's metaphor for itself gives considerable deductive data about the family climate, structure, interaction patterns, themes, roles, and missing parts. The obverse is also true—knowing the structure, roles, etc., frequently points inductively toward a metaphor. In either case, the metaphor is not necessarily interpreted. It is worked with, enacted, even played with. Dramatizing metaphorical images provides clarity and intensity. Dramatizing creates circumstances that prompt transformation.

Your intervention need not be limited to verbal techniques. Extensive use of figurative and nonverbal metaphors is yet another creative way of elucidating and revising family patterns.

The manner or style you use varies. Sculpting, a nonverbal mode, opens up family images, feelings, and fantasies and animates the session. You might encourage family members to sculpt what the problem feels like to them. Doing so can bring about kinesthetic contact that may be lacking in a family. You can also have the family sculpt what the solution would look or feel like, fostering a significant start to an actual solution.

The essence of metaphoric work may not be the product arrived at as much as the manner of getting there. Shuttling between right- and left-brain functioning is the keystone of effective metaphoric work. In general, the more resistant a client is, the more effective it is to be indirect.

Metaphors, parables really, can be helpful for clients struggling with motivation or losing hope. For such clients, a metaphor or story can be told of some character, real or imaginary, successfully overcoming barriers and hopelessness with perseverance and determination. Timing, however, is exceedingly important, as is sensitivity. Beware of making your clients feel like children.

SOURCES OF METAPHORS

There are three main sources of metaphor in working with individuals and families. First, as discussed earlier in terms of Tony, Mr. R, and the T and G families, there is the individual's or family's metaphor for themselves, their own self-created image. This metaphor is the easiest to work with since it immediately directs attention to relevant and significant information for both diagnosis and treatment. Another source is the clinician's metaphor for the individual or family. Here you work from data toward the development and then introduction of a metaphor that fits. The disadvantage to this inductive approach is the risk of misreading or projecting onto the individual or family your own picture based on discrete pieces that constitute a different whole. Nevertheless, a clinician can introduce stories, myths, and fairy tales as a further rich source for valuable images.

Stories and Fairy Tales

Stories are embedded with manifold messages. They teach certain truths in an absorbing and entertaining form. They invariably present a picture of life as a struggle against difficulties. They usually suggest, however, that when one squarely meets unexpected and sometimes unjust hardships, the end is salubrious. Metaphoric tales represent the dilemmas of Everyman in imaginative and captivating form. They appeal, as in the case of Bill and his mother, Mrs. P, to the subconscious. They even suggest solutions without requiring further discursive explanation. In going beyond the surface, they enable you to extract varied meanings from them to educate, support, and liberate individuals and families. Through one telling of the fairy tale "Jack and the Beanstalk," combined with periodic reference to it, Bill, a teenage client, began to fathom and overcome obstacles to dealing with his mother and she to him without necessarily realizing that this was happening. Stories can enable clients to create alternative endings to their own dilemmas and safely explore a range of new feelings. As with the example below, stories provide an opportunity to retreat from reality to the deeper areas of the psyche to clarify difficulties, then to face and to break through them.

Bill was a fatherless adolescent of fourteen who came with his widowed mother of three years because of what Mrs. P described as "faulty communication." Their problem really had to do with her overinvolvement with him and her inability to allow him to be independent, which was expressed in belittling remarks disguising her overprotectiveness.

After some thought, I recounted my version of "Jack and the Beanstalk," one that depicts the stages of development an orphaned boy naturally goes through to become a separate individual. Mrs. P was able to recognize from the story how she was thwarting her son. She learned also what Bill needed from her in order to grow. At the same time, Bill found in the story encouragement and support for his quest for differentiation.

The initial telling and allusion to it over time by means of a simple agreed-upon signal, the author raising his arm, stimulated in both mother and son internal and interrelational processes that improved their interaction. Bill felt permission through the example of Jack to assert himself and "put aside" his mother. Mrs. P learned from Jack's mother to tolerate his striving without foolishly holding him back and to find other means to meet her own needs.

Metaphors allow you to use fictional characters and dialogue to put into words opinions or emotions that may help clients understand their own or others' opinions or feelings. A character could indirectly state what you would like to say but might sound confrontational, creating possible resistance, if said directly. Mr. L, for example, a voracious reader, quoted verbatim from protagonists in the novels he read to impart his innermost thoughts and feelings. Also, metaphors can be fun, making therapy more enjoyable for therapist and client.

The classic story of *The Wizard of Oz* can exemplify the three steps of metaphor. The scene where Dorothy is saying good-bye just before returning to Kansas first presents to us the "surface structure of meaning" in the actual story. But this story activates many different general feelings of sadness and/or happiness, relating to thoughts about specific events such as leaving friends, accomplishing a goal, or returning home.

BENEFITS OF WORKING WITH METAPHORS

Metaphors are especially useful in therapy that seeks to alter or reinterpret the client's situation. They can make therapy enjoyable for both clients and you without diminishing its seriousness.

Working with metaphors has many benefits. Most of these center on making the therapeutic process more vivid. They can be employed also for portraying or illustrating points. They cannot be confined or reduced to narrow meanings. They provoke thought and evoke feeling at the same time. Specific characteristics that make metaphors especially helpful in therapy include:

1. Being nonthreatening
2. Operating on many, even contradictory, levels
3. Evoking more than intellectual responses
4. Appealing to the unconscious
5. Being indirectly revealing
6. Bypassing resistant postures
7. Promoting multiple responses
8. Highlighting the moment
9. Making the interaction memorable
10. Being lively, gripping, and engaging
11. Supplying infinite variety and uniqueness
12. Providing process fluidity

They supply a garden of benefits for clinicians and clients. For the clinician they can:

- Unearth and air buried material
- Plant suggestions and seed messages
- Prune and shape diagnosis
- Weed out resistance

For the client they can:

- Nourish a helping relationship
- Cultivate conditions for change
- Propagate new viewpoints
- Ripen awareness

An old saying puts it this way: "The glory of the garden lies in more than meets the eye." Gardens mirror life in so many ways, including life's teachings on growth, nurturing, obsession, heartbreak, death, pain, resilience, and, ultimately, hope. Both constantly change; both always produce surprises. Fresh starts are a part of both. And both the garden and life are reflected through metaphor in therapy.

There are no "wrong" metaphors; just different metaphors. Clients may compose them or respond to them as they feel able, and when this is realized, they may feel more free to be self-expressive. The impact of the intervention is immediate, instantaneous, and full. Metaphoric work intensifies recollection and reconstruction.

Working with metaphors has three major limitations. The first is that the client's unconscious may respond in a way that is not expected. You must always be keenly attuned to the nonverbal cues and vigilant of the associations of clients because these provide closer access to the nature and quality of their responses.

The second limitation is a caution based on an old maxim: "if the only tool you have is a hammer, everything looks like a nail." In other words, the metaphor can become a trap. Avoid the temptation to make everything fit because in doing so you distort rather than clarify the picture. Very real parts and pieces that seem not to jibe with the metaphor can be dangerously left out or ignored. A lack of awareness of your own unconscious associations may pose a third obstacle. While, to a certain degree, it is important to allow your unconscious some reign in connecting to client's metaphors, these may interfere with rather than contribute to the therapeutic process if they are disconnected from the client's primary messages.

HOW TO WORK WITH METAPHORS

As with a poem, breaking apart a metaphor by overanalyzing or interpreting it deprives it of power. Interpretation is inadequate. A more productive approach is to work with it affirmatively—encourage it, nurture it, draw it out, propel it. Transformation rather than translation is the key. Extending and enlarging the metaphor, shaping and dramatizing it, leads to alterations in clients' views of reality. Such an approach prevents clients from being bruised.

More specifically:

- Occupy yourself with the metaphor.
- Respect the richness and complexity of the image.
- Keep your remarks simple, clear, and brief.
- Stay speculative.
- Pay attention to your own associations.
- Attend to what is unspoken, nonverbal.
- Avoid jargon.
- Attempt to mirror the client's style, image, and language.

Your awareness that metaphors are pregnant with meaning is the first step toward utilizing them effectively in treatment. When you are conscious of metaphors, you can use them to convey fresh views of stagnant situations, to develop new ideas, to suggest the possibility of changing patterns, and to stir up emotions and unearth buried memories. Metaphors make it possible to discover new relationships between events, feelings, and behavior and to bring them forth with a simplicity that leads to heightened understanding. Individuals and families learn to exercise imagination and draw upon unconscious resources and allusions.

The literal meaning of a metaphor is not nearly as significant as the impression it produces. You do not really "know" what the metaphor signifies. You have hunches based upon your own experience and knowledge and information provided by clients. Relying on both the right and left hemispheres of your brain, you actively listen and fantasize, creating various individualized images from the data and history. These images, refined or revised by understanding of clients' unique patterns and themes, propose possible ways of proceeding to "play out" the metaphor. A metaphoric way of thinking for both clinicians and clients helps integrate our two spheres—one objective, analytic, and logical and the other subjective, imaginary, and global.

Figure 14.2 attempts to capture graphically how you can proceed in understanding, selecting, and then building upon a metaphor for an individual or a family. It traces one newly married couple's original statement that they often felt that their life at home was truly a "battlefield." The specific data they offered about a continual pattern of struggle, usually followed by reconciliation, led me to an association to their having to fight in order to "make peace." A series of right-brain hunches, combined with left-brain analysis of more data, led to possible metaphors: "war of attrition," "guerrilla warfare," "revolutionary war," and "civil war." This course led to a fuller understanding of both of their family of origin issues, that closeness first required conflict, and led to my metaphoric statement, "Seems you're engaged in a civil war where you're fighting to join forces," which was first met with a détente and eventuated in a cessation of the destructive cycle.

Understanding a metaphor is as much a creative endeavor as making a metaphor, and as little guided by rules. Responding, understanding, and utilizing them in your clinical practice involves responding to them in their totality. It involves rational awareness and intellectual analysis; it also involves an intuitive grasp and emotional responsiveness. Approached this way, metaphors dynamically energize the therapeutic experience.

FIGURE 14.2. Tandem Right- and Left-Brain Functioning in Forming Metaphoric Interventions

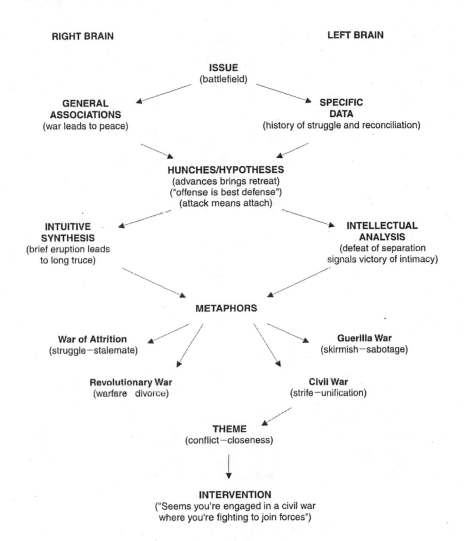

Chapter 15

The Termination Process

Human beings are not victims of traumata from birth to death;
they can find fulfillment in experiences that are hard to leave.

Jesse Taft

What we call the beginning is often the end. And to make an end
is to make a beginning. The end is where we start from.

T. S. Eliot

Any ending is tough. Ending a helping relationship is especially
so. Perhaps that is why we rarely hear people say "good-bye." Instead
we hear such expressions as, "be good," "take care," "see you later."
The very expression "good-bye," originally meaning "God be with
ye," has been abbreviated to "bye," perhaps to soften the pain of dealing with leaving and separation. As one client explained about termination:

> It means splitting, leaving, going away forever. It's feeling
> lousy, like crying, like relief from a burden, responsibility; it's
> all the things you did, and all you didn't do—right, wrong, every-
> thing but indifference, because you really cared about them.
> That's why it's so painful. That's why it's so damned hard to ex-
> press.

"Good-bye" is avoided as if it is a curse, because the words arouse
acute and threatening feelings of loss, permanent separation, and

foreshadowings of death. If "good-bye" is not uttered, the ending it signals does not have to be faced; yet, only when you and the client say good-bye, will both of you know the success of your work. I frequently share with clients a quip I heard long ago: successful helping is like successful parenting—it is self-obliterating.

Terminating the helping relationship concludes a unique interpersonal endeavor and signals a transitional process for you and your clients. In either case, it arouses pain; however, it can be, at the same time, a powerful and significant experience of growth, a marker of change. When skillfully handled, termination has the potential to put to rest past failures at endings.

NECESSARY LOSSES

Termination is not a unique occurrence in daily life or in professional functioning. To be alive is to be faced with continual separations, seldom dealt with squarely. It is no wonder, then, that terminating such an intimate association as the helping relationship evokes sadness and triggers unfinished business from previous losses and separations invariably experienced in the cycle of life from birth to death, expected (birth, first day at school, graduation) and abrupt (death, abandonment, divorce).

Judith Viorst (1986) catalogues these losses so well and concludes:

> . . . these losses are a part of life—universal, unavoidable, inexorable. And . . . losses are necessary because we grow by losing and leaving and letting go. (p. 3)

How clients and you approach termination reflects how we have dealt, probably miserably, with farewells in our lives up to this point. But this can change. You need not muddle through. Termination upsets and threatens the steadiness of your relationship; it also challenges you to discover more satisfying ways to separate. Loss, alarm, rejection, and helplessness are feelings that often overcome us when relationships end. You, however, the helper, are obliged to acknowledge, accept, and discipline your feelings so that you can speak the unspeakable "good-bye." You may know this, intellectually, yet are often so concerned with helping clients work out their feelings that you ignore your own. In not confronting your own feelings, you ultimately cheat clients of a full and shared experience. Actively address clients' central issues and feelings about termination; but first, candidly face your own.

It is easy to overlook, forget, or bypass all the painful feelings that termination arouses, but when you do, you disrupt the process and disturb clients. Do not preoccupy yourself with looking for a ready-made formula for a "smooth ending"; none exists. Furthermore, the looking distracts you from fully experiencing *this* ending.

This chapter explains how termination can simultaneously bring closure to your present relationship with the client and offer him or her an opportunity to resolve older ones. Depending upon how you approach it, termination can be a dismal undertaking or a catalyst for growth. Termination determines the degree to which therapeutic gains are maintained. When termination is a stimulating experience, it can bring clients and you to increased levels of integration and maturation.

VIEWS OF TERMINATION

Termination is the culminating stage, an end point in a total therapeutic process. It is also a discrete entity having its own distinctive stages with specific characteristics.

Termination: An End Point

Endings have their roots in beginnings. An integral part of a larger, multifaceted process, termination gives you both an opportunity to review and tie together, retrospectively, the entire helping endeavor. Reiterating and scrutinizing the results of what you set out to accomplish reinforces and stabilizes change.

A microcosm of the entire helping process, your impending departure, like your initial presence, heightens clients' anxiety. The client reexperiences a separation/individuation crisis manifested by an ambivalent pull between his or her desire for independence and wish for dependence (Webb, 1985). Termination provides more than an opportunity to reinforce gains; it offers still another chance to recognize and modify conflicts. One reason why termination is frequently so unsatisfying is your failure to differentiate between task accomplishment and relationship ending. Often, clients who report improvement in their functioning and accomplishment of contracted goals are reluctant to leave. It is the relationship with you that they want to preserve.

Clients experience the beginning of the helping process as an ending. You helped them to stop clutching at untenable patterns and assisted them to reach toward untested ones. In ending the helping process, clients confront yet another beginning, but alone, because they leave behind your support, which accelerates their fear of losing what has been gained and of facing an uncertain future. From this fear grows separation anxiety, echoing anxiety felt in the beginning. Impending termination revives old feelings and stirs up new ones. All need to be ventilated and resolved.

Termination: A Distinctive Process

Termination stands apart from other phases of the helping process, having its own phenomenology and dynamics that resemble crisis intervention. The precipitating event is any announcement of impending termination that shifts the focus of your work from resolution of clients' problems, as such, to exploration of anxiety, and the defenses against it, connected with separation. Even though clients often consider it a "little death," termination can enliven and intensify your relationship. Wanting to hold on to the familiar and comfortable, clients' motivation is renewed to accomplish much in a little time. Take advantage of this release of energy and channel it toward dealing with the reality of ending.

Consider these remarks by Harry, a thirty-four-year-old social studies teacher, when termination was at hand:

> This is a powerful place. There has been a lot of hard work and struggle. With results. It's hard to leave the center of some of your greatest triumphs. I'd like to stay. I know I have to go. You have been very important in my life and instrumental in my growth. It will be hard not to see someone you care about and trust—even my family and best friends don't know what you know.
>
> I often left your office upset, but never hopeless. Let's pull things together. I think I'm ready. No, I'm sure I'm ready.

Webb (1985) suggests that during ending, as in crisis, clients simultaneously feel happiness, exhilaration, anxiety, and loss at the prospect of being on their own. Many of the principles of working with clients in crisis, therefore, apply to termination as described by Webb.

TASKS IN TERMINATION

To assist clients to make a successful transition from being clients to being on their own, the eight tasks listed below should be carefully integrated into the process of preparing to separate:

1. Determining when to start termination
2. Evaluating progress and goal accomplishment
3. Working out conflict between acknowledging improvement and separating from help
4. Acknowledging and mourning the loss of the relationship
5. Recognizing and working through ambivalence
6. Discussing how progress can be transferred to other issues clients may encounter in the future
7. Planning how to maintain gains and continue growth
8. Letting go

SIGNS OF CLIENTS' READINESS FOR TERMINATION

What are the signs of clients' readiness for termination? In general terms, these include clients discovering their own potential, experiencing increased feelings of mastery, and demonstrating an ability to take charge of their own lives, all of which become integrated functions in their day-to-day living. Ten specific checkpoints for assessing individuals' and ten more for assessing families' readiness for termination are listed below.

Individual Checkpoints

1. Approximate freedom from initial problems
2. Relief from anxiety and unrealistic expectations
3. Improved adjustment and coping with reality
4. Increased awareness, appreciation, and acceptance of self
5. Willingness to assume responsibility for own actions
6. Decreased complaining about the unfairness of life

7. Reduced dependency
8. Expansion of personality to include previously disowned characteristics
9. Enhanced sense of humor; laughing at self
10. Recognizing that life is not simple, predictable, or controllable

Family Checkpoints

1. Family members seeing each other as distinct individuals
2. Tolerating, perhaps enjoying, differences
3. Loosening bonds
4. Resolving problems at home
5. Communicating directly and clearly
6. Developing outside relationships
7. Expressing strong positive and negative feelings
8. Risking new behaviors
9. Differentiating individuals from the family mass
10. Repairing emotional ruptures

Extraordinary Checkpoints

Sometimes, out of the blue, clients let you know, in remarkable, surprising, and totally unexpected ways, that they are ready to end their treatment. Phyllis, the woman I spoke about in Chapter 12 as having grave difficulty completing and sharing her responses to my inventory of questions, gave me, as we were four weeks into our scheduled six-week termination, a completed handwritten copy of the inventory. She commented, in what we both remarked was a double entendre, "this is now all past history."

In another example, Charlie, a six-year-old boy whom I had seen as a result of his father's imprisonment, at our last session handed me a small box, wrapped in tissue paper and tied with a bow. As I took it he asked, "Can I open it?" I handed it back to him, and he opened the bow and removed the paper. He handed the box back to me. He again asked, "Can I open it?" He opened it and again handed it to me. As I took it, he asked, "Can I take it out of the box?" Once more I handed it back to him. Charlie lifted a blue Smurf out of the box. Holding it, he said, "Can I keep the Smurf?" quickly followed by, "You can keep the box." From this exchange, I felt secure that our termination was on target. Why? Because I believed that he understood and expressed, in metaphoric terms, the process of therapy. The box, the "safe house," was returned to me. But having been in it, he had his "self" back.

SEPARATION PARADOX

Termination arouses dread and anxiety and a desire to escape the stimulation causing it; simultaneously, it triggers an impulse to turn for relief to an "attached figure," to soften the blow. Ironically, in the complex interplay between clients and you, each of you is, for the other, the figure of both separation and attachment. In this instance, you are the source of both unpleasant feelings and comfort. Because they have depended on you for relief from suffering, when clients face losing you, they will grieve. Their grief will be accompanied by a mixture of other feelings—anger, alienation, and confusion—which will be defended against and manifested only indirectly.

Clients, during termination, may feel paradoxically closer to you for sticking by them during leave-taking, while experiencing a sense of growing estrangement. This close yet more distant feeling, this dilemma of ambivalence, frequently stirs in them a natural urge to preserve the familiar and ignore the inevitable ending. While clients might be terrified by deeper feelings and pull back from them, you need to be ready and willing to plumb them since you have the responsibility to interrupt such avoidance. Deal directly with your own feelings and actions as well; otherwise, you might unwittingly collude with clients' denial, evasion, or flight.

Self-Awareness

You may feel a genuine sense of loss as work with clients ends, especially if it has been gratifying and productive. Acknowledging and reining in your own feelings about separation will free you to be more attentive to clients' feelings. The success of termination—indeed, the success of the entire helping endeavor—depends on your sensitivity to your own feelings. Among these feelings are sorrow, delight, and wish for gratitude, all of which, if unexamined, depress the exchange with clients. Taking stock of your feelings reduces the chance of interfering with clients' expression of their own.

The outcome of termination—relieving clients' fears of abandonment and helping them accept separation—depends upon such factors in clients and in you as the quality of your particular relationship, the perceived degree of success or satisfaction within it, the degree to which earlier losses of significant persons have been faced, and the level at which mastery of the separation/individuation crisis has been achieved. You will improve the chances for a successful termination when you do the following:

- Remain sensitive, flexible, empathic, and observant
- Noncritically respond to clients' needs for security
- Communicate continually in an open and direct fashion
- Interrupt barriers inhibiting expression of feeling
- Offer honest expressions and explanations
- State thoughts briefly and simply
- Answer questions
- Use concrete and familiar examples

STAGES IN TERMINATION

Termination for clients is a multiple conclusion. It marks the end of this interpersonal relationship with you as a real person, a transferred object, and a helper. Although clients react differently to this multidimensional ending, some being compliant, some oppositional, certain reactions commonly occur in progressive and predictable stages. Alert to the onset and progression of these stages, you are better able to assist clients to express feelings accompanying them that might be ordinarily withheld or repressed. You are also better able to distinguish and help them distinguish between feelings that are induced specifically by this ending and feelings that are residual, that is, originating from past relationships but reawakened and projected onto this relationship. Understanding this distinction allows you to address both.

Termination also stirs up in you emotions about clients and about your own past endings, as well as feelings about your professional competence. This phenomenon is related to countertransference issues discussed in earlier chapters. It is likely that, unrecognized, ignored, or unattended, these feelings will interfere with attending to your client's needs, feelings, and experiences and short-circuit your availability to appropriately respond to them. Be sure to take an inventory of your own feelings before unearthing your clients'.

Perspectives on Stages of Termination

Reactions to loss and its attendant feelings of grieving have been described in different ways. Certainly, your awareness of various phases in approaching ultimate termination, after inventorying your own feelings, is important. At first, clients are in a state of denial—they attempt to ward off recognition of the termination as well as feelings associated with it. After the denial breaks down, there is usually a period of considerable emotional expression. A prolonged period follows in which the reality of termination and its associated feelings are worked through.

Kübler-Ross (1969) identifies five progressive stages for dealing with loss—denial and isolation, anger, bargaining, depression, and acceptance. These stages pertain, as well, to loss sustained during the ending phase of the helping process. In the first stage, denial and isolation are erected as defenses against the reality of separation. Clients, not accepting the approaching ending, make little attempt to deal with its reality, often acting as if you never mentioned it. In the second stage, anger, clients express hostility and lash out at you or others close to them. The ending of any meaningful relationship causes distress; things will never be the same. Familiar and comfortable in their relationship with you, clients naturally want to hold onto it; anything that hints at its dissolution provokes anger. In the third stage, clients might bargain with you to maintain the relationship even at the cost of therapeutic gain. They try to make a deal to forestall the inevitable ending. Another client strategy is to present an eleventh-hour problem or crisis. A common client strategy during this stage is to negotiate a change in the relationship or modify the contract, subtly conveying that they will be irked by your refusal to agree to new terms. Depression, the fourth stage, sees clients obsessing about the loss rather than working it through. The fifth stage, accep-

tance of separation, entails putting to rest the feelings attendant to all
stages in order to avoid depositing old feelings into new relationships.

Another approach to loss and managing its effects, offered by Fox
1969, p. 316), is captured in the following chart:

Major Affect	Management of Affect
1. Sadness or grief over loss	Initial denial or other defense against impending loss
2. Anger at the worker for leaving or at self for not being able to be left	Period of emotional reaction and expression of sadness, hurt, anger
3. Narcissistic wounds based in disappointed expectations	Working through these feelings

Different in some respects from Kübler-Ross's approach, both
frameworks underscore common themes—an initial period of denial,
a period of hurt and anger, and a thrust toward resolution and acceptance. A further theme pervades the termination process but is not explicated by these writers—the constant struggle toward maturity and
independence propelling clients toward health. Although stages in-
frequently proceed according to the neat sequence suggested by these
outlines, knowing their character attunes you more fully to clients'
underlying dynamics.

How clients uniquely advance through the stages of ending and
how they manifest affects is related to the nature of their problem, the
state of their ego, the quality of their relationship with you, their emotional involvement in the helping process, and how well their earlier
separation experiences were handled. Your sensitivity and timing
will make it possible for them to ventilate feelings at successive
phases and to move on to the next. When feelings are not talked out,
they are acted out in self-defeating ways.

TERMINATION TROUBLES

Tuning into You

Good-byes are filled with a mixture of contradictory feelings; however, do not underestimate your clients' adaptive capacity. If you do, you
may stay locked in a place with them where neither of you will be free to

examine your work together and your relationship and, ultimately, break your tie. If you sincerely believe that a new whole can emerge from elements of preceding events, behave accordingly, realizing that clients' aroused acuity at this stage of your work makes them especially sensitive to the authenticity of your own reactions and behavior.

At termination, clients are exquisitely attuned to your feelings and how forthrightly you handle, project, or act them out. They may capitalize, consciously or unconsciously, on this awareness to provoke or manipulate you to continue the work. Their motive is simple—to distract both of you from the real pain of separation and to hide feelings associated with it. In provoking you to behave in certain ways, they can justifiably react. These maneuvers are ingenious, but they sidetrack you from the issue at hand, permit clients to conceal their true emotions and thoughts, or evoke guilt in you or in clients. Remember, clients' acting out requires your complicity.

Unaware of your own feelings, you are less aware of the clients' and are therefore more susceptible to manipulation. Your vulnerability is increased further when you are stressed or have conflicts of your own related to separation. You may feel, for example, that by terminating you are deserting or betraying clients whose only relationship of trust is with you. As a result, in an attempt to assuage your guilt, you may minimize your importance or that of the helping process— acting distant or, the reverse, overprotective. Intercepting this message, and alert to its underlying meaning, clients may behave in ways that cause you even more guilt. On the other hand, they may act in ways that convince you that your leaving reflects a lack of caring or results from their "bad behavior." Clients may even act out somatically, once again drawing you closer. A vicious cycle is maintained by all the interactions mentioned above that effectively defeats your appropriately dealing with the real issues of separation.

Clients do not necessarily set out to dupe you; rather, their response is usually motivated by a desire to hold on. They may idealize or patronize you. Some clients, possibly keyed into your needs for gratification, may attempt to convince you that whatever changes they made, they made expressly for you and tacitly threaten to resume maladaptive behavior unless you continue to work with them. Making it up to them to feel better yourself, offering excessive reassurance and advice, and "catching" their symptoms, risks that they will sense your inappropriateness and, indeed, revert to former patterns of behavior.

The prospect of ending the helping relationship raises clients' insecurities about being on their own. If you ignore the real issue of separation, you cheat clients; feelings go unaddressed and unrelieved. Clients therefore understandably question the validity or value of whatever work you have accomplished. When you play avoidance games with clients, you precipitate regression. A premature and sometimes abrupt rupture in the relationship may ensue, precipitating negative feelings in clients and in you.

Sometimes clients feel intimidated or helpless and act like obedient children, telling you only what you want to hear and refraining from criticism or hostility. Other times, feeling out of control or frustrated, they may blurt out anger and resentment. Accept and examine all these reactions; not doing so confirms clients' dread that no one has control and complicates the process of working through feelings by justifying their sense of futility. Your own fear of clients' hostility or your own need to be liked may lead you to ally yourself with their anger. If you do so, both you and your clients will feel victimized.

When you are unable to manage your own feelings, you may blame clients for causing you pain, and you may then respond inappropriately: directly, with abuse, criticism, or hostility; or indirectly, with displeasure or subtle discontent. A sense of rejection results, which they translate, to protect themselves, into ways to reject you, often by leaving prematurely, in effect saying, "You can't fire me; I quit."

You may feel unsuccessful, not having rescued clients from distress. You may blame and persecute them for not meeting your expectations and needs, thereby eliciting anger from clients and becoming the victim of their legitimate feelings. When not assuming responsibility for your own feelings and actions, you contribute to clients' feelings of unworthiness, helplessness, and powerlessness, all with damaging results. Catching clients' feelings, pulling away, denying or displacing your own feelings, and detaching yourself from the experience of separation leaves clients feeling abandoned, which undermines the entire helping process.

PREPARATION FOR TERMINATION

Averting Pitfalls

Devote sufficient time to termination. Whether termination is suggested by clients or by you, it should not be abrupt, but should be introduced well in advance of the actual date of departure to allow sufficient time to discuss all the facets involved—cognitive, affective, and behavioral. It is always important to give notice and reiterate, from time to time, the impending ending; importance grows in direct proportion to the length and intensity of your relationship. Clients deserve the opportunity to enter, understand, and work through, productively and systematically, each successive stage of disentanglement from the helping process and from you. Clients fear leave-taking and react to their lack of control over it. You can help them to discover strength in overcoming their painful reactions to parting. Draw upon their adaptive capacity to help them understand and deal with separation; they will not merely survive it but experience it as producing growth.

Tying Up Loose Ends

Prepare for termination by examining what you believe has been accomplished in your work together. Review progress objectively and in detail, taking account of what goals have and have not been achieved. Consult your original contract and read your case record for evidence of change. Acknowledge the specific ways in which clients have promoted their own progress; credit yourself for your own contributions. Recognize and name other factors that have positively and negatively influenced the change effort—maturation, environment, friends, etc.

Prepare clients for the end of the helping relationship in a timely, planful, and deliberate way. Good advance preparation can stabilize clients' gains and increase their degree of insight and sense of independence. Take advantage of a head start. You have already previewed how clients may react to termination by observing their responses to your absences at vacation time, at the end of difficult interviews, or when changing or missing appointments. How clients typically handled these absences gives you a clue to how they will approach this permanent break.

Avoid Avoidance

Rather than "weaning" clients, set a date for termination. Setting the date makes the fact of your ending more real and tangible. It forces both of you to attend to issues and feelings that are easily evaded, avoided, or distorted. It averts any abrupt or unexpected parting. It prepares you to affirmatively give them permission to leave, your blessing (Johnson, 1988) as it were, which strengthens your clients' belief in the therapeutic process, in you, and, most important, in themselves. It also confirms that theirs is an achievement, an arrival, a second coming of age (Johnson, 1988).

Taking Leave

Take an active role in encouraging clients to think and talk about what goals have been accomplished, problems resolved, and risks taken. When you do, you enhance their ego and support their autonomy. Empathic affirmations lead to feelings of being valued and affirmed. Encourage clients to apply new learnings in assessing themselves and their progress. When you help them visualize how they will practice new behaviors in the future, they may venture to express a conditional good-bye. They may say, "I'm not ready for this," "Not yet," "Wait a while." Look closely at what they mean. Are they really saying, "Give me time to let go"? Reviewing the contract, as well as logs, inventories, and letters written during your work, furnishes you and clients with tangible documentation of accomplishments. Ending does not have to be a unilateral, arbitrary decision because, from the outset, your contract contained mutually agreed-upon goals, expectations, and guideposts, including those for termination. The contract makes termination less confusing and frustrating. It spells out in specific terms how changes might appear and identifies end points to strive for. Rely on it for direction and remind clients about it.

During the termination process, clients say that they do not know how they feel or claim to have no feeling at all. Despite major steps forward in accepting responsibility for themselves and their actions, the threat that you will "abandon" them leaves them frightened and reluctant to follow through on their new course by themselves. Termination amplifies feelings of uncertainty, perhaps terror. When clients are not able to identify their feelings or accomplishments, name them yourself and invite their feedback. As you move through the pain of separation, model to clients that you yourself are able to plunge deeply into the intellectual, behavioral, and emotional effects of change.

Good-Bye, Alan

The following excerpt from an actual interview with Alan, an eleven-year-old inner-city school student, exemplifies some of the ideas highlighted above and shows that saying good-bye can have positive results.

CLINICIAN: You know, Alan, we've only this and one more session before I leave. I'm feeling sad that I won't see you after next Friday. How about you?

ALAN: I'm happy . . . er, sad. I'm sad.

CLIN: Have you ever lost a friend or had one move away?

ALAN: Yeah, my old friends moved to the projects, and I moved to my grandmother's.

CLIN: How did you feel when you didn't have them to play with?

ALAN: My grandmother doesn't like me playing with hurt birds who can't fly no more. Would you like one of my puppies to keep, so you could remember me?

CLIN: I'd like that, but I can't keep a puppy where I live. It's not allowed. Once I had a pet turtle.

ALAN: What happened to it?

CLIN: It died and I felt real bad. I even cried because I cared a lot for it.

ALAN: I had a goldfish that died. My grandmother gave it too much food and it died.

CLIN: Gee, how'd you take that?

ALAN: I don't know. I buried it in the yard.

CLIN: When someone or something you care about leaves you, it's hard to take, like your goldfish and my turtle.

ALAN: (nods affirmatively) I liked that goldfish and it went away.

CLIN: I'm leaving soon, kind of feel bad about that, do you?

ALAN: Could you stay here longer?

CLIN: I'm afraid it's not possible, but I'll remember you and me being friends and having this time together.

ALAN: When I go to the tutoring program, Bill takes me on trips.

CLIN: You know you've made some changes this year, don't you, Alan?

ALAN: I can talk better, more words.

CLIN: When I met you, you were very quiet and shy. Now you can say some things and express how you feel lots better; and your teacher says how good your math and writing are.

ALAN: (listening)

CLIN: When I've been in to see you in the classroom, I see your hand up a lot; that's quite a change from before.

ALAN: I still like to hustle, but I come to school more now.

CLIN: It's time to go now. I'll see you next week.

ALAN: When will you come for me?

CLIN: Same time as today. Remember when that is?

ALAN: Friday, right? After second period. (smiling)

CLIN: I'll walk you back to class now.

ALAN: I'm going to think about you.

CLIN: I'm going to remember you too, Alan.

Guidelines for Leave-Taking

In leave-taking, do the following:

- Focus on and highlight gains
- Avoid tackling new problems
- Validate and reinforce the client's problem-solving capability
- Relate to explicit and implicit positive statements and adaptations
- Cite evidence of decisions, choices, and responsibility
- Commend activity that exhibits motivation, self-direction, and self-control
- Emphasize accomplishments and initiative taking
- Comment on clients' worth and value
- Consider future expectations
- Express confidence in the client's future
- Make clear the possibility of future help
- Express interest and positive feelings for the client

Rituals and Guided Exercises for Termination

Termination is a significant transition in your clients' lives, and transitions are eased by rituals. Rituals during the end of your work can provide valuable vehicles for reaching the often contradictory emotions and thoughts that accompany such endings (Gutheil, 1993). Five elements of rituals are particularly important to bear in mind:

1. The sense of specialness
2. The connection to both past and future
3. The ability to hold both sides of the contradiction
4. The capacity to deal with emotions
5. The communication component (Gutheil, 1993, p. 167)

Evaluating your work together by systematically examining your achievement of goals as outlined in Chapter 6, using single-subject design or goal-attainment procedures, is one type of ritual. Guided exercises are also rituals and can assist you in helping clients to address separation issues. They can also foster self-awareness. In an exercise called fantasy gift exchanging, imaginary gifts are exchanged as a parting gesture. For example, I handed a fourteen-year-old male client, who had struggled and ultimately come to terms with overwhelming feelings of self-doubt, an imaginary can of "I cans" he had come to recognize: "I can do math problems," "I can ask for extra help in school when I need it," "I can score two foul shots in a row," and "I can graduate." Sam offered me, in return, a Xerox copy of his imaginary "I will" poster, listing such "wills" as "I will go to high school," "I will talk to my mother more about her ignoring me," and "I will play on the basketball team."

In another ritualized exercise, clients draw a map of the helping process to illustrate symbolically any significant accomplishments that they find it difficult to state in words. Discussing the details and detours of their map of change opens avenues to verbal sharing. In another exercise, clients imagine departing in a car. Driving away, they peek into the rearview mirror to see what they are leaving behind and are asked to describe whatever feelings are evoked. They then shift the car into reverse and return to express what they would have regretted not having said had they left without this opportunity. Exercises such as these promote introspection, reflection, and open discussion.

GOOD-BYE, FAREWELL, AND BEYOND

Discuss plans and goals with clients; invite their recommendations and prescriptions for their own future. Do not hesitate to offer advice and observations to consolidate the experience you had together, having successfully faced the unknown. Convey your confidence in their ability to meet what lies ahead of them without your continued presence.

Your final leave-taking can be extremely difficult, but can also be releasing. Be direct. Polite or mechanical platitudes get in the way of sharing intimate feelings. Prolonged hanging on inhibits the release of emotions triggered by loss. Enable clients to release their feelings about separation by being genuine and honest yourself. Saying good-bye is not a curse. Perhaps only through separation can clients become fully independent and developed. Think of "good-bye" as the departing blessing it originally meant. Say good-bye so that both of you are free to go on to the next "hello".

The following quotation, from an unknown source, summarizes the process of termination in a heartfelt way:

> Active as I am in sessions
> going with you to the marrow of emotions
> our shared journey has an end.
> Tonight, as you hesitantly leave my office
> to the early darkness of winter days
> and the coldness of December nights,
> you do so on your own.
> Yet, this season of crystallized rain
> changes, if however slowly,
> and our time and words together
> can be a memory from which may grow
> a new seed of life within you,
> not without knowledge of past years' traumas
> but rather in the sobering realization
> that in being heard a chance is created
> to fill a time with different feelings,
> And savor them in the silent hours
> when you stand by yourself alone.

References

Chapter 2

Barrett-Lennard, G. (1981). The empathy cycle: Refinement of a nuclear concept. *Journal of Counseling Psychology,* 28 (2), 91-100.

Basch, M. (1983). Empathic understanding: A review of the concept and some theoretical considerations. *Journal of the American Psychoanalytic Association,* 31 (1), 101-126.

Bowlby, J. (1975). Attachment theory, separation anxiety, and mourning. In D. Hamburg and H. Brodie (Eds.), *American Handbook of Psychiatry,* Second edition, Vol. VI (pp. 292-309), New York: Basic.

Fosshage, J. (1981). The psychological function of dreams. Paper presented at Long Island Association of Psychoanalytic Psychologists, Long Island, NY.

Frank, J. (1973). *Persuasion and healing.* Baltimore: Johns Hopkins University Press.

Greenson, R. (1967). *The technique and practice of psychoanalysis,* Vol. 1. New York: International Universities Press.

Grunebaum, H. (1983). A study of therapists' choice of a therapist. *American Journal of Psychiatry,* 140 (10), 1336-1339.

Hogan, R. (1969). Development of an empathy scale. *Journal of Consulting and Clinical Psychology,* 33 (3), 307-316.

Kohut, H. (1977). *The restoration of the self.* New York: International Universities Press.

Kohut, H. (1978). *The search for the self.* New York: International Universities Press.

Kohut, H. (1982). Introspection, empathy, and the semi-circle of mental health. *International Journal of Psychoanalysis,* 63 (4), 395-407.

Kohut, H. (1984). *How does analysis cure?* Chicago: University of Chicago Press.

Rogers, C. (1958). The characteristics of a helping relationship. *Personnel and Guidance Journal,* 37 (1), 6-16.

Winnicott, D.W. (1986). *Holding and interpretation.* New York: Grove Press.

Chapter 3

Atwood, G.E. and Stolorow, R.D. (1993). *Faces in a cloud: Intersubjectivity in personality theory.* Northvale, NJ: Jason Aronson, Inc.

Buber, M. (1970). *I and thou.* New York: Simon & Schuster.

Coady, N.F. and Wolgien, C.S. (1996). Good therapists' views of how they are helpful. *Clinical Social Work Journal,* 24 (3), 311-322.

Compton, B. and Galaway, B. (1979). *Social work processes.* Homewood, IL: Dorsey Press.

Edwards, J.K. and Bess, J.M. (1998). Developing effectiveness in the therapeutic use of self. *Clinical Social Work Journal,* 26 (1), 89-105.

Frank, J. (1973). *Persuasion and healing.* Baltimore: Johns Hopkins University Press.

Grunebaum, H. (1986). Harmful psychotherapy experience. *American Journal of Psychotherapy,* 40 (2), 165-176.

Kadushin, A. (1976). *Supervision in social work.* New York: Columbia University Press.

Kohut, H. (1973). *The analysis of self.* New York: International Universities Press.

Marziali, E. and Alexander, L. (1991). The power of the therapeutic relationship. *American Journal of Orthopsychiatry,* 61 (3), 383-391.

McCall, E. (1988). I tell homeless kids, "love you, baby." *The New York Times,* November 1, A19.

Rogers, C. (1958). The characteristics of a helping relationship. *Personnel and Guidance Journal,* 37 (1), 383-391.

Strupp, H. H. (1977). A reformulation of the dynamics of the therapist's contribution. In A.S. Gurman and A.M. Razin (Eds.), *Effective psychotherapy: A handbook for research* (pp. 1-22), New York: Pergamon Press.

Unzicker, R. (1988). To be a mental patient. *Pilgrimage,* 14 (4), 89.

Chapter 4

Gutheil, I. (1992). Considering the physical environment: An essential component of good practice. *Social Work,* 37 (5), 391-396.

Hammond, D.C., Hepworth, D. H., and Smith, V.G. (1978). *Improving therapeutic communication.* San Francisco: Jossey-Bass.

Chapter 5

Blythe, B. and Briar, S. (1985). Developing empirically based models of practice. *Social Work,* 30 (6), 483-488.

Fox, R. (1987). Short-term goal oriented family therapy. *Social Casework,* 68 (8), 494-499.

Seabury, B. (1979). Negotiating sound contracts with clients. *Public Welfare,* 37 (2), 33-38.

Chapter 6

Beck, A. (1979). *Cognitive therapy of depression.* New York: Guilford.

Bloom, M., Fischer, V., and Orme, V.G. (1995). *Evaluating practice: Guidelines for the accountable professional.* Boston: Allyn & Bacon.

Cohen, M. (1988). *Suggested outline for process recording.* Unpublished manuscript.

Elks, M.A. and Kirkhart, K.E. (1993). Evaluating effectiveness from the practitioner perspective. *Social Work,* 38 (5), 554-563.

Fox, R. and Gutheil, I. (2000). Process recording: A means for conceptualizing and evaluating practice. *Journal of Teaching in Social Work,* 20 (1/2), 39-56.

Gabor, P., Unrau, Y.A., and Grinnell, M.N. (1997). *Evaluation for social workers: A quality improvement approach for the social services,* Second edition. Boston: Allyn & Bacon.

Ho, M.K. (1976). Evaluation: A means of treatment. *Social Work,* 21 (1), 24-27.

Proctor, E.K. (1990). Evaluating clinical practice: Issues of purpose and design. *Social Work Research and Abstracts,* 26 (1), 32-40.

Rubin, A., and Babbie, E. (1997). *Research methods for social work.* Belmont, CA: Wadsworth.

Tyson, K. (1995). *New foundations for scientific, social and behavioral research: The heuristic paradigm.* Boston: Allyn & Bacon.

Urbanowski, M. and Dwyer, M. (1988). *Learning through field instruction: A guide for teachers and students.* Milwaukee, WI: Family Service America.

Chapter 7

Cowger, C.D. (1994). Assessing client strengths: Clinical assessment for client empowerment. *Social Work,* 39 (3), 262-268.

Chapter 8

Angell, G.B.. Dennis, H., and Domain, R. (1998). Spirituality, resilience, and narrative: Coping with parental death. *Families in Society: The Journal of Contemporary Human Services,* 79 (6), 615-630.

Bugental, J.F. (1965). *The search for authenticity.* New York: Holt, Reinhart and Winston.

Camus, A. (1969). *Lyrical and critical essays.* New York: Alfred A. Knopf.

Canda, E.R. (1988). Spirituality, religious diversity, and social work practice. *Social Casework,* 69 (4), 238-247.

Canda, E.R. (1989). Edward R. Canda's response. *Social Casework,* 70 (2), 572-574.

Flach, F. (1997). Resilience: The power to bounce back when the going gets tough! New York: Hatherleigh Press.

Frankl, V.E. (1992). *Man's search for meaning: An introduction to logotherapy,* Fourth edition. Boston: Beacon Press.

Garmezy, N. (1994). Reflections and commentary on risk, resilience, and development. In J. Haggerty, L. R. Sherrod, N. Garmezy, and M. Rutter (Eds.), *Stress, risk, and resilience in children and adolescents: Processes, mechanisms, and interventions.* Cambridge, England: Cambridge University Press.

Harvey, M. (1996). An ecological view of psychological trauma and trauma recovery. *Journal of Traumatic Stress,* 9 (1), 3-23.

Herrenkohl, E.C., Herrenkohl, and Egolf, R. (1994). Resilient early school age chil
dren from maltreating homes: Outcomes in late adolescence. *American Journal of*
Orthopsychiatry, 64 (2), 301-309.

Kobasa S.C., Maddi, S.R., and Kahn, S. (1982). Hardiness and health: A prospective study. *Journal of Personal and Social Psychology,* 42 (1), 168-177.

Kobasa, S.C., Maddi, S.R., Puccetti, M.C., and Zola, M.A. (1985). Effectiveness of
hardiness, exercise and social support as resources against illness. *Journal of*
Psychosomatic Research, 29 (5), 525-533.

Kobasa, S.C. and Puccetti, M.C. (1983). Personality and social resources in stress-
resistance. *Journal of Personal and Social Psychology,* 45 (4), 839-850.

Liem, J., James, J.B., O'Toole, J.G., and Boudewyn, A.G. (1997). Assessing resilience in adults with histories of childhood sexual abuse. *American Journal of*
Orthopsychiatry, 67 (4), 594-606.

May, R. (1969). *Existential psychotherapy.* New York: Random House.

McQuaide, S. and Ehrenreich, J. (1997). Assessing client strengths. *Families in So-*
ciety, 78 (2), 201-212.

Moran, P.B. and Eckenrode, J. (1992). Protective personality chararacteristics among
adolescent victims of maltreatment. *Child Abuse and Neglect,* 16 (5), 743-754.

Rank, O. (1950). *Will therapy and truth and reality.* New York: Knopf.

Rutter, M. (1990). Psychological resilience and protective mechanisms. In J. Rolf,
A.S. Marten, D. Cicchetti, K.H. Neuchterlein, and S. Weintraub (Eds.), *Risk and*
protective factors in the development of psychopathology. New York: Cambridge
University Press.

Saleebey, D. (1996). The strengths perspective in social work practice: Extensions
and cautions. *Social Work,* 4 (3), 296-305.

Saleebey, D. (1997). *The strengths perspective in social work.* White Plains, NY:
Longman.

Sartre, J.P. (1960). *Existentialism and humanism.* London: Methuen.

Siporin, M. (1992). Strengthening the moral mission of social work. In P.N. Reid and
P.R. Popple (Eds.), *The moral purposes of social work.* Chicago: Nelson-Hall.

Wolin, S.J. (1991). The challenge model: How children rise above adversity. Ple-
nary address at the Annual Meeting of the American Association of Marriage
and Family Therapists, Dallas, November.

Yalom, I. (1980). *Existential psychotherapy.* New York: Basic Books.

Chapter 9

Alexander, F. (1956). *Psychoanalysis and psychotherapy.* New York: Norton.

American Psychiatric Association (1994). *Diagnostic and statistical manual of mental*
disorders, Fourth edition. Washington, DC: American Psychiatric Association.

Bandura, A. (1986). *Social foundations of thought and action.* Englewood Cliffs,
NJ: Prentice-Hall.

Brenner, C. (1973). *An elementary textbook of psychoanalysis.* New York: International Universities Press.

Bugental, J. (1976). *The search for existential identity.* San Francisco: Jossey-Bass.

Fenichel, O. (1945). *The psychoanalytic theory of neurosis.* New York: Norton.

Frankl, V. (1963). *Man's search for meaning.* New York: Basic Books.

Frankl, V. (1969). *Will to meaning.* New York: World Publishing.

Freud, A. (1966). *The ego and the mechanisms of defense.* New York: International Universities Press.

Freud, S. (1915-1917). *Introductory lectures on psychoanalysis.* London: Hogarth Press.

Fromm, E. (1941). *Escape from freedom.* New York: Rinehart and Winston.

Hall, C. (1973). *A primer of Freudian psychology.* New York: New American Library.

Hartmann, H. (1964). *Essays on ego psychology.* New York: International Universities Press.

Lazarus, A. (1981). *The practice of multimodal therapy.* New York: McGraw-Hill.

May, R. (1981). *Freedom and destiny.* New York: Norton.

O'Leary, K. D. and Wilson, C.T. (1987). *Behavior therapy: Application and outcome,* Second edition. Englewood Cliffs, NJ: Prentice-Hall.

Shapiro, D. (1965). *Neurotic styles.* New York: Basic Books.

Wolpe, J. (1969). *The practice of behavior therapy.* New York: Pergamon Press.

Yalom, I. (1981). *Existential psychotherapy.* New York: Basic Books.

Chapter 10

Ackerman, N. (1966). *Treating the troubled family.* New York: Basic Books.

Aponte, H. (1972). Structural family therapy. In Gurman, A.S. (ed.), *Handbook of family therapy.* New York: Brunner/Mazel.

Bowen, M. (1978). *Family therapy in clinical practice.* New York: Jason Aronson.

Framo, J. (1982). *Family interaction.* New York: Springer.

Guerin, P. (1976). *Family therapy.* New York: Gardner Press.

Haley, J. (1977). *Problem-solving therapy.* San Francisco: Jossey-Bass.

Kerr, M. and Bowen M. (1988). *Family evaluation.* New York: Norton.

Madanes, C. (1984). *Behind the one-way mirror.* San Francisco: Jossey-Bass.

McGoldrick, M. and Gerson, R. (1985). *Genograms in family assessment.* New York: Norton.

Minuchin, S. and Fishman, H. (1981). *Family therapy techniques.* Cambridge, MA: Harvard University Press.

Napier, A. and Whitaker, C. (1978). *The family crucible.* New York: Harper and Row.

Satir, V. (1983). *Conjoint family therapy.* Palo Alto, CA: Science and Behavior Books.

Zuk, G. (1981). *Family therapy: A triadic-based approach.* New York: Human Sciences Press.

Chapter 11

Dutton, M.A. and Rubinstein, F. (1995). Working with people with PTSD. In Figley, C. and Charles, R. (eds.), *Compassion fatigue: Coping with secondary traumatic stress disorder in those who treat the traumatized* (pp. 82-100). New York: Brunner/Mazel.

Faber, B. (1983). *Stress and burnout in the human service professions.* New York: Pergamon Press.

Figley, C. (1995). *Compassion fatigue as secondary traumatic stress disorder, compassion fatigue.* New York: Brunner/Mazel.

Fox, R. (2000). Grasping life: Five stories of will-filled men. In Norman, E. (ed.), *Resiliency in Social Work.* New York: Columbia University Press.

Fox, R. and Carey, L. (1999). Therapists' collusion with the resistance of rape survivors. *Clinical Social Work Journal,* 27 (2), 185-201.

Fox, R. and Cooper, M. (1998). The effects of suicide on the private practioner: A professional and personal perspective. *Clinical Social Work Journal,* 26 (2), 143-157.

Freudenberger, H.J. (1980). *Burn-out: The high cost of achievement.* New York: Anchor Press.

Greenberg, J. and Mitchell, S. (1983). *Object relations in psychoanalytic theory.* Cambridge, MA: Harvard University Press.

Kernberg, O. (1975). *Borderline conditions and pathological narcissism.* New York: Jason Aronson.

Koeske, G. F. and Koeske, R. D. (1989). Workload and burnout: Can social support and perceived accomplishment help. *Social Work,* 34 (3), 243-248.

Maslach, C. (1982). *Burnout—The cost of caring.* Englewood Cliffs, NJ: Prentice-Hall.

Maslach, C. and Jackson, S.E. (1981). The measurement of experienced burnout. *Journal of Occupational Behavior,* 2.

McCann, I.L. and Pearlman, L.A. (1990a). Vicarious traumatization: A framework for understanding the psychological effects of working with victims. *Journal of Traumatic Stress,* 1 (3), 131-149.

McCann, I.L. and Pearlman, L.A. (1990b). *Through a glass darkly: Understanding and treating the adult trauma survivor through constructivist self development theory.* New York: Brunner/Mazel.

Orr, D. W. (1954). Transference and countertransference: A historical survey. *Journal of the American Psychoanalytic Association,* 2 (3), 621-670.

Pines, A.M. and Maslach, C. (1978). Characteristics of staff burnout in mental health settings. *Hospital and Community Psychiatry,* 29 (4), 233-237.

Racker, H. (1957). The meaning and uses of countertransference. *Psychoanalytic Quarterly,* 26 (2), 303-357.

Scully, R. (1983). The work setting support group: A means of preventing burnout. In B. Faber (ed.), *Stress and burnout in the human service professions.* New York: Pergamon Press.

Chapter 12

Fox, R. (1983). The past is always present: Creative methods for capturing the life story. *Clinical Social Work Journal,* 11 (4), 368-378.

Lazarus, A.A. and Lazarus, C.N. (1991). *Multimodal life history questionnaire.* Champaign, IL: Research Press.

McGoldrick, M. and Gerson, R. (1985). *Genograms in family assessment.* New York: Norton.

Spence, D. (1982). *Narrative truth and historical truth.* New York: Norton.

Chapter 13

Cameron, J. and Bryan, M. (1995). *The artist's way: A spiritual path to higher creativity.* Los Angeles: Tarcher Putnam.

Fox, R. (1982). The personal log: Enriching clinical practice. *Clinical Social Work Journal,* 10 (2), 94-102.

Holman, W.D. (1998). The fatherbook: A document for therapeutic work with father-absent early adolescent boys. *Child and Adolescent Social Work Journal,* 15 (2), 101-115.

Pennebaker, J.W. (1997). *Opening up: The healing power of expressing emotions.* New York: Guilford Press.

Rico, G.L. (1983). *Writing the natural way.* Los Angeles: J.P. Tarcher.

Chapter 14

Atwood, J.D. and Levine, L.B. (1991). Ax murderers, dragons, spiders and webs: Therapeutic metaphors in couple therapy. *Contemporary Family Therapy,* 13 (3), 201-217.

Fox, R. (1989). What is meta for? *Clinical Social Work Journal,* 17 (3), 233-244.

Lankton, S. and Lankton, C. (1983). *The answer within: A clinical framework of Ericksonian hypnotherapy.* New York: Brunner/Mazel.

Siegelman, E.Y. (1990). *Metaphor and meaning in psychotherapy.* New York: Guilford Press.

Chapter 15

Fox, E. (1969). The termination process: A neglected dimension in social work. *Social Work,* 41 (4), 315-326.

Gutheil, I. (1993). Rituals and termination procedures. *Smith College Studies in Social Work,* 63 (2), 163-176.

Johnson, C. (1988). *When to say goodbye to your therapist.* New York: Simon & Schuster.

Kübler-Ross, E. (1969). *On death and dying.* New York: Macmillan.

Viorst, J. (1986). *Necessary losses.* New York: Fawcett Gold Medal.

Webb, N. (1985). A crisis intervention perspective on the termination process. *Clinical Social Work Journal,* 13 (4), 329-340.

Index

Page numbers followed by the letter "i" indicate illustrations.